ALBERT SCHWEITZER'S MISSION

Healing and Peace

With Hitherto Unpublished Letters from Schweitzer, Nehru, Eisenhower, Khrushchev, and Kennedy

BOOKS BY NORMAN COUSINS

The Healing Heart
The Words of Albert Schweitzer
Anatomy of an Illness as Perceived by the Patient
Human Options
Dr. Schweitzer of Lambaréné
The Improbable Triumvirate
The Physician in Literature
Who Speaks for Man?
The Celebration of Life
Present Tense
In Place of Folly
Modern Man Is Obsolete
The Good Inheritance
"In God We Trust": The Religious Beliefs and Ideas
 of the American Founding Fathers

ALBERT SCHWEITZER'S MISSION

Healing and Peace

With Hitherto Unpublished Letters from Schweitzer, Nehru, Eisenhower, Khrushchev, and Kennedy

NORMAN COUSINS

W · W · NORTON & COMPANY
New York · London

Copyright © 1985 by Norman Cousins
All rights reserved.
Published simultaneously in Canada by Penguin Books Canada Ltd., 2801 John Street,
 Markham, Ontario L3R 1B4
Printed in the United States of America.

The text of this book is composed in Janson. Composition and manufacturing by the
 Maple-Vail Book Manufacturing Group.

First Edition

Library of Congress Cataloging in Publication Data
Cousins, Norman.
 Albert Schweitzer's mission: Healing and peace, with hitherto unpublished letters
from Schweitzer, Nehru, Eisenhower, Khrushchev, and Kennedy.
 Includes index.
 1. Schweitzer, Albert, 1875–1965—Political and social views. 2. Nuclear war-
fare—Moral and ethical aspects. 3. Missionaries, Medical—Gabon—Correspon-
dence. 4. Theologians—Europe—Correspondence. 5. Musicians—Europe—
Correspondence. I. Schweitzer, Albert, 1875–1965. II. Title.
CT1018.S45C68 1985 172'.42 85–7145

ISBN 0-393-02238-2

W. W. Norton & Company, Inc., 500 Fifth Avenue, New York, N. Y. 10110
W. W. Norton & Company Ltd., 37 Great Russell Street, London WC1B 3NU

1 2 3 4 5 6 7 8 9 0

To Joan Kroc,

whose commitment to the Schweitzerian ethic of reverence for life has made a difference for the better in the lives of more people than she may ever know.

Contents

Acknowledgments

O nce again (having done so in the forerunner of this volume), I want to emphasize my debt to Clara Urquhart, who was my bridge to Albert Schweitzer. She brought me to Lambaréné. As my interpreter, she shaped my words to the occasion; she also provided creative advice at times when I wasn't sure of the proper approach or the next move. More than that: She was a full partner in the total undertaking described in this book. I must also express my thanks to Jean Anderson, who brought the letters together, arranged and annotated them, and supplied the kind of systematic editing and attention such an effort requires. George Brockway made valuable suggestions about the form and balance of the book. Ali Silver, who was Albert Schweitzer's right hand for many years, gathered copies of Dr. Schweitzer's correspondence from the archive at his home in Gunsbach and performed the additional service of translating a large number of those letters for inclusion in this book. Vicki Rintels and Gabriela Anicker did additional translation. Susan Sakala and Jane Britar helped with the word processing.

My wife Ellen kept me going throughout.

Editor's Note

I n the early years following the death of Albert Schweitzer in 1965, several biographies appeared about the towering figure who achieved eminence as a philosopher, theologian, physician, musicologist, and organist. Since that time, an entire generation has come of age and needs to know that such a man lit up the moral imagination of people in many lands. No person of his time furnished more evidence of the possibilities of creative human development or the altruistic reach of an individual human being.

This book, then, is an attempt to call attention to the work and thought of a man who was widely regarded as one of the most influential persons of his time. Part I is an adaptation of the book *Dr. Schweitzer of Lambaréné* (1960), which I wrote following a visit to his jungle hospital. Part II consists of hitherto unpublished correspondence relating to the cause that dominated the last half-dozen years of Dr. Schweitzer's life; namely, the need to free the world of nuclear terror.

In the half-decade preceding his death, I received forty-five letters from Dr. Schweitzer, most of which were directed to his concern over the accumulation of nuclear force. The correspondence also radiated out in several directions, with President Dwight D. Eisenhower, Prime Minister Jawaharlal Nehru, Premier Nikita Khrushchev, and President John F. Kennedy. These letters are related to the dominant theme of this book and are therefore included. In toto,

this correspondence does more than provide important material for the historical record; it has particular relevance for our own time.

For two decades, from 1963 to 1982, the raw edge of the nuclear issue was blunted. Indeed, there was a sense that people were adjusting to things that should admit no adjustment. Young people came into a world in which nuclear weapons pre-existed and were taken for granted, along with television sets and computers. But statements by some government officials to the effect that nuclear war was survivable produced an eruption of popular indignation. The result was something of a return to the spirit of the late fifties and early sixties, when public opinion enabled President John F. Kennedy to pursue his quest of a treaty barring atmospheric testing of nuclear explosives. President Kennedy credited an aroused public with the support he needed for Senate ratification of the treaty.

If the role of the public on the nuclear issue was important at that time, its relevance is no less vital today. In the two decades since the treaty outlawing nuclear testing was ratified, some 50,000 more nuclear explosives have been accumulated in the world's arsenals. The number of nations possessing the capability to make nuclear weapons has expanded steadily, confronting the world's people with the reality that any conflict anywhere could put a nuclear torch to the human habitat.

This problem was anticipated by Albert Schweitzer, as his letters demonstrate. It is a problem that no one can afford to delegate. For this is a problem, as President Eisenhower recognized, that governments by themselves are incapable of reducing to manageable proportions. Dr. Schweitzer argued the problem is solvable because the means of solution are within the scope of human intelligence and conscience. It is not enough, however, to say that our species is smart enough to survive. The proposition must be demonstrated. It is to that end that I hope this volume may serve a useful purpose.

N. C.

Note: Readers will note that the impersonal reference to Dr. Schweitzer throughout the manuscript takes a capital "D" as in the sentence: "When I came into the room,

the Doctor was standing at the piano." It was customary in Lambaréné to refer to Dr. Schweitzer in French as "Le Grand Docteur." The form used in translation is suggestive of the original and is not intended to reflect an excessive or objectionable veneration of someone who was quite human. Also, I realize that the general use of the term "man" or "his" when applied to humankind is grossly imperfect and I apologize to anyone who prefers the terms "his or hers" or "humankind" or "persons." In holding to the old convention, I intend no disrespect to half of the human species. As soon as a form is devised that does not sound clanking or that does not call attention to itself, I promise to use it. Language, like other forms of human relationships, has the obligation to reflect increasing awareness of human sensitivities.

Part I

—

A Visit to Lambaréné

At the end of dinner each evening at his jungle hospital in Lambaréné, French Equatorial Africa, Dr. Albert Schweitzer would fold his napkin, announce the number of the hymn to be sung, get up, and walk over to the upright piano on the other side of the room. He would arrange the hymn carefully on the music stand, study it for a moment, then start to play.

I doubt whether I shall ever forget my shock and disbelief when, the first evening of my visit, I saw him approach the upright. Earlier in the day, while exploring the hospital on my own, I had wandered into the dining room where Dr. Schweitzer and his staff of fifteen ate each day. The first thing that caught my eye was the piano. It must have been at least fifty years old. The keyboard was badly stained; large double screws fastened the ivory to each note. I tried to play but drew back almost instantly. The volume pedal was stuck and the reverberations of the harsh sounds hung in the air. One or more strings were missing on at least a dozen keys. The felt covering the hammers was worn thin and produced pinging effects.

Before coming to Lambaréné, I had heard that under equatorial conditions of extreme heat and moisture one doesn't even try to keep a piano in tune; you make your peace with the inevitable and do the best you can.

Even so, when I saw Dr. Schweitzer sit down at the piano and prop up the hymnbook, I winced. Here was one of history's greatest

interpreters of Bach, a man who could fill any concert hall in the world. The best grand piano ever made would be none too good for him. But he was now about to play a dilapidated upright virtually beyond repair. And he went at it easily and with the dignity that never leaves him.

I knew then that I would never be able to put out of my mind the image—painful in one sense, exalting in another—of Schweitzer at the old upright in Lambaréné. For here was the symbol, visible and complete, of everything he had given up in order to found a hospital in Africa. Renunciation by itself may mean little. What is renounced and the purpose of the renunciation—those are important. In the case of Albert Schweitzer, renunciation involved a distinguished career as organist and pianist; it extended to the intimate study and analysis of the nature of music in general and the organ in particular; it embraced a detailed understanding of the life and meaning of Johann Sebastian Bach. In all of this work there was the meticulous pursuit of perfection. Yet this did not exhaust the renunciation. There was a record in theology, philosophy, and history, in each of which Schweitzer had made major contributions as teacher and author. Solid foundations had been built for a lifelong career in any of these fields.

I wrote a moment ago that I felt not only pain but a certain inspiration in the image of Schweitzer at the old piano. For the amazing and wondrous thing was that the piano seemed to lose its poverty in his hands. Whatever its capacity was to yield music was now being fully realized. The tinniness and chattering echoes seemed subdued. It may be that this was the result of Schweitzer's intimate acquaintance with the piano, enabling him to avoid the rebellious keys and favoring only the cooperative ones. Whatever the reason, his being at the piano strangely seemed to make it right.

And, in a curious way, I discovered that this was to be true of almost everything else at Lambaréné. Schweitzer's being there made it right. Much of what you saw for the first time at the hospital seemed so primitive and inadequate as to startle. But when Dr. Schweitzer walked through the grounds, everything seemed as it should be. More than that: the profound meaning of Lambaréné

suddenly came to life. And I was to learn that there was a reason behind everything at Lambaréné.

I was also to get close to one of the things that drew me to Lambaréné—not Schweitzer's purpose, which was clear enough, but the sources of that purpose.

"You must come to Lambaréné," Emory Ross had said early in 1955. "There is something there that I can't capture for you in words, but it will mean much to you when you come near it."

Emory Ross was the head of the Schweitzer Fellowship in the United States. He was a former missionary devoting his life to advancing the cause of the African people. He had helped to build schools in various parts of Africa; he had brought promising African students to American colleges and universities; he had raised thousands of dollars for Dr. Schweitzer's hospital in Lambaréné.

After being with Emory Ross for only a minute or two, you felt you were with a country doctor whose knowledge and skill could put him at the head of almost any hospital in the country but who preferred to sit at the non-specialized bedsides of people who needed him. Emory Ross's manner was extraordinarily kind and reassuring; you never left him with the feeling that half of what you wanted to talk to him about had been left unsaid. Dr. Ross had known about my occasional correspondence with Dr. Schweitzer on world issues. In particular, he knew of my efforts to persuade Schweitzer to take a public stand on the world issues raised by nuclear weapons.

For a dozen or more years after the first atomic bomb was dropped on Hiroshima, there had been one voice that might have had a powerful effect on the biggest issue of the age, but that voice was silent. I knew that Albert Schweitzer had deliberately avoided political issues in order to confine himself to the fundamental and overriding moral questions of concern to the entire human community. But such an overriding question now existed. It was whether the conditions that made human life possible on this planet could be maintained.

Could anyone who was concerned about the problem of ethics in modern civilization exempt himself from such a question? Albert

Schweitzer believed in the sacredness of human life. Was there no moral issue if man's genes were to be twisted, if the air he breathed was to be fouled, if unborn generations were to be punished for his present failures?

The crisis could not be easily met by the political leaders of the nations. For the requirements of sovereignty too often came first. The political leader was the spearhead of that total sovereignty, its chief presiding officer. In order that the entire human grouping be served, it would become necessary to go beyond the nation; indeed, it would be necessary to create the means whereby the nation would find security through means other than massive armaments or coalitions. A man like Albert Schweitzer might enable people to develop a consciousness of their relationship to each other. Alongside the real threat to life on earth, the razor-sharp distinctions between peoples on earth had to be replaced with new connections and even new institutions.

If this in fact was not a fundamental issue, then the man who would see its fallacy was Albert Schweitzer. But if Albert Schweitzer agreed that the problem of nuclear war was real and universal, then it was important and proper for him to speak. And if his reluctance to speak was the result of humility or doubts as to whether his words would be heard, then one could at least attempt to remove these doubts.

My discussions with Emory Ross strengthened the view that it would be worthwhile to try to persuade Dr. Schweitzer to speak out. Ross would write to Dr. Schweitzer to find out if he would invite me to come to Lambaréné. He had already sent Dr. Schweitzer editorials and articles from *The Saturday Review*. He believed that the doctor, being isolated from day-to-day developments, would welcome an opportunity for a direct exchange of views.

There was something else on Emory Ross's mind.

"If you do go, you can help me in another effort I have been making for some time," he said. "I am worried about Dr. Schweitzer's unpublished manuscripts. I believe he has completed one of them. It is a major theological work; he has already titled it *The Kingdom of*

God. The other work he refers to is a philosophy of civilization. It is a very long work; he says it is a long way from being finished.

"What worries me," he continued, "is that something could happen to those manuscripts. Who knows, they might even be eaten up by the goats in Lambaréné. Or the ants. Then there is the climate to worry about. If we can just rescue those manuscripts. . . ."

Dr. Ross wrote Dr. Schweitzer. The response came in the form of a visit to me from Clara Urquhart, friend and confidant of the doctor and a frequent visitor to his jungle hospital. Clara Urquhart was a wisp of a woman, with dark luminous eyes and one of the most serene expressions I have seen on any human being anywhere. She had much to relate about Schweitzer—about his work and manuscripts, and, in general, about his state of mind. She said that Dr. Schweitzer was reluctant to break his vow of many years to avoid taking stands on public issues, but that he had read considerable material on the nuclear issue, including articles and editorials from *The Saturday Review.* He welcomed the letter from Emory Ross and was happy to invite me to come to Lambaréné.

"As for your main mission to get him to speak out on nuclear testing," she said, "you must not be discouraged if at first he resists." Later, I was to discover that no five words were more characteristic of Clara than "you must not be discouraged." She never underestimated the difficult but never made the mistake, either, of confusing the difficult with the impossible.

I asked about the manuscripts.

"I've been after him for years about it," she said.

"Can anything be done? Should anything be done?"

"Recently," she continued, "he promised me he would do some work on the manuscripts. He came to his room early in the afternoon and began to write. I returned an hour later and peeked into the room. The Doctor was no longer there. A breeze had blown some of the sheets of the manuscripts off the desk. An antelope had wandered into the room. Some of the sheets had been trampled upon. I had no way of knowing whether any had been eaten.

"I gathered up the papers and smoothed them out. Right then, I

became determined to see this through.

"When the Doctor returned to the room I told him what had happened. He shrugged. I said that even though he was reluctant to finish the manuscripts, the least he could do was to attend to the physical safety of his papers.

"Unlike previous occasions, when he brushed that kind of talk aside, this time he said nothing. My guess is that he is about ready to change his mind. I hope you will accept his invitation to come to Lambaréné. If you want an accomplice in your projects—the nuclear issues and the manuscripts—I'd like to volunteer."

You didn't have to be with Clara Urquhart very long to know that this slight, dark woman possessed a rare combination of intensity of feeling with calmness of manner. She knew how to establish the level of rapport in ten minutes that would take some people ten weeks. Also, she had the art of absolute relevance. When she listened, you had the feeling that all her energy was being mobilized in absorbing every sound and capturing your total intent. And when she spoke, she would address herself with precision to your questions or the things that interested you—and frequently to the thought behind your questions.

She had brought with her some photographs she had taken at Lambaréné over the years. Many of them were being incorporated in a book about Schweitzer shortly to be issued in London. Several of the photographs were intimate portraits of Dr. Schweitzer. They showed a face of vast power and purpose. It was lean and strong, with lines associated with expressiveness and sensitivity rather than with age. The eyes were set wide apart; they were like steel lanterns in the rugged landscape of his face.

Other photographs were of the people associated with Schweitzer at the hospital. These were people I wanted to meet, and I said so.

"When are you leaving for Lambaréné?" Clara Urquhart asked. I said I thought very soon.

Dr. Ross had told me that months would go by without the Doctor's being able to touch his manuscripts. Worse still was the fact that there were no carbon copies. The Doctor wrote in longhand on

faded sheets of paper. He was in the habit of hanging them on nails in his room; Dr. Ross spoke of the hazards of moisture, wandering goats, possible fire, and just plain loss.

"I tremble when I think of what would happen if some of that manuscript should come undone," he said.

We discussed various means of persuading the Doctor both to take the time necessary to finish his books and to provide for the safety of the manuscripts. We also considered various methods for making duplicate copies, and we agreed to investigate the comparative merits of microfilming, duplicating machines, and plain photography. None of these devices, of course, could be used without the permission and cooperation of the Doctor himself. And here we anticipated trouble. Emory Ross emphasized that Dr. Schweitzer was a perfectionist who was severely reluctant to part with anything he wrote that was not absolutely final and complete.

"It's too easy for the Doctor to say no to me. You've got to go and put it to him. It won't be easy. If his mind is made up about something, it takes some real powers of persuasion to move him. Even if we don't succeed, it is important that you go. It will be an experience you'll never forget."

In the weeks that followed, Dr. Ross and I met with other members of the Schweitzer Fellowship. I recall with particular pleasure a luncheon with Erica Anderson, Jerome Hill, and Eugene Exman. Erica Anderson had just returned from Lambaréné where she had worked on a film biography of Dr. Schweitzer. She had also just completed, in collaboration with Eugene Exman, vice-president of Harper & Brothers, a picture-and-text book about Dr. Schweitzer and the hospital.

A picture formed in my mind of Schweitzer as an austere and remote figure who could be approached only with the greatest care. I found it interesting that even those who knew him best had to conjecture about his responses to situations. They had to plan any action involving him as carefully as they would the strategy for a military campaign.

Erica Anderson's eyes were sparkling with the challenge. "I think

maybe the best thing to do would be just to go there," she said. "As for the manuscript project, tell the Doctor what you want to do. But just don't turn up with a lot of equipment showing. I made the mistake of doing that once and ought to know."

The planning for the trip began. I had two more meetings with Clara Urquhart before she left for London. At one of these meetings she had a long checklist of questions to be asked and things to be done.

"How's your French?" she asked. "The Doctor does not speak English though he reads it with little difficulty and understands far more than he admits."

"My French is about the way you describe the Doctor's English."

"What about German?"

"Nil."

"You must not be discouraged," she said. "The Doctor is accustomed to communicating with English-speaking visitors through an interpreter, in German."

When I asked who would do the interpreting, Clara Urquhart said this was all part of the work of the "accomplice's" job that she had volunteered to perform.

Her plan was to leave for London and Rome to see some friends, then to return to her home in Johannesburg for a month. We could meet in Johannesburg, perhaps, she said, then go to Lambaréné. Meanwhile, she would write to Dr. Schweitzer to say that we were definitely coming.

"You'd better make up your mind to stay for a full week or more," she said. "The Doctor says that short visits make him nervous."

I agreed to stay for as long as was required to do the job.

"Now," she said, "comes the most important matter of all. You've got to promise that you won't be disillusioned."

I smiled.

"You mean a hospital ward without bedsheets, lack of sanitation, and all that sort of thing?" I said. "Please don't let it worry you; I know all about it. It was this kind of argument that seemed to me all along to miss the main point about Schweitzer."

"There's something more important than that," she replied. "I'm talking about Schweitzer himself."

This startled me. "Why is there any danger that I or anyone else would be disillusioned about Schweitzer?"

"Some people are. They come to Lambaréné with an image of a sweet and saintly St. Francis feeding the birds and they see instead a driving man fighting the jungle and African lethargy and they do not remain for a sufficiently long period to see or sense the goodness and power underneath. They go away feeling hurt and unhappy."

I was touched by her concern but still puzzled. What was there about Schweitzer that created "hurt and unhappy" feelings in people? Whatever the answer, I couldn't guarantee Clara Urquhart what my feelings would be after I met him.

"Of course not," she said. "I just want to be sure you'll stay long enough to get over some first impressions that may not be so favorable."

"Such as?"

"Such as the fact that those who do not know the Doctor will think that his manner toward the indigenous black is unfeeling and authoritarian.

"Such as the fact that his views seem to reflect little confidence in the Africans to whom he has given his life. Schweitzer has deeper and wider dimensions than anyone else I have met. If evaluated from a superficial viewpoint the image is distorted. For better or for worse Schweitzer is a patriarch. I remember saying to him that he was an enlightened despot—to which he replied: 'An enlightened despot is able to give the greatest amount of freedom.'

"If one fails to remember that his basic motivation is reverence for life—he might seem arbitrary in his dealings with those around him. Just wait and observe for the first few days."

Before long, I was on my way to Lambaréné.

The air connection from Brazzaville to Lambaréné in French Equatorial Africa was probably the most hazardous regularly scheduled

flight in the world. It was operated by Air France over jungle mountain country. But the safety record of this particular run was close to the top among the world's airlines.

The men who flew the DC-3 on these jungle hops had earned a high reputation in the society of world airline pilots. The African "airports" at which they stopped had no radio beams for guiding planes through fog and rain, no light towers or signal beacons flashing across the sky, no neon ground markers or flares, no paved landing strips to pick out from the air—just a clearing with a dirt or grass strip. There were no sprawling cities to help a pilot get his bearings, no air terminal buildings or anything approaching them—generally, just a single small structure that served as an open shelter. Jungle country tends to look pretty much alike when you fly north from the Congo. Yet these airmen had a homing-pigeon touch at the controls that was the talk of their trade.

While we were waiting at the Brazzaville airport for the announcement that our plane was ready, Clara Urquhart called out to a tall, slender young man of about thirty who had just walked into the terminal building. She identified him as Dr. Frank Catchpool, from the staff of the Schweitzer Hospital.

Dr. Catchpool was obviously deeply pleased to see her. It developed that she had made the original arrangements with Dr. Schweitzer for Dr. Catchpool to go to Lambaréné. Frank Catchpool was an English citizen and a Quaker who, like many others, had been inspired by Dr. Schweitzer's example. When he first met Clara in London, he inquired about the hospital and his chances for joining the staff. Clara wrote to Dr. Schweitzer and the matter was arranged.

Now, at the Brazzaville airport, Clara was able to chat with him for the first time since he had been at Lambaréné. We learned that he had been at the hospital a little more than a month. He had come to Brazzaville five days earlier, he said somewhat ruefully, because of a little dog.

It all began about a week ago, he explained. One of the managers of a nearby French lumber camp had brought his pet dog, breed

anonymous, to the hospital. The dog had been suffering for some weeks with a persistent cough. Dr. Schweitzer's hospital turns away no patients, regardless of color, species, or previous condition of servitude. And so the manager put his dog under Dr. Schweitzer's care. The staff held a consultation; the consensus was that a bone was stuck in his throat. There being no X-ray machines in operation at Lambaréné, the diagnosis could not be confirmed. In any event, it was decided to operate.

Dr. Catchpool, who had had some previous experience, volunteered to apply the anesthetic. He cautioned the other surgeons and nurses about the astounding power in the sudden moves of even a small animal at the time the anesthetic is applied.

His apprehensions were all too accurate. Just as the anesthetic was applied to his mouth, the dog jerked free and bit Dr. Catchpool on the arm. A second attempt was successful, and the small obstruction was removed.

That evening, Dr. Catchpool's arm began to swell and showed discoloration. There being no anti-rabies serum at the hospital, Dr. Schweitzer ordered both Dr. Catchpool and the dog to depart immediately for the hospital at Brazzaville, the former to receive anti-rabies injections, the latter to be put under observation. And now, four days later, both patients were returning to Lambaréné, the doctor having had his shots, and the dog having developed no symptoms of rabies. The dog was now in a crate that was already checked in and waiting to be loaded.

"I wish I could say I didn't feel pretty silly about this whole business," Dr. Catchpool said. "Dr. Schweitzer must have a rather poor opinion of me for having allowed myself to get into this mess. Here I am at the hospital only a few weeks and I get immobilized by a little dog."

Clara said she was certain that Dr. Schweitzer had only the most sympathetic understanding of the situation.

"That brings up something else," he said. "I'm afraid I don't know where I stand with the Doctor. We've hardly spoken, except for the most routine things. I haven't wanted to go directly to him and tell

him about the kind of work I'd like to do at the hospital or to discuss other things on my mind. I just haven't got the heart to take up a moment of his time."

"You must not be discouraged," Clara said. "You recall that I asked you not to form any judgments until you had been there at least a month. Give yourself a little more time. Many of the things that are troubling you now will fall into place. What kind of work have you been doing at the hospital?"

Dr. Catchpool grinned.

"I'm the chief electrician and engineer," he said. "I diagnose faulty wiring and operate on sluggish generators."

"I'm sure what you are doing is most essential," Clara said. "Besides, if I may say so, some of this at least is your own fault. You insisted that I say nothing to the Doctor about your excellence as a physician or your very high recommendations. The Doctor is disposed to take people at their own evaluation of themselves. And I'm sure that when you got to Lambaréné, you persisted in underrating yourself. But you must not be discouraged. Your chance will come."

An attendant came over to announce that our plane was ready. Dr. Catchpool went off to look after the dog. Clara and I collected our hand luggage and boarded the plane. A moment later Dr. Catchpool joined us.

The air distance between Brazzaville and Lambaréné is perhaps no more than four hundred miles on a straight line. But the planes fly a zigzag route in order to cover the various jungle air stations en route to Lambaréné. The flight therefore generally requires from five to six hours. I memorized the colorful names of the jungle towns at which we stopped so I could tell Ellen and the girls about them when I returned—names like Djambala, Mayumba, Tchibanga, Mouila.

At each stop, curious children from surrounding villages would gather near the open shelter close to the landing strip. They would cluster together and stare with open-eyed wonder at the gleaming steel bird. At Tchibanga two children at the edge of the crowd were having a short game of catch with a rubber ball. I walked toward

them and made the kind of throwing motion that indicated I wanted to be invited to join in. One of them tossed me the ball. I threw it back, then he smiled broadly and put some muscle into his next pitch.

I looked at the other children. They seemed astonished to observe a white man obviously enjoying himself in a game with black children. Then, suddenly, a clamor went up as at least fifty youngsters called out to join the fun. I would toss the ball into a sea of waving arms and out it would come again. One boy, about twelve or thirteen, sprang high in the air and caught the ball with one hand. Then he ran off at a distance of about forty yards so that he could show me how far he could throw. This in turn set up a cry from at least a dozen others who wanted to do the same. Almost before I knew it, children were streaking all over the airport clearing. It made me think of one of those bullfighting festivals when the spectators come swarming down into the arena to try their luck with the brave bulls.

The two African policemen stationed at the field seemed agreeable enough when the game of catch had started innocently a few minutes earlier. But now the point of diminishing returns in their good will was just being reached. I beckoned to the youngsters that the game was over, handed the ball to its young owner, and thanked him.

Then I opened my camera and asked my ball-playing companion for the privilege of his photograph. Instead of ending the clamor, this merely set a new stage for it. In a matter of seconds, the crowd closed in on me and pinned me to the spot as each child called out for his right to be photographed.

All this while, Clara and Dr. Catchpool stood on the far side of the crowd, close to the plane. They were enjoying themselves hugely. Clara's expression as much as said: "You got yourself into it; now get yourself out of it."

Finally, the two African policemen made it clear to the youngsters that the big steel bird was ready to go into the sky again, and they helped to detach me from their midst. I doubt whether I shall ever forget the high-pitched deafening yells of *au revoir* and the wildly

waving arms of the children as I boarded the plane.

"I hope you noticed how the children drew back at first when you approached but how quickly they responded when they saw that you wanted to make friends," Clara said after the plane had leveled off in flight.

It was, I agreed, very striking.

"You will find that this same thing is true of Africans of all ages almost everywhere on the continent," she said. "There is that initial hesitation. They are not sure what you want or intend to do. They are conditioned to react almost chemically against a white skin. But once you make it clear that you approach them as friends, the response is warm and hearty, almost overwhelming."

She paused, and her words seemed to hang in the air for a moment.

"Let me amend that a bit," she said. "I suddenly realize that this is the kind of observation I would have made almost automatically only a few years ago. But it is no longer true; at least, not to the same extent."

"In three or four minutes we ought to be able to see the hospital from the plane," said Dr. Catchpool from across the aisle in the Air France DC-3. "These pilots are very thoughtful fellows. When they know that some of their passengers are going to the Schweitzer Hospital, they generally make a run over the place."

Dr. Catchpool was right. We flew over the Ogowe River, which connects the south Atlantic with the interior of the middle Congo. From the air, the Ogowe was a light muddy brown. Here and there along the river, we could see small African villages. Then there was a cluster of buildings, with a church tower in the center. Dr. Catchpool identified this as the town of Lambaréné.

Then, suddenly, Dr. Catchpool called out and pointed to the hospital. It consisted of a series of long, narrow buildings close to the river. Red rooftops interrupted the jungle only briefly. Immediately beyond was the deep and endless green.

The Lambaréné airstrip, like all the others we had seen en route from Brazzaville, was just a dirt clearing in the jungle. The "terminal" was a large lean-to in which waiting passengers could shelter themselves from the sun. There were, of course, no mechanical installations or gasoline trucks for servicing the plane.

The reception committee at the airport consisted of Dr. Jan van Stolk and Mme. Oberman. Clara introduced us. Dr. van Stolk was the senior staff doctor at the Schweitzer Hospital. He was a native Hollander who had gone to medical school in the Union of South Africa and who had left a growing practice to come to Lambaréné. He was about thirty-two.

Mme. Oberman had worked with Dr. Schweitzer some months each year for about four years. She, too, came from Holland. (Many of the members of the staff, I later learned, came from Holland.) She worked in a general supervisory capacity, taking care of the needs of the hospital personnel.

The entire party got into the back of a truck and sat on benches along the sides. I was thankful for the overhead canvas. It was noon and the equatorial sun was living up to its reputation.

We drove for perhaps a mile and a half over a bumpy dirt road, alongside which were scattered African dwellings. Then we came to a clearing, just beyond which was the river. At the narrow wooden dock was a long pirogue, the sturdy and graceful native canoe specially built to withstand the powerful currents of the Ogowe.

Our bags were loaded into the pirogue by a half-dozen young men who comprised our crew. I sat up front near Mme. Oberman. Behind us were Dr. van Stolk and Clara and the young men who sang in rhythm to their strokes with the paddles. The trip to the hospital is against the current, and so we stayed close to the shoreline. I marveled at the staminia, power, and good spirits of the young Africans as they paddled us upstream. And I recalled something that Dr. Schweitzer had written in one of his early books, *On the Edge of the Primeval Forest*. Shortly after he founded his hospital in Lambaréné, it became necessary to make an emergency canoe journey into the interior. For hour after hour, the African natives insisted on

staying at their paddles. It was an endurance feat that made a profound impression on the Doctor, and he resolved to remember it every time he was tempted to regard the Africans as shiftless or lacking in energy.

I recalled, too, that it was on his canoe trips that Dr. Schweitzer felt that conditions were most congenial for the exercise of the moral imagination. This I could readily understand. There is a total awareness of nature, if only because the contrasts are so compelling. The stillness over the water is made dramatic by the cries of the birds in the jungle. The sky is a silver sheath sparkling in the sun in contrast with the soft filtered light of the forest. The power of the current in the center of the stream contrasts with the easy play of the waters near the shore. I could understand why Dr. Schweitzer wrote that he could never take a canoe up or down the river without reflecting on the importance of reverence for life.

"The Doctor loves the river," Mme. Oberman said as if reading my thoughts. "Perhaps you will have a chance to take a ride with him in a canoe. When you do you will marvel at his expression, at his concentration."

I asked Mme. Oberman if the Doctor was in good health; some reports I had heard recently were disturbing.

"You will see for yourself," she said. "He is in fine health. His energy is high and he is in good spirits. Watch now; soon we will see the hospital."

The hospital is around a bend in the river and you do not have a good view of it until you swing around and come toward it downstream. In order to do this your canoe continues perhaps a third of a mile or more on the opposite shore beyond the hospital so that when you cross the river the current will not carry you beyond the dock.

As the canoe swung into midstream, I discovered some figures dressed in white walking down the hill from the hospital toward the small dock. Clara waved toward the shore. When we were about three hundred feet from the dock, I recognized the Doctor. He was at the edge of the dock now, waving to us. Then, when the canoe

was within perhaps fifty feet, he began to call out directions. It was like a ferry being eased into her slip by commands from the bridge.

"A gauche! A gauche!" the Doctor cried out. "Lentement!" Then, sharply, "Arretez!"

He stooped and grabbed the prow, then eased the canoe alongside the dock. The Africans held the pirogue firm, and the Doctor reached over to help us out, one at a time. As he took my arm, he introduced himself, then went over to greet Clara warmly. He turned to Dr. Catchpool and inquired about both the health of the doctor and the health of the dog. Dr. Catchpool replied that he was well and that he had brought the dog back apparently none the worse for the experience.

The Doctor then took my arm and escorted me up the hill to the hospital. The lane was narrow and we threaded our way past some small shacks and enclosures on the hillside. The ground underneath was moist and slippery and had the consistency of a chickenyard. The reason was readily apparent. Almost everywhere I looked there were chickens, ducks, goats. Dr. Schweitzer halted the procession to permit a mother hen and a half-dozen baby chicks to cross the path. "I'm falling behind on hospital affairs," he said. "I didn't even know she was expecting."

Then the path opened out on a courtyard, with low-lying wooden structures. The building on the left was mounted on concrete piles about six or seven feet above the ground. This was where the doctor and the immediate members of his staff lived. Directly opposite were some utility and storage buildings, also set on concrete piles a few feet off the ground.

At the foot of the steps leading to the Doctor's quarters was Mrs. Schweitzer. I had been told she was not well and was able to get about the hospital grounds only with the greatest difficulty. The Doctor introduced me. Mrs. Schweitzer spoke in English; she was most gracious, apologizing for the fact that she was unable to accompany me to my room, and saying she hoped I would drop by for a chat after I got settled. We resumed our walk, the Doctor leading the way past several other frame buildings, each with its dark-red

corrugated-iron rooftop. One could hardly see the sky because of the thick benevolent overhead shelter from the trees. In a moment we were walking along the porch of a long single-story bungalow consisting of about twelve rooms for members of the staff.

The Doctor opened the door to my room, bid me rest a while and then come to the dining room for lunch. He apologized in French for the fact that he didn't speak English and said that the only place in the world where he would dare to speak English was Edinburgh, for the people there had a habit of speaking very slowly.

I thanked the Doctor and began to tell him how privileged I felt in being able to be with him at his hospital. He cut me short with a wave of his hand, saying with a smile, "Pas des compliments."

The room was far nicer than I had expected. Walls and furniture were painted white. The room was only six or seven feet wide but it had everything one might need: small writing table and oil lamp, bookshelf, wooden cabinet for clothes, and a stand for water basin, pitcher, and toilet articles. The bed was an iron four-poster, fairly narrow, with a thin mattress. It was firm, just the way I like it, and did not sag.

One end of the room was screened in and opened out on the slope going down to the clinic and the hospital wards. Beyond was the river Ogowe, shimmering in the midday sun. Some Africans in their pirogues were drifting downstream. It was warm, but not uncomfortably so. I was delighted with my first fifteen minutes in Lambaréné.

I looked closely at the Doctor as he chatted with Clara across the luncheon table. His skin was pink and firm. His eyes were clear, his manner was alert. He was in excellent health. It seemed to me unbelievable that this vigorous, fully functioning man was about to mark his eighty-second birthday. When he had led me up the walk from the docks to my bungalow I had to step quickly to keep pace.

He asked about his various friends in the United States by name, beginning with Emory Ross, and I was happy to be able to tell him that they were all in good health. When he asked about Erica Anderson and Jerome Hill, who had just produced the motion picture

about his life, I told him that I had seen a preview of the film and felt certain that it would be well received. I added that he was well on his way to becoming a movie idol in the United States.

He smiled. "Well, who knows, I may be famous yet."

One of the attendants came into the room with a baby gorilla clinging to her neck. She sat down on a bench in front of the wide window. The doctor beamed every time he looked over at the gorilla. For the next few minutes he discussed gorillas and their high order of intelligence, saying that gorillas were much closer to man in the scale of evolution than they were to the chimpanzee. Then he got up and walked over to the bench and took the baby gorilla in his lap. He put his head down so the gorilla could play with his massive head of unruly gray hair. Now and then the gorilla would tug fairly hard and the doctor would wince, but say nothing. He had the look of an adoring grandfather.

That first afternoon, after lunch, I had a chance to talk to Dr. Margaret van der Kreek, a lovely young woman of about thirty from the Netherlands. She was chief of surgery at the hospital. She preferred to be addressed as Dr. Margaret, although her colleagues referred to her as "La Doctoresse." I could readily understand why Clara had called her one of the most beautiful women in the world. There was nothing mechanical about her appearance. Light-colored hair was combed straight back and held in place by a simple ribbon. She wore no lipstick or other makeup. Yet she possessed an unmistakable quality of classic loveliness of both feature and expression. I wondered abut this attractive creature—how she happened to go into medicine and surgery, why she came to Lambaréné. Here was the raw material from which legends were fashioned.

A young African mother, her face heavy with apprehension, carried in a five- or six-year-old girl and set her down next to La Doctoresse. The child was wide-eyed and fearful. She clung to her mother's faded skirt with both hands.

La Doctoresse knelt down alongside the child and spoke to her reassuringly, then stroked her head as, speaking through an interpreter, she asked the mother the trouble. The mother said the child

had persistent fever. Still kneeling and speaking softly, La Doctoresse took her stethoscope and applied it to the child's chest. Then, very deftly, she put a tongue depressor in the child's mouth. The little girl coughed involuntarily, then cried out. La Doctoresse reached behind her and took a little wooden doll from one of the drawers in her desk. She made small clucking sounds as she held the doll alluringly in front of the little girl. While the child scrutinized the doll, La Doctoresse lifted the child's dress and examined the lower part of her body.

Then she smoothed the little girl's dress and told her that it was all over and that she would soon be well again. The child smiled shyly, still holding the doll. La Doctoresse told the mother the child had malaria but that it could be brought under control. The child was assigned to a place in the wards, and La Doctoresse wrote out instructions for her care and a prescription to be filled by the hospital apothecary. Then she asked the African interpreter to have the woman repeat everything said to her, just to be sure she understood.

In keeping with the custom at the hospital, the woman was asked whether she could afford to pay anything. Dr. Schweitzer believed that people are more respectful of advice, especially of a medical nature, if they have to pay for it.

The woman was prepared for the question. She opened her hand and offered La Doctoresse one hundred francs (the equivalent of about twenty-five cents), an amount that was slightly above the average. La Doctoresse thanked her, then carefully made a notation of the revenue in the accounts book in which the daily fees from patients were entered.

I could see that the woman had something to say to La Doctoresse but was choked up. The heavy apprehension in her face was gone; now there was measureless relief and gratitude. I wondered what went through her mind as she looked at this white goddess with the golden hair who had such knowledge and skill as only the most gifted of men were supposed to possess. I could tell the woman was struggling for a correct way to make known her feelings. Then she reached out and lightly touched Dr. Margaret's arm. It was a simple gesture

but profound in intent. Dr. Margaret responded with the smile not
of a doctor but of one woman communicating with another in a universal language.

It was time now to close the clinic for the afternoon. Dr. Margaret
marked some notations in the accounts book, then closed her desk.
We walked up the short hill to the bungalow where the staff lived.

"You must see my garden," Dr. Margaret said. "The jungle flowers are just now coming up."

In front of the porch leading to her room, Dr. Margaret had built
a small wire enclosure of perhaps no more than six by eight feet.
Inside, protected from the goats and other wandering animals, were
the young shoots of jungle flowers. I couldn't identify them nor do
I remember their names; but Dr. Margaret named them for me one
by one as she ran a finger around the tender buds. What I do remember vividly is the joy and pride that this lovely woman took in creating a tiny sanctuary for a few flowers.

It was late afternoon. The sun had lost its fever and a small wind
came up from the river and eased the heaviness in the air.

Dr. Margaret sat down on one of the porch steps. It had been an
exhausting day, and now she rested her head on her hands and
breathed in the coolness.

"Do you like Lambaréné?" she asked. "It has all the things that
are difficult to find outside. A chance to concentrate on your work;
quiet when you need it; and, most of all, freedom from all the nonessential things that fill one's life."

"Non-essentials?"

She looked at me sternly.

"Surely you must know," she said. "The non-essentials of life in
Europe and America. The endless running around in circles to do
things that seem a matter of life and death at the time but that you
can't remember two days later. The business of struggling with a
checking account at the end of the month to make sure there's enough
to cover all the things that we bought but that we don't even know
where to put. And the desperate way we try to entertain ourselves.

"Here at Lambaréné, we do nicely without the frills. We have a

purpose and we apply ourselves to it. We never have to ask ourselves whether we are really needed. We are never at wits' ends for what to do with our time. When our work is over for the day we can sit down and rest or we can make our tea and talk among ourselves or we can read and we can think. It is very good. Do you find this strange?"

I told Dr. Margaret that I had nothing but admiration for the people at Lambaréné and for their ability to come to terms with life.

"It may take you a little time to understand Lambaréné," she said. "So many people come here just for overnight and go away appalled. You know, there's a reason for everything at Lambaréné, but it takes a little time to find it out."

I said that I had been carefully indoctrinated by Clara and that I would do my best to get to know the real Lambaréné.

"That is good," she said. "Maybe you will not make the mistake of judging this as you would a modern hospital. It is a jungle village with a clinic. If Dr. Schweitzer had put up a fully equipped modern hospital of the kind you see in large cities, I am not sure the natives would come to it. They would probably be afraid of it. They must understand something before they give themselves to it. The hospital here they understand. It is very simple. If a person gets sick and the local remedies are of no use and the sickness stays on, the entire family gets into a pirogue and paddles—sometimes many, many miles—to the clinic here at Lambaréné. When they arrive, they find an African village very much like the one they left. If the patient has to be hospitalized, we assign the entire family to a cubicle in one of the shelters. The people go into the woods for their toilet and take care of their own refuse. They get their water from the wells. They cook their own food. They can get fish from the river. We give them bananas and some rice. They get the rest from the trees. We do the diagnosis and supply the medicines and check up on the progress of the patients. When they get better they go home."

"Do you manage to establish any real contact with your patients?" I asked. "Do you find yourself getting caught up in the lives of the

people you treat so that you have a real emotional stake in what happens to them?"

Dr. Margaret looked up. "It is true that there are many patients. So very many patients. Each day they come. It is hard to keep track of them, and many of them we see just once. But at the time they stand before you and tell you their story you make the contact. I think this has nothing to do with Lambaréné necessarily. It comes with being a doctor. A person comes to you and describes his ailment. You observe him carefully. You watch closely for a little sign that will tell you what you must know. And the patient will not have confidence in you if he senses that the contact has not been made."

I asked the question I had wanted to ask her since I first saw her in the dining room for the staff. I asked how it was she came to Lambaréné.

Dr. Margaret reached over the wire fence and ran her hand lightly along one of the young shoots. She said she had wanted to be a doctor ever since she was old enough to think about what she wanted to do with her life. Her father was an artist, her mother a poet. She grew up in an atmosphere of kindness, graciousness, and intelligence. She was aware that the great happiness enjoyed by her parents in their relationship to each other and her own resultant happiness were not the lot of all people. Her family suffered no deprivations, not even during the depression; and her father felt the obligation to do what he could to help others when he could.

All this created a determination in her to serve. Medicine seemed an effective way. Then she read about Dr. Schweitzer and his work in Africa. She doubted that the Doctor would accept her, but she decided she would get the most comprehensive medical and surgical training available and then volunteer. She knew that many of the persons on the Lambaréné staff came from Holland; at least she could get one of them to write a letter of introduction.

After she completed her internship the introductory letter was written to Dr. Schweitzer.

"Then very soon after that came his reply," she said, reliving the experience in her brightened expression. "He would take me. His letter was amazing. Dozens of details. He put each one down. How I was to travel, what the timetable was, where I was to change trains and so forth, what my work would consist of in Lambaréné, how I was to go about making arrangements for passports, and the kind of clothes I would probably need. And there was an air of great kindness in everything he said.

"It is now two years since I arrived. At first, like most of the others who came, I was puzzled by many things, sometimes even disappointed. But the more I stay the more I understand and the stronger is my admiration for the Doctor. I know now why things are done the way they are.

"People know the Doctor as a great philosopher and theologian. I am lucky to know him as a human being. It is fantastic all the things he does every day and the things he manages to keep in mind. He has been after me for several months to take a holiday. I have been putting it off but finally I will leave. Next month I go to South Africa. A surgeon, Dr. Jack Penn, visited the hospital here recently. There are new techniques in reconstructive surgery I want to learn. Dr. Penn invited me to work at his hospital. After I accepted, Dr. Schweitzer took it on himself to make all the arrangements for passport and visas. Only two days ago, he went in the pirogue to the village and filled out the forms. He brought back the forms for me to sign. Then, because there was some hurry in the matter, he took the pirogue again to the village and didn't return until long after dinner. Maybe he spent six or seven hours that day to save me the trouble. No detail escapes him. Everything has to be just so; and whenever he comes across something that he knows will be especially burdensome, he never asks someone else to do it, though we pray that he will, but goes ahead quietly and does it himself."

"Who will do your work while you are in South Africa?" I asked.

"Right now, we are very fortunate at the hospital. We have enough doctors. You have met Dr. van Stolk. He comes from Holland, too. He is very young but he is very talented and he is very precise. Dr.

Schweitzer leans on him heavily. Dr. Friedmann is a completely dedicated man. He has a fine background of experience. We have teamed up in the clinic and there is nothing about the operation of the clinic he does not know. You probably have heard that Dr. Friedmann lost all his relatives in the concentration camps of Germany during the war. He is not embittered. He asks only to be allowed to serve because he himself was spared. Then there is Dr. Cyril Coulon. He, too, is young. His wife is with him. Soon they will have a baby. They will have it here at the hospital. Mrs. Coulon is such a fine young woman. The Coulons have worked in the jungle before. They are Dutch. They have gone out by themselves into the jungle villages to help supply medical help. Now they are here to help Dr. Schweitzer. Dr. Coulon knows the Africans well; he is a great asset to our staff. Dr. Catchpool you have already spoken to on the plane. He has not been here very long. He has done no medical work so far but I can tell that he has had excellent training. He is a sensitive man. There will be no shortage of doctors while I am gone. When I come back, Dr. van Stolk will go on leave for six months. There is always a great deal of rotation going on."

Dr. Friedmann came up the path and greeted us. He was soft spoken and there was shyness in his manner. He had an enormous jet-black mustache; it made me think of some of the photographs of Schweitzer at the age of thirty. When Dr. Friedmann sat down on the stoop and crossed his arms on his knees I could see, on the inside forearm, the number tattooed on him at the concentration camp. He would carry the number as long as he lived. He noticed that I was staring at it.

"Just a souvenir; you're welcome to look at it," he said, holding up his arm.

I told Dr. Friedmann that La Doctoresse had been telling me about her approaching holiday and about the things that led to her decision to come to Lambaréné.

"Actually, it is not much different from the rest of us," he said. "Some of us may have come here because we were in good circumstances and didn't feel quite right about it; others because they were

in difficult circumstances yet managed somehow to survive, and they wanted to find some way of acknowledging their debt. But always it is the debt. And always you will find that somewhere we happened to read something by Albert Schweitzer that opened up a big door in our mind and made us know we had to come."

Just then, we heard explosions of joy from the far end of the porch. Three or four of the nurses were holding bright-colored dresses to themselves, their arms clasping the garments to their waists and their chins pressing against the necks of the dresses. They swirled around and squealed ecstatically.

"Dr. Margaret, come quick," one of them shouted. "Clara brought each of us a dress."

Clara was leaning against the porch railing near the end of the bungalow. Even at a distance I could see that she was deeply pleased.

Dr. Margaret jumped to her feet with the bright alertness of a child being offered a surprise gift. She ran down the porch. Clara reached into a box and took out a long blue cotton dress and handed it to Dr. Margaret, who exclaimed her thanks and then rushed into her room to try it on. Three minutes later she emerged, smiling and radiant. The dress fit perfectly.

"Look at Margaret!" exclaimed Trudi Bochsler, the nurse in charge of the lepers. "She looks like a movie star. Only more beautiful."

Then the other young women rushed into their rooms to try on their own new dresses. When they returned, it almost seemed as though the place had been touched with magic. Each woman proclaimed her delight with the appearance of the others. More appealing than anything else were their expressions of satisfied wonder as they danced up and down the porch, their dresses swooshing and swirling.

"How does it feel to be Mrs. Santa Claus?" I asked Clara. She was beaming.

"You have no idea how much they hunger for the chance to dress up and do the attractive things most young women take for granted," she said. "It's so easy to forget that even dedicated women like this— women of serious purpose and high intelligence—are still warm and

wonderful and full of eagerness and feminine charm."

Albertina van Beek Vollenhoven, a nurse in charge of one of the wards, spun around and clapped her hands. "Tonight we will have a party," she exulted. "We will surprise Dr. Schweitzer. We will wear our dresses to dinner. And we will fix our hair."

Albertina was auburn-haired. Even in the early evening light I could see that her face was flushed with excitement. Yet there was an essential quality of composure about Albertina that seemed to cause her to draw back as soon as she saw she had become the center of attention.

But Albertina never had the chance to develop any second thoughts about her suggestion, for the others seized upon it with whoops of agreement. They would wear their new dresses to dinner, they would put ribbons in their hair—and, some of them would use lipstick. They would all gather in the dining room several minutes early and would be in their places when the doctor walked in.

The plan was a complete success. When Dr. Schweitzer walked into the dining room, the women—scrubbed, shining, bright-eyed—were all wearing their new dresses. They were sitting in their customary places, trying to make it appear that nothing special had happened.

The Doctor, in a split second, took it all in. His eyes danced behind the craglike brows. I could see he had a vast delight.

"Thank you for letting me come to your banquet," he said in the manner of a man who had just arrived at the Queen's ball. Then, when he sat down and the customary silence occurred so that he could say grace, he said that he was so overwhelmed by all the beauty around him that he had forgotten all the grace prayers he ever knew.

The Doctor leaned forward in the manner he adopted when saying grace, and the entire table became silent. I couldn't help noticing that the prayer of thankfulness had a special meaning for everyone on the staff.

The Doctor finished saying grace and looked up.

"I, too, have a contribution to make to the festive banquet," he announced. "A case of wine that was sent here some time ago and

has been waiting for just such an occasion as this. It is a very fine burgundy. We will all dine superbly tonight and drink to each other's health. And tonight—there will be butter!"

The mood of the staff that evening, like the wine itself, had a delicious sparkle to it. Only a few hours earlier, nothing out of the ordinary had been anticipated. Then, suddenly, the evening had been transformed into a surprise party—and each person was the guest of honor.

I looked around the long table. The men were obviously pleased with the sudden assertion of femininity by Dr. Margaret and the nurses. Three of the four male doctors were young and unmarried. While the men were certainly not unaware of the young women on the staff at any time, their appreciation under ordinary circumstances was subordinated to the unending demands of the hospital. For the main part, their relationship was professional. But now, for the moment at least, the circumstances had changed. The dining room was transformed into a small banquet hall.

It was interesting to see the way the occasion affected the conversation. Usually the people on the staff spoke about the work of the day or about matters related to the hospital. But now, appealing nonsense was in order.

"Dr. Schweitzer, we want you to settle a bet," Dr. Margaret said. "Trudi and I have just been talking about champagne and how it is made. She says it is made just like wine and I said it can't be because of the fizz and the sparkle in it."

Dr. Schweitzer was equal to the occasion. For almost five minutes he expounded on champagne—how it was developed historically, what goes into it, why it is expensive, what kind of water is necessary, how it is bottled in order to keep the carbonation, etc. It was an astounding tour de force on the one subject in the world that he might be expected to know least about.

Neither Dr. Margaret nor Trudi had been completely correct and the bet was declared a stand-off.

Then the conversation somehow veered off into playwriting and acting, and from there into exploration and geology, and finally into

furniture-making. On each subject the Doctor would listen carefully and then come forward with a surprising wealth of observation backed with historical information, dates, and intricate detail. With respect to furniture, the Doctor identified the soft woods and the hard woods, and spoke vividly of their uses, the relative expense in their manufacture, and the competitive problems in the world market for fine woods.

Whenever the conversation seemed on the verge of getting too heavy, the doctor restored the mood of gaiety with an amusing anecdote, which invariably had a point to make. One of these anecdotes grew out of a question on the declining powers of observation of older people.

"Naturally, it all depends on the person you are talking about," he said with mock seriousness. "When I was a boy of sixteen, I was very much under my grandfather's thumb. One day a cousin of my age of whom I was very fond came to visit me. We wanted to leave the house for a certain purpose but feared Grandfather might not give us permission. And so we told him we wanted to visit our uncle some blocks distant, and he said we might go.

"When we were out of viewing range from the house, we turned sharply and went in the direction of our real destination—a beer tavern. After we were there about ten minutes a man sat down at our table. It was our grandfather.

" 'An old man isn't as blind as you might think,' my grandfather said. 'And sometimes he is just as thirsty as younger men. Why didn't you invite me to come with you in the first place? Now pour me a drink.' "

Then Dr. Schweitzer looked at me with a twinkle in his eye.

"I'd better be careful," he said, "or Mr. Cousins will think I do nothing except tell funny stories."

The meal came to an end. The Doctor reached up and took his napkin out from his open collar, folded it carefully, and put it in his holder. The hymn books were passed out and the Doctor announced the number of the hymn to be sung that night.

It was then that I experienced the shock of watching him sit down

to play the dilapidated old upright piano. But all the others were long accustomed to both the sight and sound, and it did not diminish the general festive air of the party. And so tonight they sang with added spirit, still flushed with the brightness of the occasion. The Doctor finished the hymn, returned to his place, and read the Lord's Prayer in German. Then, the dinner over, the staff went to the small side tables, carrying extra cups of coffee and tea, so the mood would not be broken, and they could chat and relax in the cool of the evening.

The Doctor said goodnight and went back to his room to submit himself to the inevitable tyranny of his correspondence.

I walked back to my room, turned on the oil lamp, and wrote home to Ellen and the little girls. I was eager for them to know about a place called Lambaréné and the people who worked there, for nothing is more essential to young people than to have their natural idealism nourished—and this I felt I could give them through what I had seen in my first day at Lambaréné.

Long after I turned off the small light from the kerosene lamp, I lay in bed listening to the sounds from the open wards a short distance away. There was a hacking cough, and then a child's cry. They were contrasting sounds to the ones I had heard a short time earlier in the dining room, but it was part of the human mixture and it was real.

The next morning, I rose early in order to see the hospital starting up on a new day. African women, wearing their blankets or faded colored cloth in wraparound style, were carrying water jars on their heads and were on their way to and from the wells. Some of them had babies riding on their hips in a sort of side-saddle arrangement. In front of many of the rooms or cubicles in the open wards women were cooking over homemade burners. I noticed one woman squatting close to an improvised stove consisting of a large pit in which she was making a banana-and-milk stew for her family. The milk

was her own. She deftly worked each breast close to the pan, sending streams of her milk into the stew. Here was the eternal woman in the oldest drama in the world—giving her totality to the cause of life near her, infinitely resourceful, inventive, responsible. The banana-and-milk stew sent up its steam and the woman sang softly.

I continued down the path past the long rows of open rooms. African women were helping to wash the ill members of their families. A father of about thirty was playing with his little girl, throwing her into the air and catching her just above the ground. My homesickness was too much; in no time at all I managed to join the party and both of us entertained the youngster.

To my great relief, I was still able to perform the trick I used to play on my own youngsters: reaching behind their ears and finding all sorts of strange objects—pennies, pencils, rubber bands, and buttons. Then the three of us walked down to the dock, the child riding between us on our outstretched arms as we skimmed her over the ground.

The African father's name was George Malthen. I spoke to him in French and learned that his wife had just suffered a miscarriage. He had brought her and their child to the hospital just one day earlier. There were no complications, and she was now resting comfortably. Dr. Margaret had told him that in another two or three days she would be well enough to go home.

I asked where home was. He said it was up the river perhaps eight miles from the hospital, where he worked at a lumber camp. He had had enough schooling to learn to read and write French, but that was all. He lived with his wife and child in a compound built by his wife's grandfather, who was still alive.

Two years earlier his wife's sister had died during childbirth. The baby had been thought to be overdue and the local midwife tried to induce labor. Then, when the women's condition became serious, the witch doctor, or fetisher, was brought in. The woman was given potions and made to do strange things. Then external force was used on her abdomen. The woman went into labor and died.

George Malthen said he resolved then that he would never let

anything like this happen to his own wife. And when, several days ago, his wife began to bleed, her mother summoned the fetisher who told his wife to do strange things if she wanted to save her baby. When George said he wanted his wife to go to the Schweitzer Hospital, the fetisher warned him not to interfere or he would cause him to turn into a vampire at night and kill his own child.

"He told me he would cause me to kill again and again and then I would be killed myself."

"Were you frightened?"

"Yes, I had much fear. The fetisher, he is a powerful one. But I could think only about my wife and what had happened to her sister."

"And what will happen when you return to your village?" I asked.

The father said nothing for a moment or two. His eyes were fixed on a pirogue not far away. "I have not thought much about that yet. The fetisher told me not to come here. I don't know what the fetisher will try to do to me. I will try to be strong. I have seen people under the spell of the fetisher do terrible things. Other people who have disobeyed him have lost their minds or have died. It is a strange power he has. I must be strong."

As he spoke, I thought back on something Clara had told me about the witch doctors at Lambaréné. They would hover at the perimeter of the hospital, weaving their spell on the patients or members of their families as they came within range. Generally, the witch doctors wore Western clothes, complete with white shirt and tie, though the outfit would be somewhat frayed and unpressed. Occasionally, they would affect the long diplomat's frock, wing collar, and black tie—again of a distinctly secondhand origin. Each would warn the patients to leave the hospital and place themselves in the fetisher's hands. The usual threat has to do with visions of human beings transformed into vampires in the middle of the night and sucking the blood of loved ones, sometimes until death.

Once, the entire leper village was tied up when a witch doctor of obvious persuasive ability caused virtually the entire African population to refuse any treatment. Patients went on a no-treatment sys-

tem. Dr. Schweitzer was angry and he was all for finding the fetisher and settling the matter once and for all.

Even before the Doctor got to him, however, Clara had managed to persuade the fetisher to call off the strike. Clara is about five feet tall and looks as though she barely weighs one hundred pounds. I had an image in my mind of this lovely, dainty little lady confronting the African witch doctor in his stained diplomat's frock, trying to convince him to rescind his authority and abdicate. Later, Clara refused to tell exactly what transpired at the meeting or what superior magic she herself had brewed in order to persuade the African to cease and desist. Whatever it was, it worked, and the patients submitted to treatment and diligently took their medicines.

When I asked Clara at least to tell me how she felt during her parley with the witch doctor, she knitted her brows. "I was terrified," she said, "that what the Africans said about him might be true. I expected at any moment that he might get a big hex out of his black bag and turn me into a vampire right on the spot." She shivered, then smiled. "Now let's not talk about it any more."

The rational-minded Westerner finds it easy to scoff at the hold of the fetisher over many Africans. But before we give ourselves too much credit, we ought to take into account the countless millions spent each year in America and Europe on mediums, bogus doctors, tea-leaf readers, numerologists, stargazers, to say nothing of snake oil, cure-all drugs, and quack potions for revitalizing the blood. Both the quacks and the witch doctors can point to people they have treated who have become well again. The human body has an amazing capacity for overcoming both natural illness and mistreatment by those who profess to cure. Indeed, even in the West, doctors today are amazed that people should have been able to undergo without too much apparent harm the kind of medical treatment that not so long ago was considered routine. We need also to remind ourselves that George Washington's physician tried to treat his patient for a cold by bleeding him. It may or may not be a coincidence that Washington died shortly thereafter.

In any event, the witch doctor has had—and still has—vast power

in many parts of Africa. And his exploits are sufficiently dramatic for him to maintain the myth of his magic. While standing on the dock talking to George Malthen about his own experience, I recalled an incident that had been told me by Laurens van der Post of the Union of South Africa, one of the most sensitive and skilled writers to deal with the terrifyingly complex subject of Africa. His *The Dark Eye in Africa* is a poetic and rich presentation of the human situation in contemporary Africa.

Colonel van der Post had been in New York several weeks before my departure for Lambaréné, and discussed some of his own experiences with witch doctors in the southern part of Africa. He liked to visit African villages in the remote interior. Knowing the ways of the tribes, he would wait with his African guide and companion just outside each village until, eventually, one of the elders would come out to look him over, and, if he were lucky, to bid him enter.

On this particular occasion, van der Post and his guide had to wait several hours. Finally, they were confronted by the witch doctor, who was apparently torn between the natural curiosity and friendliness of the villagers, which led them to want van der Post to come in, and his own need for a sense of superiority, which led him to try to keep van der Post out.

The witch doctor casually said he would permit van der Post and his guide to enter on condition that they would agree to a test of comparative magic that the fetisher would name.

Van der Post readily accepted.

"The fetisher smiled in triumph," van der Post told me, "then bid me follow him. Inside the village a large crowd quickly surrounded us. The fetisher announced that the white man had accepted his challenge. Then the fetisher handed me his staff; it was about four feet long. He told me to instruct my African guide to keep the staff planted on the ground.

"This was to be a test of power. The fetisher said he would cause the staff to rise despite anything my African guide could do to keep it on the ground. My job was to exert all the influence I could on my African guide to keep the staff from rising.

"I had known Joseph, my African companion, for a long time. He was with me all the way. He understood exactly what he was to do. He stripped to the waist, revealing a gleaming and powerful torso. Then he took the staff and plunged it into the earth as far as it would go. He spread his legs apart to assure his balance, grasped the top of the staff with both hands, and anchored it firmly to the ground.

"I announced we were ready for the challenge.

"The witch doctor seemed unimpressed with the sight of my companion leaning on the staff with his full two hundred pounds. Then the witch doctor began his magic incantations. He made large swirling motions with his arms above the straining, sweating body of my guide, clinging to the staff.

"Then the witch doctor, in African, began to chant: 'Let the staff rise! Let the staff rise!' Some of the villagers had their drums with them and took up the beat. Within a minute or two, hundreds of people joined the chant. The drums beat louder.

"I watched my companion. Joseph was sweating profusely. His eyes seemed somewhat glazed and they were fixed on the witch doctor who continued his swooshing and swooping motions. And all the time the witch doctor kept chanting, 'Let the staff rise! Let the staff rise!'

"I began to feel uncomfortably warm. My shirt suddenly seemed to have the weight of a winter overcoat. And all the time the drums got louder and louder, merging with the chanting of the crowd. The volume of the sound was unbelievable.

"Joseph kept the staff pinned to the ground. I thrust my wet face next to his and shouted to him above the din to hold on. His muscles were taut and knotted with strain. His eyes were bulging in their sockets. The staff seemed secure under his weight.

"The chant approached its crescendo. Its beat was irresistible. Strange words began to form in my throat and on my lips. Almost before I realized it, I found myself intoning hoarsely with the others, first in a husky whisper, then in full voice: 'Let the staff rise! Let the staff rise!'

"The cords were standing out on Joseph's neck and shoulders. His

arms and hands were quivering. There was a moment of agony on his face, then the staff began to waver in his hands. The witch doctor swooped even closer. The staff in Joseph's hands began to rise.

"He held on to it with all the remaining strength he could muster, but it was no use. The staff rose perhaps eight inches above the ground, Joseph clinging to it all the way. Then the witch doctor clapped his hands. The drums stopped, and the spell was broken. Joseph relinquished his grip and the staff fell to the ground.

"The people began to disperse. There was neither elation nor triumph in their manner. What had happened had been entirely expected and predictable. The only excitement would have been if the witch doctor had failed.

"As for the witch doctor himself, he couldn't have been more friendly. Now that he had demonstrated the inferiority of the white man, there was nothing more to prove; and he bid me welcome. We couldn't have enjoyed greater hospitality at that village that night if we had owned it.

"The next day, several hours after we had left the village, I decided to speak my mind to my African guide and companion.

" 'Joseph,' I said, picking my words carefully, 'how did you ever let yourself fall for that old hypnotism trick? That staff rose from the ground only because you lifted it. You were hoodwinked by one of the oldest witch doctor tricks in Africa.'

" 'Colonel,' he replied, 'I'll be glad to tell you why I couldn't hold that stick to the ground if you tell me why you kept screaming in my ear to let it rise.' "

Walking around the hospital with George Malthen, I could understand why some visitors came away with negative impressions.

The idea of a hospital creates instant images in the mind of immaculate corridors, white sheets, total sanitation. These images were badly jolted when one saw the hospital at Lambaréné for the first time. Countless numbers of goats wandered at will all over the place;

even when they were not visible their presence was perceptible. The ground was made moist and slippery by an equally large number of chickens. Hanging heavily in the dank air was the smoke from the dozens of crude burners used by the Africans for their cooking. There was also an inexplicably sweet and somewhat sticky smell—perhaps from the cooking or from fallen and fermented fruit.

The sanitary facilities were at an absolute minimum. There were only two outhouses, one for each sex. The sewer underneath was open and sometimes the wind blew from the wrong direction.

There were no bedsheets. The Africans brought their own blankets. There were no "wards" as the term is used elsewhere. There were long, bungalowlike affairs with small cubicles. When a patient came to the hospital, he was generally accompanied by his entire family. The mother did the cooking, as she would at home. The children were usually on their own.

The difficulty, of course, was with the term "hospital" as applied to the Schweitzer colony. It created false images and expectations by outsiders. The proper term should have been "jungle clinic," as Dr. Margaret had explained. Dr. Schweitzer did not come to Africa for the purpose of building a towering medical center. He came in order to meet the Africans on their own terms. What he built was an African village attached to a functional medical and surgical clinic. The Africans were attracted to Schweitzer because of the man himself and because this was a village and a way of life familiar to them rather than a forbidding building where they would be cut off from their families and frightened by a world of total whiteness, of people and walls and machines. Modern medicine has come to accept the emotional security of the patient as a vital part of any therapy. Dr. Schweitzer knew this almost a half-century earlier when he made his plans to serve in Africa.

Most visitors who stayed long enough became aware of these things. While they might never be able to accept completely all the crudeness, as least they developed a working perspective. Some visitors, however, could hardly wait to get back to Europe or America in order to make known their discoveries. I had read at least four arti-

cles by disillusioned visitors to Lambaréné who misunderstood and
misjudged Dr. Schweitzer and what he was trying to do in Africa.

In addition to exposing the lack of sanitation, the articles would
invariably talk about the gruffness of Dr. Schweitzer, especially to-
ward the Africans. They would be disturbed especially by his ref-
erences to the "noble savage." These were some of the things that
Clara Urquhart had cautioned me about before I left for Lambaréné.
I, too, was surprised when I first noticed it, but after a while I real-
ized it was more apparent than real.

The Doctor would bark out his orders to the Africans and scold
them when they were doing something wrong. The impression he
gave was that he was dealing with children. There did not seem to
be sufficient respect in his manner toward the Africans. But this was
not the complete story. To get the full picture, one must realize that
Schweitzer also treated most whites as his "small brothers" and one
had to find out how the Africans themselves interpreted his manner.

I watched the Africans closely as they worked under Dr.
Schweitzer's orders, pushing back the jungle or gathering up stray
pieces of lumber or moving crates of medicines. When he appeared
to be arbitrary or gruff in what he told them to do they would smile
broadly and carry out his instructions. Sometimes when he called
out sharply, he would have a glint in his eye which they would catch
and it would amuse them.

In talking to one of the African leper workers at some length, I
learned that those who had been with the Doctor for any length of
time had no trouble in understanding him. They knew he was some-
what short-tempered when things did not go just right; but they
knew something, too, about the pressures under which he worked.
And what was most important to them was that they knew the stern
manner did not reflect any displeasure by Dr. Schweitzer.

Even when the Doctor seemed to lose his temper, it was only for
the moment, the leper said. Sometimes, if he had been too severe,
he would go out of his way later to make amends. Once he scolded
the wife of one of the patients. Fifteen minutes later he beckoned to

her when no one was looking, said he was sorry, and gave her thirty francs.

"We do not become angry," the leper said. "How could we? Could a man become angry at his own father for telling him what to do?"

The fact that Dr. Schweitzer's role at Lambaréné was that of father—with respect to patients, their families, the workers, the white doctors and nurses, and even the visitors—is vital to any understanding of his manner. He had a sense of total personal responsibility for everyone and everything at Lambaréné. Time was his most precious commodity and he was no longer able to expend it in lengthy and cordial explanations for what he would like to see done. When, for example, he ordered the staff and visitors to wear pith helmets, he did not have time to explain that when he first came to Lambaréné he had to deal with serious cases of sunstroke suffered by white people who had insufficient respect for the striking power of the equatorial sun. Once he had to take an overnight trip by canoe to attend the wife of a French planter who became seriously ill because she thought it was unnecessary to wear a helmet when the sky was overcast. She hadn't understood that even the diffused rays of a hidden sun can cause trouble. Dr. Schweitzer did not intend to use all his time in Africa treating white people for sunstroke; his purpose was to provide medical treatment for Africans. And it became a little wearisome having to go through detailed explanations to each new visitor. Hence his "take-my-word-for-it" approach, whether with respect to sun helmets or other matters, each of which had its reasons.

At Lambaréné I realized that the criticism of Dr. Schweitzer's relationship with the Africans missed an important point. The somewhat arbitrary or patriarchal manner was not reserved for blacks only. Once, while Dr. Schweitzer was superintending a jungle-clearing operation, he ordered the blacks to rest. Then he turned to three white members of the staff and to me and said, "Now it's your turn." We obediently took up the work, pulling stubborn weeds from the trunks of nearby trees. After about ten minutes we looked as though we had been working ten hours. Our white shirts and khaki

pants were drenched. All the while the Africans stood by, looking on us with boundless compassion and appearing desperately eager to spare us further effort. Then the Doctor said we could stop; he just wanted us to have some respect for the requirements of physical labor in Lambaréné. He had made his point.

Not infrequently, his seeming brusqueness was leavened with humor. When he escorted Adlai Stevenson on a tour around the hospital, the former presidential candidate noticed a large mosquito alighting on Dr. Schweitzer's arm and promptly swatted it.

"You shouldn't have done that," the Doctor said sharply. "That was my mosquito. Besides, it wasn't necessary to call out the Sixth Fleet to deal with him."

Clara gave me another illustration of the fact that his sternness knew no color lines. Once, he became particularly exasperated at an African who was putting boards of lumber in the wrong place. He mumbled that he could almost slap the man. Clara, who was standing nearby, was shocked and said so to the Doctor.

"Well, Clara," he said, "I don't think I am going to slap him. But if I should do so, I want you to close your eyes and imagine that I am slapping a white man. In that case, it will probably be all right with you."

By 7 A.M., the sun had claimed the sky and the moisture was heavy in the air. I was halfway down the path leading to the dining room when Dr. Catchpool fell in alongside me.

"Better not let Dr. Schweitzer catch you without a helmet," he said. "He's very sensitive on this subject. He's had some experience with other people who saw no reason for wearing a helmet when they were going to be outside for only a few minutes. He's had to hospitalize them, and if there's on thing that annoys the Doctor, it's taking care of people who have no right to be sick."

In the dining room at breakfast, a few minutes later, Dr. Schweitzer

referred to the matter. He instructed Clara to be sure to get a helmet
to fit me from one of the extras in Mme. Oberman's possession.
Clara nodded knowingly, then whispered to me that the Doctor meant
business.

Breakfast consisted of thick homemade bread, jam, warm milk,
coffee, and bananas. The Doctor ate somewhat more heartily than
the rest. He supplemented the regular fare with an avocado pear and
an egg.

Toward the end of the meal, I told Clara that I hoped we might
have a chance to spend a few minutes with the Doctor. I didn't want
to impose on his time, but I did have a few commissions that I felt
ought to be performed as soon after my arrival as possible. During
the course of a correspondence with President Eisenhower, whom I
came to know when he was president of Columbia University, with
which I had a warm personal history, I had mentioned that I hoped
to be able to visit Dr. Schweitzer in Lambaréné at about the time of
his eighty-second birthday. The President proceeded to write a let-
ter of birthday greetings to Dr. Schweitzer which he asked me to
deliver. In that letter he spoke of his high admiration for the Doctor,
saying that he had derived much inspiration from his work and his
thought, and felt the world was greatly in need of the kind of con-
tribution he had been making. He ended by wishing the Doctor
many more years of effective service to the human community. I
had another message for the Doctor from Prime Minister Jawaharlal
Nehru, whom I had seen on his visit to the United States in the fall
of 1956 and who was most eager to have conveyed to the Doctor his
deep admiration and affection.

I had a third commission. A fifteen-year-old boy by the name of
Marc Chalufour in Concord, New Hampshire, was engaged in a
crusade to save an old organ in his church from being replaced with
an electronic instrument. He felt the old organ could be repaired
and that it was sacrilegious to let it die—especially since he did not
feel the new machine was really an organ. When, through one of his
teachers, who was a friend of mine, he happened to learn of my

coming visit to Lambaréné, he asked if I might deliver a letter from him to the Doctor. He felt that if he could enlist the Doctor in his crusade, he might win his fight.

I knew I would feel better when these various commissions were out of the way. And so I asked Clara what she thought would be a convenient time to act. When the Doctor got up from the breakfast table, Clara followed and spoke to him on his way out. Then she nodded to me, indicating the matter was arranged.

As I emerged from the dining room, Clara handed me a pith helmet that had just been given her by Mme. Oberman. It was a little large and I had the feeling I was walking around inside an inverted laundry basket, but it served the purpose.

In the compound not far from where we stood, the Doctor was giving working instructions for the day to perhaps two dozen Africans. First there had been a roll call and now the Doctor was dividing the men into different groups, one of which was to collect stray lumber around the place, another of which was to repair the porch on one of the long bungalows occupied by the staff, and still another of which was to carry on the war against the jungle, cutting, pruning, weeding, pushing back. I could readily see the truth of the remark that had been made in connection with Lambaréné, that if you left the jungle to itself for two months, it would close in over you and you would have to tunnel your way out.

Dr. Schweitzer completed his instructions and motioned to Clara and me to follow. He went up the several steps to his quarters, which were at one end of the long bungalow facing the compound. Just to the side of it was a fenced-in area for several antelopes.

The Doctor's room, like all the others, was open at both ends, covered by a wire screen and supporting woodwork. On the far side he had his desk, part of which was under a mound of papers and books. Opposite it was a medium-sized bookcase. The Doctor asked us to be seated, then sat on a stool at least as old as the hospital. I made a mental note of the fact that nowhere at Lambaréné had I seen an upholstered chair or anything even resembling a sofa or couch.

Dr. Schweitzer apologized for the fact that we did not have a talk

the previous afternoon. He pointed to a pile of forms on his desk.
"All this is to be filled out," he said. "Now the French government
has asked us to prepare complicated forms for each patient at the
hospital. Miserable paperwork. Also now we have to fill out work-
man's compensation forms for the working people who come to the
hospital. Dozens of items for each patient. And I hardly know what
to do with these." He lifted his head in the direction of one end of
his desk, indicating a large bundle of new mail.

"My paper work is killing me," he said slowly. "Week by week
the mail gets larger. Mlle. Ali and Mlle. Mathilde help me as much
as they can. Even so, we keep falling farther and farther behind.
Many of them are important letters which must be answered. Some
of them are from theologians who raise significant questions in con-
nection with things they may have read that I had written at one
time or another. The least I can do is to try to answer them. I am
maybe fourteen months behind with part of my correspondence.
Some of the letters involve the work of the hospital—people who
volunteer to work here.

"While the turnover is not excessively large, we do have to bring
in new people now and then. The nurses and doctors here have to
take a leave of absence after a year or two just to rest up after the
exhausting work in this climate. And so new people keep coming.
Before a new nurse arrives at the hospital, some twenty-seven letters
have to be written. It is important, so very important, to be sure
about these things. It is not like a girl coming to the city from the
country to get a job. It is a long way from Europe and America to
Lambaréné. And the only way I have of finding out what I must
know about each person is through letters—most of all the letters
the person herself writes, but also what I can learn from other peo-
ple.

"After it is decided that a nurse or doctor is to come here, then
the real work begins. I must be very clear and very complete in the
instructions. Passports, visas, enroute accommodations.

"But we will not talk any more about this. Are you comfortable
in your quarters?"

I said I was very comfortable indeed. I told the Doctor I was eager to take care of some matters, and handed him the letter from President Eisenhower. He opened the letter carefully, then read it without translation.

"A letter from the President of the United States," he said slowly, then read it again. I could see that he was moved by what the President had written. Then he looked up and smiled.

"Do you know," he said, "that if, eighty-two years ago, my dear mother had been told by someone that her little baby would someday receive a letter from the President of the United States, she would have had the surprise of her life. This is a very kind letter from the President. I will take great pride in returning the greeting."

Then I conveyed the cordial good wishes of Prime Minister Nehru. At the Doctor's request, I told him about the Prime Minister's recent visit to the United States, and the importance attached to it by President Eisenhower. I referred to the fact that in the past few years some misunderstanding had developed between the United States and India. This was not merely a matter of differing foreign policies. Public opinion in both countries had been growing apart. In America, the mistaken notion existed that India had ranged itself on the side of the Soviet Union against the United States, especially as it concerned the decisions made in the United Nations. In India, a large segment of public opinion took the view that the United States was insensitive to the independence movement in Asia and Africa, and that we were determined to preserve the interests of the colonial powers in that part of the world.

The result of both these views was that the two peoples of the world whose national historical experience had so much in common and who, by standing together, could contribute so mightily in the building of essential bridges between East and West were drifting apart. Hence the significance of Mr. Nehru's trip to the United States. Both the President and the Prime Minister had developed an instant mutual admiration and respect.

In talking to the Prime Minister before he returned to India, I learned that the exchange of views with the President had cleared

up many matters in his mind. At the same time, he was able to impress on the President the reasons for the positions taken by India with respect to affairs in Asia and the Middle East.

The Prime Minister attached the utmost importance to the uprisings in Poland and Hungary. What happened in Hungary, he said, would have a profound effect everywhere, especially amoung young people who would now realize that communism could no longer be the headquarters for their natural idealism. And even though the uprisings were suppressed, there would be profound internal changes in the Communist world, he felt, changes that would inevitably move away from the old dictatorial shape of things. People were demanding something better than what they had known; they were demanding greater liberty and a better life. There was no way for this demand to be resisted. He was therefore hopeful that, given world peace and a little time, there would be long steps forward for a large part of the world community.

Dr. Schweitzer listened carefully. He recalled the time he had met Nehru in Lausanne in 1936. He was impressed by the interesting combination in Nehru of the contemplative man and the man of action. And he was fascinated by the way Nehru complemented Gandhi.

But enough of politics, he said. There was work to be done around the hospital and he invited me to tag along if I wished.

There was still the matter of Marc Chalufour and his crusade to save the church organ. I decided to bring it up another time. As for the main reasons I had come to Lambaréné—safeguarding copies of the Doctor's unpublished and unfinished manuscripts, and the possibility of direct action by him on the matter of world peace—these would have to wait for an hour when there might be some easing of the pressures of the hospital. But the more I learned abut the hospital and about Dr. Schweitzer, the more pessimistic I became that such an hour might be found.

In any event, I accepted the Doctor's invitation to accompany him as he discharged his morning chores. The first job we had was to move planks of lumber that had been stored in several places to the

porch of a bungalow that was now under repair. The wood was the finest mahogany in the world. Its use as floor boards was dictated by two factors: first, the abundance of maghogany in the general area of Lambaréné, making it inexpensive; second, the need for the hardest woods as protection against termites. Much of the hospital, in fact, had been built with the kind of hardwoods that in Europe and the United States were reserved for the most costly cabinets or luxury paneling.

The Doctor worked alongside the Africans as the wood was transported by hand and placed in neat piles under the bungalow porch being repaired.

Our next job was to get rid of crates of medicines that had spoiled because they were improperly packed before being shipped. Shippers in Europe and the United States, apparently, have little experience in preparing medicines for storage under equatorial conditions. In addition to the heat and the moisture, medicines have to contend with raiding ants. Large crates would arrive with labels saying they had been specially sealed to guard against heat and moisture; but within three weeks after arriving at Lambaréné they had to be repacked. Even sealed metal drums sometimes failed to do the job. I watched two such drums containing millions of cathartic molasses tablets emptied into wheelbarrows for dumping into the river because they had spoiled or turned into tar.

Then several large packages of asprin had to be dumped. There was some evidence indicating successful ant raids into the aspirin stores. Judging by the size and activity of the ants at the hospital, I would have supposed that they were in no need of pain killers. In any event, they kept coming back for more. The ants, who have an appetite for paper, made it necessary to do double labeling on each bottle. In fact, almost everything connected with the medicines required two or three times as much work as it would in a temperate zone. Every bottle, for example, had to be resealed with paraffin after it arrived.

Ideally, of course, a hospital should have large refrigeration facilities for its medical supplies. This was especially true with respect

to the new antibiotics. But there was very limited refrigeration equipment at the Schweitzer Hospital. For the most part, the medicines had to be stored in the empty space underneath buildings that were so situated on the hillside that they had relative protection against the sun. Sometimes the Doctor had to get down on his hands and knees and crawl through the dirt in order to check on the medicines and help move them as might be required.

After two hours of working alongside the Doctor I was ready to throw in the towel. The Doctor's shirt was wringing wet. His hair lay in moist gray clumps on his forehead.

Again I had to keep reminding myself that the Doctor was entering his eighty-third year. Just trying to keep up with his stride as he hurried from place to place was a feat of endurance. I could hardly wait for the afternoon siesta.

When I entered the dining room, I felt fully at home for the first time. For I knew that the look of severe midday fatigue on all the faces of the staff was reflected on my own. The Doctor, too, showed the effects of his exertions. Yet it was astounding and wonderful to see the way even a brief respite and a good meal enabled him to recoup his energies. After he had had his soup and was halfway through his cheese and noodles the color began to come back to his face. By the end of the meal he was sitting straight in his chair, his eyes were twinkling, and he had some stories to tell the staff that lifted their spirits.

"I have an announcement to make," he said. "Civilization in all its glory has finally come to Lambaréné. As you know, there are only two automobiles within 75 miles of the hospital. Today, the inevitable happened: the cars collided. We have treated the drivers for their injuries. Anyone with a reverence for machines may treat the cars."

Then he turned to Albertina.

"How is your pet monkey doing these days?" he asked.

"Not very well," Albertina replied. "I set him free in the morning but he has a terrible habit of wandering too far and has increasing difficulty in finding his way home."

The Doctor smiled. "Maybe he drinks too much," he said.

The doctor seemed in fine spirits, his sense of humor in full flower.

"Some of you have asked why I haven't reported on my trip to Europe a couple of months ago," he said. "No particular reason. I'd been meaning to get around to it. The highlight of the trip was a visit to the Royal Palace in Copenhagen for dinner. The invitation came from the Queen. They sent an oversized car for me—far larger than I could use. The palace, as you might imagine if you remember your storybooks, was quite magnificent—gleaming marbled corridors, glass chandeliers.

"We sat down at the royal table. It was mahogany with a highly polished top and seemed to go on forever. They put me at the head of the table, with the King and Queen at each side of me.

"I looked down at my plate and tried to repress a shudder. There was a herring on it. I happen not to like herring. My sainted mother had always said to me: 'Albert, you must never leave anything on your plate.' But my stomach had also instructed me: 'Albert, don't send anything down here we can't use.'

"What to do? I hit on a plan. It worked. When the King and Queen were talking to each other, I quietly and deftly pocketed the herring.

"Two days later, there was an account in the newspaper of my visit to the Royal Palace. It quoted the Queen: 'We were very pleased to have Dr. Schweitzer for dinner. But I must say that the King and I were somewhat surprised at the strange habits he had picked up from his jungle companions. Not only did he eat the head of the fish, he even ate the bones of the fish. There was nothing left on his plate.'"

I was to learn that humor was as much a part of the nourishment in the dining room as the simple food on the plates.

On my way out of the dining room I asked Clara when she thought we might discuss with the Doctor the two main purposes that brought us to Lambaréné. She said we might have to wait another day or two, perhaps longer; when the right time came, the Doctor would come to us.

Walking toward my room, I passed the Doctor's quarters. Through the wire screen I could make out his silhouetted form perched over his correspondence. For the rest of the afternoon I stayed in my room, taking care of office matters that had been airmailed to me from *The Saturday Review* in New York. Like everything else in the world, my job had been revolutionized by the air age. There is hardly a place in the world that cannot be reached by person or mail in forty-eight hours. I have had airmail bundles of work from New York only two and a half days old delivered to me in a Moslem village fifty miles from Dacca in East Pakistan. On another occasion, a postman on a bicycle met me coming out from a small Japanese inn near Nagasaki and handed me page proofs of the forthcoming issue of *The Saturday Review*. And now in a jungle hospital in Africa, I was no farther away from my office than I would have been twenty years earlier in Colorado.

The airplane has made it not only possible but necessary for an editor to move his desk from place to place in the world. Indeed, the airplane itself has become an efficient and productive office. Nowhere outside of a plane have I found such ideal working and thinking conditions. When at my job in New York, my main business each day is to preside over interruptions. I have little time for reading, less time for writing. Sequence is annihilated. One takes things as they come, and they come in short, uneven bursts. Once, I became sufficiently objective about my job to keep track of everything that happened in the course of an average day. I discovered that the telephone rang on the average of once every six minutes; that there were at least six visitors each day, three of whom came by previous arrangement; that the important business that had to be transacted with the staff had to be squeezed into less than an hour and a half. In between the telephone and the appointments, I would work on my unanswered-mail folder, which weighed heavily on me even when out of sight. I would type my replies on the back of each letter for retyping by my secretary on office stationery.

On a plane, however, especially when we are high above the clouds, the fragmentation disappears. Sequence comes to life again and the

mind has a chance to reorganize itself for consecutive thought. The meal tray serves as an excellent stand for my typewriter and an empty seat beside me becomes a side table for working papers. I estimate that one hour in the sky is the equivalent of about four hours on land in terms of actual output.

There are, of course, distractions. The sky itself. Even so, it is the kind of distraction that nourishes thought. For nowhere else in the world is there grandeur like this. Sometimes, when flying above a storm, vast, clearly defined cloud masses catch the light of the sun; the result is a Grand Canyon of color multiplied by infinity. Once, flying from Seattle to San Francisco, I saw three distinct cloud levels, with clear sky in between. Each level had its own character. The first was a massive purple floor, swelling and bulging when we were close to it. The second layer was full of tunnels and canyons, exploiting every gradation of gray and black. The third level abandoned itself to color, with gentle formations suggesting lakes of gleaming silver, or long lemon-colored slopes meeting a light green-blue sky.

Another time, flying from Beirut to Karachi, we darted in and out of vast thunderheads, each of which looked as though it were made up of the combined masses of all the mountains in the world. The thunderheads each ran up to forty thousand feet, growing fatter and more menacing on their way up, and then, suddenly, flattening themselves out on the top, connecting with each other to make a giant white roadbed. Underneath were the long caverns, deep gray on one side, streaked blue on the other. For more than an hour, we rode through the caverns until we finally hit a long open clearing.

I need not even mention the sunsets. The combination of the setting sun, the winds, and the swift movement of the plane changes the landscape so rapidly that no two minutes are the same. It is a developing wonder and makes a moving picture that stays in the mind. And, if you catch the late sun just right as you fly west, it will cause thin golden threads to spin off the propellers.

As I say, these are nourishing distractions, and I welcome as many of them as I can find. Indeed, I have made a hobby of collecting

skyscapes, and now have some two dozen in my memory box to think back upon. It is the kind of hobby that went naturally with the kind of job that has the world for its locale.

On my third morning at Lambaréné, after breakfast, I crossed the small compound from the dining room to the porch of the Schweitzer quarters in order to pay my respects to Mrs. Schweitzer. She was seated in a dilapidated beach chair. In her hand was a long bamboo rod which she used to fend off some of the animals that would otherwise disturb her rest. In particular, there was one bird she had to guard against. He looked like a cross between a raven and a parrot. He would come swooping down and alight on your shoulder or back of your neck. If you weren't used to this sort of thing, it could be somewhat unnerving, for it would happen very suddenly and you hardly knew what hit you. Generally, it would be accompanied by a sudden flapping of wings and occasionally a nip of the ear. This bird was totally gregarious and it was hard to persuade him that his attentions were not always the ultimate in human enjoyment. Mrs. Schweitzer like to doze in her chair. So long as she held on to the bamboo rod, the bird respected her solitude. But when the rod was absent, the bird invariably interpreted it as an invitation to a shoulder.

The first time I saw Mrs. Schweitzer I could see she was not well. The blue veins stood out in her forehead and seemed stark against the pure whiteness of her skin. She had lovely gray-brown eyes but they seemed to look at you through a mist. When she spoke it was with considerable effort. Her breathing was labored. Despite her difficulties, she would not allow anyone to treat her as an invalid. She insisted on coming to the dining room for lunch and frequently for dinner. It was easy to see how much of a struggle it was for her, even with the aid of a cane, to negotiate the two dozen or so steps across the compound and climb the short stairs to the dining room. Once, I saw Mrs. Schweitzer start out across the compound, her

weight bent forward on the cane and her whole being struggling for breath. I rushed to her side and took her arm. She looked up at me, somewhat puzzled, as though I did not know the rules of the game at Lambaréné. Then she smiled and thanked me but said she was in the habit of getting around by herself. She expressed the hope that I might come to visit her on the porch and talk to her.

"You know," she said, "I am so interested, so very much interested, in what is happening in the world, and here one does not often get a chance to talk about it. The Doctor is very busy with the hospital and all his other work and I do not want to tire him by asking him about things. So there is very little talk. And I am hungry for talk, especially about the world. It would be very nice if you could come to visit with me; that is, if you are not too busy."

I accepted the invitation gratefully. And now, the next day, I visited Mrs. Schweitzer on the porch. She bid me draw up a chair and told me she would do her best to protect me against the bird now making short circles above my head in preparation for a landing.

She apologized for the fact that she was unable to escort me to such parts of the grounds as I might like to see. Many years earlier, she had had a skiing accident that had broken her spine; in recent months she found it increasingly difficult to get around. Hence the cane and her seat on the porch.

"It makes me feel so foolish," she said, "this being so helpless. I ought to be working with the Doctor. He is an amazing man. I really think he is working harder now than he did twenty years ago. And twenty years ago I was afraid he was killing himself with work. He has always said that he has a favorite prescription for anyone over sixty who does not feel well—hard work and more hard work. As you can see, it is a prescription he follows himself.

"I am only sorry I cannot work hard, too. We have been working here a long time . . . more than forty years. I used to be able to help the Doctor; but in the last few years it has no longer been possible for me to do so."

I asked Mrs. Schweitzer which place she considered her real home— Gunsbach or Lambaréné.

"Actually, there are three homes," she said. "When I was young, shortly after I was married, I contracted tuberculosis, so we went to live in the Black Forest of Germany, where the climate was considered helpful for people in that condition. We liked it very much, so very much that we kept a home there even after I was cured.

"Then there is the home in Gunsbach—in Alsace, as you know. At first it was very much a home, but we spent less and less time there. And whenever we returned, there would be so many people who wanted to see my husband that I came to regard it more as an office than a home.

"And so, of the three places, this place seems most like home to me. It is very hot here in Lambaréné; it is very moist and there isn't much more than a bedroom to our own quarters. But this place to me has been our main home for more than forty years."

When I asked about their daughter, Mrs. Schwitzer said that she wasn't sure that Rhena had the same feeling about Lambaréné being a home for her.

"You see," she said, "when Rhena was small, the Doctor did not feel that Lambaréné was a good place in which to bring up a child. And so we sent her to boarding school. In later years, when she was fully grown, she came here for a visit—for a few weeks. She is now married, to Jean Eckert of Zurich, an organ builder, and she of course has her own home."

Mrs. Schweitzer then got up from her chair and went inside. After a moment she reappeared, holding the family album. One of the early photographs showed the Albert Schweitzers with their little girl. Albert Schweitzer was young and sturdy, with black wavy hair, a thick mustache, and an unwrinkled face. Helena Schweitzer was pretty and vivacious; her features were thin and sensitive but there was great strength and directness in the face. Rhena had large dark eyes and held her mother's hand. She wore the expression so familiar to parents of little girls—part shyness, part curiosity, part uncertainty, part feminine delight in being asked to pose.

Another photograph showed Dr. Schweitzer at the age of thirty-seven or thirty-eight. This was about the time he was getting ready to come to Lambaréné. He was in a reflective mood. His wide-set

eyes had caught a distant light and seemed to carry him outside the frame of the photograph. His chin was resting on his closed right hand. There was a quizzical look around the mouth. There was no trace of whiteness in the hair.

Then there was a picture taken of Rhena and her husband just after they were married. Mr. Eckert was alert and well groomed. Right after this were other family pictures of the Eckerts, the most recent of which showed their sixteen-year-old boy, Philippe, who had recently been very ill but who was fast recuperating. Mrs. Schweitzer said the Doctor was very fond of Philippe.

"Here," Mrs. Schweitzer said, "you were interested in our home in Gunsbach. This is a picture of the street and this is a picture of the house itself. It is a nice house, not pretentious, but very sturdy and comfortable.

"I like these pictures. I turn to them very often. Those early pictures were taken so many years ago that it is hard to remember exactly how many. Now we do not take pictures any more.

"I know I am talking like an old woman. But it is true. I am old. I am very old. And now I have very little to do except to look at these pictures and old letters and think back upon our life together.

"You will forgive me? Thank you, I am so eager to hear about your own family. Clara has told me about your wonderful wife and your children—four or five girls, which?"

I took out a small group photograph showing Ellen and three of the four girls. I did not happen to have a picture of the youngest girl.

Mrs. Schweitzer lingered a long time over the photograph, asking me to describe each child. This I did with relish and supporting anecdotal material. Then, at her request, I told her about our home and the openness and sense of freedom it afforded the children. She eagerly devoured the information about my family and made me promise to send additional photographs from time to time.

I feared I might be intruding on her rest, so I got up to leave. She made me sit down again, saying that it had been a long time since she had had the opportunity to talk to anyone so fully. Besides, we

hadn't even mentioned the world situation. What about the political situation in the United States? What about the struggle between East and West? What about communism? What about atomic energy?

"You must understand," she said, "that there aren't many visitors from the United States. And those who come do not stay for very long. They have urgent business, or so it seems, with the Doctor, and there isn't much opportunity to talk to them."

For the next hour I answered Mrs. Schweitzer's questions as best I could—and she had comments of her own to make now and then.

"It is so terrible," she said. "The world gets rid of one monster like Hitler but there are always others waiting in the wings to take his place. Isn't it strange? Human beings allow themselves to become all twisted under the influence of these men. I have seen it happen to many people I knew in Germany. I have seen the change that came over these human beings. I have seen decent people turn into killers and sadists."

She was of Jewish origin; she knew what she talked about.

"Anyway, we do the best we can and we work for better things. I don't know why I say 'we.' My time is over. I am too old. But I can hope. No one is ever so old that he cannot hope—even if his hopes are for others. I have done much such hoping in my life—and some of the hopes have come true. In recent years for me there has been not much to do except to hope—and to look at the pictures and think back."

Mrs. Schweitzer did not come to dinner that night. I feared that our conversation had been a drain on her energies, but Clara told me that she had been coming to dinner with decreasing frequency in recent weeks.

I next saw Mrs. Schweitzer at lunch the following day. She was at least fifteen minutes late in coming to her place. For the longest time after she sat down she had difficulty in getting her breath. Her lips were a stark blue. But she smiled graciously and did her best to engage in conversation. All she had for the noonday meal was a cup of tea. When she got up to leave she beckoned to me. Once we were

outside she said she hoped I would visit her again on her porch. It meant so much to her, she repeated, to talk to people who have just come from the United States.

I had several visits with Mrs. Schweitzer while I was at Lambaréné. I came to admire her pride, her resourcefulness, her tenacity, her continuing interest in the outside world.

Two months after I returned from the hospital at Lambaréné, I picked up a newspaper and learned that Mrs. Schweitzer had died. Her life had not been an easy one, but it had known purpose and hope and grace.

On the afternoon of my fourth day at Lambaréné, Dr. Schweitzer came to my room and said he hoped it might be convenient for us to talk. He said it would be nice if we could be incommunicado from the rest of the hospital for about two hours. We found Clara who suggested that we meet in her room which was out of sight from the main hospital paths.

Dr. Schweitzer seated himself on the bed, his arm resting on the white metal tubing on the lower end. I don't recall how we happened to get on the subject of philosophy, but for at least two hours he discussed his debt to the great thinkers in history.

At one point, he stopped short, saying that one did a disservice to philosophy in general and certain philosophers in particular if one had nothing to offer them except praise. He pointed out, as Bacon and others have done, that the uncritical acceptance of Aristotle for many centuries actually had the effect of retarding speculative and systematic thought. There was a tendency to view Aristotle as the be-all and end-all of philosophy, with the result that hardly anyone felt there was any point in further exploration or development.

"Philosophy will never be complete and can never be complete, by the very nature of philosophy. The human mind is capable of infinite growth. There are endless adventures in creative thought

ahead of us. It is only when men bow low before great thinkers and proclaim them to have said the last word that philosophical growth becomes arrested.

"Aristotle wasn't the only one. There was Kant. He was such a giant that men who should be working on the philosophical frontiers drew back and confined themselves to endless interpretations and theorizing about Kant. It was important, of course, for qualified thinkers to analyze Kant, but they had a tendency to make this analysis an end in itself. And since Kant was regarded as the last word, the new words were delayed in coming."

Then Dr. Schweitzer ran his fingers through his long, shaggy hair— one of the most characteristic of his gestures.

"I can't blame all this on Kant, of course," he said. "But I can blame him for being so much system and so little compassion. One can't expect philosophers to be romanticists, but it is important to remember that the philosopher must deal not only with the techniques of reason or with matter and space and stars, but with people. After all, it is the relationship of man to the universe, and not solely the relationship of one galaxy to another, or one fact to another, that should occupy such an important part of the philosopher's quest. There is such a thing as being too detached. I fear this may have been true of Kant."

There were other things in philosophy that bothered Dr. Schweitzer. Philosophical catchwords, for example. The way a phrase would be picked up and used almost automatically whenever a man's name would be mentioned, as though the phrase described the sum total of his life and thought.

He spoke of Descartes.

"One would think that Descartes lived just to emit a line of staggering profundity: 'I think, therefore I am.' How rare are the full-bodied examinations of his work. There has been too much genuflecting before *'Cogito, ergo sum'*; too many philosophical monuments have been erected in its behalf.

"I find it difficult to be impressed by 'I think, therefore I am.' One

might as well say, 'I have a toothache, therefore I exist.' These catchwords are tricky things. I don't think they serve the cause of creative thought in philosophy."

Then he looked up and said, "I have been negative enough. Too negative. There are philosophers whom I like and who have exercised strong influence on my own thought. Hegel, most of all. A man of reason. But also a man with a deep respect for the possibilities of the human being, especially the capacity to embrace important new concepts. Hegel is a philosopher who understands the mind concerned with the problems of its own growth.

"As for a school of philosophical thought, I acknowledge my great debt to the Stoics. To my mind it is the greatest formal philosophy in human history. To the extent that I can be identified with any one school, I should be proud to be related to the Stoics. There have been other influences, of course. I have a high admiration for the English philosophers of the late seventeenth and eighteenth centuries. They were imaginative but precise. They were concerned with man's estate.

"I have also found myself influenced by the early Chinese philosophers. There is an intense human quality in their thought. They never allow themselves to get too far away from their speculations about the nature of man or the purpose of man. And it is only logical that out of all this thought should come such a creative naturalism."

Dr. Schweitzer stared at the opposite wall. He said that these real influences in his philosophical thought were sometimes overlooked in the appraisals by others. It would be said, for example, that the Buddhist influence in his work was pre-eminent. This was a mistake.

"The mistake is natural enough," he said. "There is a disposition to think that because I am so deeply concerned with the need for reverence for life that my philosophy must be Buddhist, especially in connection with the Buddhist emphasis on the importance of animal life. But there is much more to Buddhism than that; and I hope there may be more to my own philosophy than that.

"A moment ago I was talking about the need to be careful of phil-

osophical catch phrases. It is true that no single phrase of my own philosophy is more representative of my thinking than 'reverence for life.' But the phrase is related to a whole line of thought. Rather than have people speculate on whether this phrase connects me to this philosophy or that, I would have them look into the purpose and the meaning of my work as a whole, such as it is.

"Christian theology has found it difficult to come to terms with my thought, though Christians have not."

He paused as he made this distinction.

"I have the feeling that the Christian theologians are reluctant to come in through the door I have tried to open. I have tried to relate Christianity to the sacredness of all life. It seems to me this is a vital part of Christianity as I understand it. But the Christian theologians, many of them, confine Christianity to the human form of life. It does not seem to me to be correct. It lacks the essential universalization that I associate with Jesus. Why limit reverence for life to the human form? As I say, I have tried to open the door; I hope the Christian theologians will come in."

I asked Dr. Schweitzer whether these philosophical ideas were reflected in the two books I understood were now close to completion.

He replied yes, these ideas were reflected in the two books, but they were not necessarily the main theme. And he proceeded to describe the two unpublished works. He had published two of four volumes which together he called *The Philosophy of Civilization*. The last two volumes were not quite completed. They were a continuation of the work which had appeared more than a quarter of a century ago. Another book now in manuscript form would be called *The Kingdom of God*. It would be a fairly short book. It would contain his ideas about Christianity and the reality of the human spirit in general.

"In the early 1930s I was determined to finish the two last volumes of *The Philosophy of Civilization*. But I kept being diverted. We were in a period of considerable building at the hospital in Lambaréné and I found myself putting off my writing from month to month.

"Then, in 1938, I decided to leave Lambaréné in order to work for at least a year on the books. But even before we arrived in Europe—in fact, while we were crossing the Bay of Biscay by boat—I learned that Adolf Hitler had just made a speech in which he tried to reassure the world that his sole aim in everything he did was peace. The speech was such a patent cover-up that I realized the war was not far off. I put all thoughts of my book aside and concentrated on planning for the hospital's needs in the event of war. I obtained a large stock of medical and other supplies, knowing that we would be largely cut off from Europe. Then I returned to Lambaréné in order to prepare for the war."

He knitted his craggy brows and I could tell that he was reliving the anxieties of the late thirties, when the heavy clank of the iron heel grew louder and nearer with each passing day.

The war came and only occasionally, at night, was he able to work on the books. And then, at war's end and in the years that followed, a whole new crop of problems sprang up at the hospital, resulting in yet other postponements for his serious writing. First of all, he said, additional buildings were needed. Then there was the biggest single new project since the hospital started—his leper village, built with the money he received from the Nobel Peace Prize. And, of course, his visit to the United States in 1949 in connection with the bicentenary celebration at Aspen, Colorado, of Goethe's birth.

"Interruptions—important interruptions—but interruptions all the same," he said. "I worked for months on the Goethe lectures to be given in America. I worked for almost half a year on the Nobel acceptance speech."

I asked if the original Nobel acceptance manuscript was still available; I felt that any number of book publishers would feel privileged to issue it. Perhaps some of the matter might be adapted for article purposes. In that case *The Saturday Review* would like to put in a bid for the material right now.

Dr. Schweitzer said he had not looked at the material for some time, but would, at a later date, send me a copy. He feared, however, that it might need a great deal of work. And he shuddered

when he thought of all the other work that claimed priority. Here he was telling me of the difficulty he was having in finding time to finish his two major manuscripts and now, just in the act of talking about it, another book was being mentioned.

"Perhaps I had better do what I can, when I can and if I can, on the *Philosophy* and the *Kingdom*. Even though it has been some years now since I have been able to do any sustained writing on these books, my mind has kept ticking away like an old clock a long time after the key had been lost. The central ideas have been developing in my mind; I have a fairly good idea of what it is I should like to say; now all I need is time to say it."

His reference to time jolted me into the awareness of my own responsibility for having taken up so much of his afternoon. I told the Doctor that there was much I wanted to discuss with him, especially as it concerned his manuscripts; but perhaps we should leave it for another time.

He said he had understood from Emory Ross that I had some mission or other in connection with his manuscripts but the whole thing was very mysterious. He smiled and got up to leave.

"Tomorrow, at four o'clock, I will come here again to Clara's room and we will talk. And the mystery will be no more."

As he walked out the door he turned around and cautioned me to wear my helmet at all times. He said it would take him too long to give all the reasons why it was necessary for me to do so but he hoped I would take his word for it. I told him that by now I was completely indoctrinated.

After he left, Clara said she had a feeling we would get what we came for. She was deeply pleased to see the Doctor so relaxed.

"It's been a long, long time since he has talked this fully about philosophical matters with anybody. He needs it. It is a busy but lonely life here for him at Lambaréné. Always it is the pressure of the hospital. And he does not have the chance to exchange ideas in the fields that mean so much to him. He will come tomorrow and we will put the two propositions to him."

But at four o'clock the next afternoon, Dr. Schweitzer did not

come. Fifteen minutes later we were in the middle of an equatorial squall. I had a large umbrella and I asked Clara whether I ought to take it to him. Clara said that even though the Doctor had no umbrella and seldom used a raincoat he would not be stopped by the heavy rain. This troubled me and when, at four-thirty, the Doctor had failed to arrive, I put on my raincoat and set off after him with the umbrella.

He was not in his bungalow. I learned that he was out in the rain, looking after a new shipment of medicines, making sure they were in a dry place. When he came to his bungalow and saw me standing there with outstretched umbrella, he shook his head slowly and said he hoped I had not thought he had forgotten our engagement.

We walked together to Clara's room. He took off his helmet, hung it on the bedpost, then seated himself on the bed as he had done the day before, resting his arm on the metal tubing. He started off by lightly scolding the both of us for having thought it necessary to come after him. I exonerated Clara and said I had come to fetch him because of the storm. He put me at my ease at this, saying that even old ducks can shed water.

"Now then," he said, "there are some matters you wish to take up with me?"

There were two such matters, I replied. One of them concerned the manuscripts. The other matter was of a more general nature. I would like to defer it until we had had a chance to discuss the first.

"Very well, then," he said, "let us proceed with the first matter. Emory Ross has asked me to give it my most careful and favorable attention. I almost have the feeling of approaching doom."

His face lighted up with a big smile. This put me at ease. I told Dr. Schweitzer that his friends in America and throughout the world, in fact, were deeply concerned about his unpublished manuscripts. They felt it a matter of the most urgent importance that these works be completed and issued. In this latter connection, I said there was serious apprehension over the physical safety of the manuscripts.

"All right," he said, "we will discuss the manuscripts. So that you will know fully all there is to know about them, I will review the

situation as it stands at this moment. As I told you yesterday, there
are two unpublished manuscripts. Having mentioned *The Philosophy
of Civilization* at our meeting yesterday, we will now discuss *The
Kingdom of God*.

"No one has seen this book and I have not talked about it. This
book is practically complete. The thesis is that Christianity has veered
away from Christ. Christianity has constructed an elaborate dogma
but it has not really comprehended that the mission of Jesus was to
enable every man to discover the Kingdom of God in himself. Jesus
wanted to prepare man for the Kingdom of God; it was his dominant
concern. But Christianity, as it has developed, has been more con-
cerned about the forgiveness of sins and the resurrection than it has
been about the thing that was closest to Jesus—the fact that mankind
must understand the meaning of the Kingdom of God. Jesus did not
claim to be the Messiah. He claimed to be none of the things that
have been claimed for him. He claimed only to know the reality of
the coming of the Kingdom of God.

"There is not much more to say about it. An author is really a
poor person to talk about the central ideas in his book."

I asked where the manuscript of *The Kingdom of God* was.

"Right here in a trunk at the hospital," he said.

"When will *The Kingdom of God* be ready for publication?"

"As well ask a hen exactly when she expects to produce her egg.
I do not know. There are so many things for me to do here at the
hospital. Everything is changing. Now that the Africans have all
become French citizens, our whole relationship to the patients is
different. Now there are elaborate forms to be filled out for the
administration. Each African who wants workman's compensation
has to have detailed information supplied about him.

"Formerly, I would just dash off a short note, sign my name to it,
and that was that. Now it's endless. And if I say that a patient has
been treated and is ready to go back to work, he may become out-
raged for he would like to stay away from his job yet get paid for it.
Little by little, all the joy is going out of our work."

(I recalled reading that when he first came to Lambaréné, Dr.

Schweitzer wrote to his friends in Europe, saying that he wished they could come to see his joy when a patient left for home after being treated at the hospital—well and smiling.)

"And this is not all," he continued. "There is so much work to be done. Little things that have to be done that no one else will do. Look at that curtain. It should have a rod at the bottom, too, so it won't blow into the room when the wind is strong. I must really get to it.

"A few years ago, I thought that my long-range problems at the hospital were in the process of being solved. I had a doctor here who could take over and keep the hospital going after I died. And I felt that I would soon have the time I needed to finish my books. But it became necessary for him to leave—the reasons are long and complicated—and then I had to take the entire burden of the hospital again. The doctors who are with me now are very good but they are very young and so I cannot relinquish the supervision of the running of the hospital.

"It takes two years before a doctor is really on his own here at Lambaréné. There is so much to learn that can only be learned by experience. When a doctor first comes out, we have to go through certain stages. They all have the same ideas for bringing in electricity and for doing this thing and that—things that many years ago we had decided against for specific reasons—and one has to be patient."

I remarked that the wonder to me was not that he had been able to write so little but that, under the circumstances, he should have been able to write at all.

"The published writings have turned out to be helpful friends," he said. "As I may have told you earlier, the first buildings at this hospital were paid for by Johann Sebastian Bach. The royalties from my book on Bach, that it. Who knows, perhaps these other works, if I am able to complete them—remote as this may now appear to be—may be similarly helpful."

I asked if we could revert to his *Philosophy of Civilization*. What led him to conceive of it and write it?

"Just before the First World War," he said, "I received an invita-

tion from the London representative of Harper & Brothers to do a book on my philosophy. I started work on it, finishing it shortly after the end of the war. Then I sent it to Harper's, which apparently lost its old enthusiasm for the project, saying they were very sorry, and they returned it. I guess the idea of a book by anyone with a German background—even a French-speaking German from the Alsace—was not too popular in those days.

"And then I sent the book to my publisher in Berlin. And he, too, had no taste for the manuscript. Finally, I didn't know what to do with it, so I asked my friend Emmy Martin, who was going to Munich, to dispose of it any way she wished—on almost any terms.

"Emmy took the manuscript under her arm one day to a publishing house named Beck. I don't think she knew that Beck was primarily interested in legal books, but she went in anyhow and asked to see Mr. Beck. She was told that Mr. Beck was out but that the bookkeeper would see her. He was Herr Albers. Emmy introduced herself. Her hands trembled as she held the manuscript, and with an air of defeat she said she supposed that there would be no interest in a book on philosophy.

"Herr Albers took the manuscript, leafed through some of the pages, and said nothing for ten minutes. Then he said that Emmy couldn't have the manuscript back. He wanted to read the entire thing.

"When Emmy Martin wrote to me that Beck would take my book, I was overjoyed. On my next trip, I went in to meet Herr Albers who was to become my close friend for many years— until his death by suicide during the Hitler regime."

At this point Dr. Schweitzer interrupted himself.

"Are you sure that you are interested in this sort of thing?" he asked.

I assured Dr. Schweitzer that nothing could interest me more.

Dr. Schweitzer looked at me closely, smiled slightly, and said he did not want to seem like a garrulous old man. He continued.

"It was just about that time that Albers had persuaded his associates to publish another very long book, this one by a writer named

Oswald Spengler, who gave his work the ominous title *Decline of the West*. And so now Beck had two non-legal heavy philosophical works on his current list.

"One day, the three of us—Albers in the center, Spengler on one side, myself on the other—were going out to lunch together. And I burst out laughing, and said he reminded me of a butcher out walking with his prime oxen.

"There was much trouble before my book was published. All the money Beck made on Spengler was wiped out by the runaway inflation. And my own book was held up because the printing press had been requisitioned by the government in order to turn out more paper money. Finally the book appeared and I was pleased when I learned that it would be translated into other languages.

"But *The Decline and Restoration of Civilization*, as the book was called, was actually only part of a much larger whole. And it is the last part of this larger work that I have had such difficulty in finding the time to work on. Most of my time was spent in building up the hospital. Then one day, during the early thirties, two doctors who were here at the time came to me and insisted that I work at the hospital during the mornings only and that the afternoons and evenings I give to my manuscript. It was wonderful. I was able to accomplish a great deal. In fact, I even had time to undertake a collection of various autobiographical papers. And so, *Out of My Life and Thought* was born. It was this book, I am told, that called my ideas to the attention of people who had not heard of me before."

That was how I happened to hear about him, I said. Because of my interest in the organ a friend had sent me a copy of the book in 1938, with a slip marking the chapter on organ building. And I remembered what a pleasant discovery it was to find among the moderns someone who still used the Aristotelian system for exploring a subject. The way Aristotle explained plant life was the way Dr. Schweitzer's chapter on the organ treated the art and science of organ building—what kind of wood to use in the pipes, where to place the organ, where to place the choir, what kind of nave was

most suitable—dozens of factors that had to be correlated before an organ was built and installed.

While we were talking about *Out of My Life and Thought* one of the nurses came in to ask a question about some drugs that were needed. He disposed of the matter, then resumed.

"I was saying that after *Out of My Life and Thought* appeared, I began to make interesting connections in many places. I received an invitation to give the Gifford Lectures in Edinburgh, which I accepted. I was glad that I did so, for I worked on the lectures for almost two years and derived much intellectual stimulation from it.

"Then came World War II. You will recall that I told you yesterday that I happened to be on a boat passing through the Bay of Biscay, when I became convinced that the war was near, upon hearing that Adolf Hitler had just assured the world that all he wanted was peace. I then returned to Lambaréné in order to prepare the hospital for carrying on its work even though it might be cut off from a large part of the world in the war years. I was able during that time to give little sustained attention to my writings. Now I don't know whether I shall ever finish the *Philosophy*."

"How much more work is there?" I asked.

"Once again, the mother hen: I have no idea. There is more work to do here at the hospital than ever before. More patients. More new buildings. More letters. And the forms to fill out, of course."

"Where is the manuscript of your third volume of *The Philosophy of Civilization?*"

"It is also here at the hospital—in my trunk."

It was at this point that I told him that his friends were worried about the condition of these manuscripts. I understood that there were no duplicate copies. There were hazards of fire, flood, decay—any one of a number of things that could happen to his work. We believed that it would be wise to have photographic copies made of the manuscripts. And it was for this purpose that I had come with Clara with special camera equipment that would enable us to have film negatives made of all his unpublished work.

He looked somewhat startled at this.

"It would take many, many hours," he said.

I assured him that his own presence would not be necessary, that Clara and I would team up to carry out the project, and that all that would be needed would be the manuscripts.

He said he would consider this and give his answer the following day.

I moved on to the next point and told him that a publisher in New York had authorized me to offer him an advance against royalties of twenty-five thousand dollars for his manuscripts.

"Two things about this," he said.

"The first is that Goethe taught me a lesson that has become a stern rule. Goethe made the mistake of committing himself to deliver books by a certain date without being absolutely certain that he could fulfill the commitment. It tore him apart. He became the prisoner of his own promises. It affected him deeply. I don't want that to happen to me.

"The second thing is that I have learned from the Niebelungen to keep one's loyalty to one's associates. I already have several publishers in the United States who have worked with me."

This matter was discussed rather fully, and I told Dr. Schweitzer that I felt that at whatever time the manuscript would be ready, we could go to his own publishers and receive from them some idea of their own capacities and desires in the matter.

"This, too, I will think about," he said. "But now let us discuss the other matter."

I took a deep breath, then plunged in. I approached the question of world peace at its largest, discussing existing world tensions in the context of an age that had available to itself total destructive power. No people and no nation were really secure. And the race for security, inevitable under conditions of world anarchy, had the paradoxical effect of intensifying the insecurity. For the new weapons placed a high premium on surprise. Yet the nations felt they had no choice except the pursuit of military strength in a lawless world.

But far more serious was the fact that man was now able to tamper

with his genetic integrity. Through radioactivity he was in a position to pursue and punish the unborn generations. He now had the power to change and cheapen the nature of human life. This was power of an ominous order indeed.

I watched Dr. Schweitzer carefully as Clara, speaking very slowly in German, relayed my message. His eyes were closed and his brows were knit. He sat with his head bent forward.

I asked Clara to emphasize that I realized I was not saying anything that he did not know far better than I. My reason for bringing up the subject was that I felt there was no one in the world whose voice would have greater carrying power than his own.

When he asked what it was that we would have him do, I said we had nothing specific to suggest other than that he might feel free to express his concern to the world.

At this moment, Dr. Margaret rapped on the door. She apologized for interrupting but there was an emergency case—a woman with an extrauterine pregnancy who had just been brought to the hospital. An immediate operation was necessary but the woman was already too weak to undergo surgery.

Dr. Schweitzer stood up to leave.

"Dr. Margaret has come at just the right time," he said. "It is good to be reminded now and then that even in a world struggling with the momentous issue of war and peace the individual has problems.

"We will talk further."

There was only one place at the Schweitzer hospital where electricity was available. This was the operating room, where there were modern overhead surgical theater lights. The electricity was furnished by a generator. When the motor was turned on, the throbbing noise alerted everyone that the operating room was going into action. During the night, an African medical orderly was assigned to the river landing. When an emergency case arrived and it appeared that surgery would be necessary, he switched on the noisy genera-

tor. The effect was that of a gong in a fire station. Doctors and nurses would swing out of their beds like firemen, jump into their clothes, and do everything except slide down a brass pole.

Not long after midnight on the day Dr. Margaret came to Clara's room to tell Dr. Schweitzer about the woman with the extrauterine pregnancy, the generator started up. Instantly, I could hear activity in some of the rooms. There were hurried footsteps on the porch. The steady throb of the generator continued for perhaps an hour and a half, or two. Then the motor stopped and after a while I could hear the shuffling footsteps on the porch of the doctors and nurses trudging back to their rooms. I didn't need the sounds to tell me how exhausted they must have been. It was 4:30 A.M. In another two hours the hospital would be starting on another day. I wondered how many on the staff were too tired even to sleep. The air was heavy and the act of breathing was almost a conscious one. Little wonder that Dr. Margaret showed darkness under her eyes and at times seemed to walk with a stoop. She was no different from the others; fatigue was their constant companion.

About a half-hour after the doctors and nurses returned to their quarters, I heard strange voices coming up the hill. At first, the sound was a low rumble. Then, all at once, the voices, now sharp and insistent, seemed to be collected at the end of the porch. These were African voices and they were angry. I got out of bed quickly, put on my khaki pants, and went out on the porch. Not far away in the dim light I could make out some two dozen people in a cluster.

I walked toward the group and perceived the small, slight form of a person who was apparently saying something to the Africans in subdued tones. It was Clara. One of the Africans had stepped forward and said that the group wanted La Doctoresse to produce the body of the woman who had just died on the operating table. They had been instructed by the witch doctor to obtain the body in accordance with their customs.

In a voice that indicated understanding but also strength, Clara said that La Doctoresse was sleeping; she was exhausted from her night's work. Under no circumstances should she be awakened. Then

Clara stepped down from the porch and approached the tall African who was spokesman for the group. For a second I feared for her safety—but only for a second. Clara was saying something to the tall African that caused him to nod, then turn around and speak to the group in a native tongue. There was a brief exchange, but the voices became increasingly moderate, and then the tall African said something to Clara, politely and almost in a whisper, and turned away and started down the hill. The others followed him.

Clara sat down on the steps. I could tell from the way she did it that she had spent herself emotionally. I know she didn't want to talk about it, so I said nothing and went back to my room.

Later, at breakfast, sitting next to Dr. Coulon, I learned what had happened.

The woman had been brought into the hospital late the previous afternoon. The case had instantly been diagnosed as an extrauterine pregnancy. That is, fertilization had taken place outside the uterus. The embryo had been allowed to develop long past the danger point. Apparently the woman's parents had insisted on witch-doctor treatment, but when the pain became fiendish, the woman's husband took the matter into his own hands, put his wife into a pirogue, and paddled thirty miles to the hospital.

Dr. Coulon said that all the doctors had agreed on the need for an emergency operation to save the young woman's life. But the woman had lost so much blood by the time she had arrived at the hospital that La Doctoresse felt any immediate surgery would almost certainly kill her. Under the circumstances, they decided on immediate transfusions in the hope that the patient might regain sufficient strength to endure an operation.

At about 2:00 A.M. it became clear that the decision to operate could be put off no longer. The embryo had ruptured and an immediate operation became mandatory, however small the chance for success.

La Doctoresse did the operation assisted by the others. The patient died during surgery. It had affected La Doctoresse deeply.

"After something like this, it is natural that a doctor should torture himself with doubts," Dr. Coulon said. "Would the patient be

alive if we had operated earlier? Perhaps we should not have oper-
ated at all? Was there something that should have been done that
hadn't been done? I know that Doctoresse did everything possible,
but I know how she feels."

This sort of experience was not new to Dr. Coulon. He had stud-
ied graduate medicine at the Union of South Africa. Then he became
an itinerant jungle doctor. He worked in the African villages. The
only apothecary available to him was what he carried in his bag.
Surgery would generally be performed in the open, on a flat board.

When he arrived at Dr. Schweitzer's hospital, he marveled at the
facilities.

"People come here from New York and are appalled at the crude-
ness and the startling lack of modern sanitation and instrumenta-
tion," he said. "When Mrs. Coulon and I came to the hospital after
working in the open jungle, it was as though we had come into a
fairyland. It was wonderful. There was a ward in which patients
could be kept under observation. There was a good supply of mod-
ern medicine, including the newest antibiotics. There was an oper-
ating theater, with overhead electric spot. There was a wide variety
of operating instruments. I couldn't have been happier."

I asked Dr. Coulon about the mortality statistics at the hospital.
He said that the mortality might be high by Western standards, but
that one had to keep in mind that a larger number of the serious
cases had been brought to the hospital too late for effective medical
or surgical care.

All this time we had been conducting our conversation at the
breakfast table in very low voices. The death of the young woman
after such a long fight to save her had darkened the spirits of the
staff. Even Dr. Schweitzer, who ordinarily could be counted on to
keep a mood from becoming too heavy, remained silent through the
meal. Dr. van Stolk and Dr. Friedmann came in late for breakfast.
Neither had shaved. The Doctor nodded to them; they ate quickly,
saying little.

After breakfast, on the way back to our quarters, Clara spoke to
me about the incident earlier in the morning on the end of the porch.

She had been awakened by the voices and she had intercepted the group before they could get to La Doctoresse's room. The Africans lived in the constant presence of death. Even so, its mysteries gave birth to many dictates and rituals. And one never knew at the hospital when the fact of sudden death would cause a group to act in an inexplicable and apparently hostile way.

I asked what she had said to the group to cause it to turn back.

She said she had tried, as simply and sincerely as she could, to give them some idea how Dr. Margaret and the others had fought to save the young woman's life.

"I told them that only La Doctoresse had the authority to release the body," she said, "and that when she did so she would turn it over to a member of the family as was the custom, and not to a crowd. For if the body were turned over to a crowd every time it asked for it, people would lose their confidence in the hospital staff. I said I was certain the tall African could see this.

"These are basically very kind people and they respond to kindness," she continued. "Somehow they had gained the notion that the young woman had been sacrificed in some way or another. I knew if I could make them see how Dr. Margaret had given of herself to save the young woman, and how unkind it was to make demands on her now that she had finally earned some rest, they would change their minds. The leader of the group must be a very fine man; just before he left he said he was sorry that they had awakened me and sorry that the group had wanted to disturb La Doctoresse. As I say, these are wonderful people."

A young African woman carrying a baby walked up to Dr. Margaret. There was a slight hesitation in her manner but it was obvious she had something to say.

Dr. Margaret put her at ease. Then the mother exclaimed that her baby was all well again and she was eager to have La Doctoresse share her joy.

Dr. Margaret took the child and cradled him in her arms and held him close. He couldn't have been more than six or seven months old. She then handed the little boy back to his mother, turned to us,

and said she was going down the hill to release the woman's body to the family, so that it could be brought back to the village for burial in accordance with tribal customs.

I went back to my room to take care of some more work that had been mailed to me by the office. But I couldn't put my mind to it. I was thinking of the hospital and of the young people who had come there to help Dr. Schweitzer. I wondered whether they had been prepared for the drama that was waiting for them—for the pain of occasional defeat and the constant challenge of unpredictable human response. Life at the Schweitzer Hospital involved much more than the glamour of being associated with one of the great figures in history. It meant hard work, fatigue, heartbreak. All this came with the decision to be a doctor, of course; but there was an extra dimension at Lambaréné that was almost beyond anticipation.

And what about the Africans themselves? How did they feel about the young men and women in white who had a method of treating them and their families far different from the treatment their own customs sanctioned or dictated? Why, when death occurred, was there such a powerful tug of reversion? Did they regard this inability of a white doctor to save a black life as proof of the fallibility of the white man, and as punishment for the Africans for having wandered outside that which was part of them?

I looked out the screened door and saw a small procession in single file led by Albertina going up the hill. Mme. Oberman was walking behind Albertina, followed by two Africans carrying picks and shovels. Behind them two Africans were carrying a litter on which an object of human size was wrapped in ferns and large leaves.

I put down my work and followed the procession along the narrow path leading up the hill toward the leper village. A little more than halfway toward the village, Albertina led the procession on a path off to the right. Very shortly we came to a clearing; it was a burial ground for those persons who had died at the hospital and had no relatives or friends to claim them. In accordance with the custom of the Africans who lived in this part of the Continent, the dead are carefully wrapped in long ferns before they are laid to rest.

A VISIT TO LAMBARÉNÉ

Two Africans were at work preparing the grave. Their picks and shovels cut easily into the soft rich ground. Albertina and Mme. Oberman stood off to one side. When the grave was ready, Albertina read from the Bible while the body was put to rest. She continued the prayers for several moments and closed the book. Then the Africans filled in the grave again, working steadily. When they were through, they looked up at Albertina, who said a final prayer. Then we walked in single file down the narrow path again.

As we neared the bungalow and the path widened, Albertina waited for me to catch up with her. She told me that the man who had just been buried had been deranged and had been put in an isolation cell. For days he had refused to eat, yet there was something about him that Albertina liked and admired. So far as anyone knew, he was alone in the world. He had come to the hospital on his own, unusual for a mental case. As his condition became progressively more acute, he seemed to know that he had come to the right place. He would have periods of agony and violence, which necessitated his isolation, but he would also have moments of apparent clarity.

Only the previous evening, when Albertina came to look after him, she found him in a rational and quiet mood. He beckoned to her and told her that he thought he was going to die. He reached out and took her hand and said he was grateful to her for taking such good care of him. Then he lapsed into silence for a long time. Albertina could tell he was slipping. After a few moments he said in a low voice that he had always feared that he would be alone when he died. But now he was not alone because of Albertina, and he was content and grateful.

He asked Albertina to pray for him, which she did. Before she was through, he passed away.

And now, on the way down the hill again, Albertina was telling me about the man.

"Sometimes I wonder," she said, "whether my coming here makes sense—whether I am doing anything that is really useful. Then something like this happens, and my doubts no longer seem so terrible."

In the days that followed, I was to learn that Albertina fulfilled a dual role at Lambaréné—nurse in charge of the psychiatric ward and ministerial assistant to Dr. Schweitzer.

There was no chapel at Lambaréné. Sunday services were held in the open air. The Sunday I was there I was directed to the long, narrow compound in front of the hospital clinic. The Africans sat on the steps or in the doorways of the small wooden structures in order to get the protection of the shade. Albertina stood in the hot sun; she wore her customary white pith helmet. During most of the service she read from the Bible. There were a few hymns and the voices of the small African choral group off to one side were heard above the rest.

Like everything else in Lambaréné, the services were simple but effective. After Albertina gave the final benediction, the Africans chatted with each other. A number of them were dressed in their Sunday best: several men wore long pants and clean shirts, instead of the customary shorts and frayed undershirt. The women, for the most part, wore colored cotton dresses and their hair was neatly done.

Albertina exchanged pleasantries with the people who went up to her after the services. Then she walked slowly up the hill to her room. I watched her until she disappeared from view. Here was a young woman of about twenty-eight or thirty, tall, slender, attractive, intelligent, compassionate. She had defined a mission for herself in life. It was not an easy one. It involved a constant drain on her energies—physical, mental, emotional. Her satisfactions were centered in her exertions. Most of what little time she had to herself she spent in study—reading intensively in the field of mental disease and psychiatric treatment.

The more I thought about Albertina and the other young people on Dr. Schweitzer's staff, the more I realized their importance and the greater was my admiration. It took purpose of a very high order to work at Lambaréné. The glamour of the work, such as it is, eventually fades. Those who came expecting to spend most of their time communing with Dr. Schweitzer, or working valiantly alongside him,

soon discovered that Lambaréné was no playground for the human spirit. The contact with the Doctor, except at mealtime, was necessarily brief. For the most part a staff member was on his own—that is, if he did a competent job. If not, the Doctor stepped in and attempted to set him straight. Then, if his work was still substandard, the Doctor might switch him to something else. He didn't waste time on idle flattery or trying to keep up appearances; there was too much that had to be done, too little time to do it. More than a few people never made the grade at Lambaréné and came limping home.

That is why Dr. Schweitzer tried to be so careful in screening applicants—why it required a prolonged exchange of letters and detailed checking before a person joined the staff. As a result, an extraordinarily high percentage of the people who came to Lambaréné stayed for years.

Some of the staff members, for example, had served for a quarter-century or more. To be sure, not all of them made their acquaintance with Dr. Schweitzer by mail. A few knew him in Europe and followed him to Africa to serve in any way he wished them to. Mlle. Mathilde Kottman, general supervising assistant who had a total dedication to the Doctor, had come to Lambaréné from Alsace about 1923. Mlle. Ali Silver, from Holland, general secretary and personal assistant to the Doctor, and who helped to translate letters from and into English, had served the Doctor for over ten years. Mme. Oberman, who was in charge of billeting, had worked with Dr. Schweitzer on and off for forty years. Mme. Emma Haussknecht, who died in 1956, was the second person to join the Schweitzers at Lambaréné.

While I was at the hospital, considerable excitement attended the departure of one of the nurses, Maria Langendyk; she had served at the hospital for sixteen years. And now she was leaving for a rest in Europe. She had completed the term of service she had set for herself.

When I walked into the dining room on the evening before Maria's departure, I could tell that something special was happening. Dr. Schweitzer was wearing his black clip-on tie; some of the younger

nurses were wearing lipstick; and there was butter on the table. Clara told me about Maria, a tall woman of about forty-five, with dark hair, dark eyes, and a face of quiet strength. Maria had come to the hospital, as did the others, asking nothing except the privilege to serve. But her service was now coming to an end. She had spent almost one-third of her life with Dr. Schweitzer. This dinner was now in her honor.

Halfway through the meal, just outside the window on the far end of the room, a choral group began to sing. It was a passage from Handel's *Messiah*. The choir was most unusual in the range of its voices. I was able to pick out perhaps a dozen children's voices and the voices of perhaps eight or ten grown-ups, some of which were deep and strong. The singing was superbly blended.

Clara whispered to me that the voices belonged to African lepers and that they had been trained by Trudi Bochsler, the young nurse in charge of the leper village about a third of a mile from the main body of the hospital. They had now come to serenade Maria and wish her Godspeed.

I was profoundly impressed by the singing and told Clara so. She said she hoped she might be able to persuade Trudi to have these same lepers put on a repeat performance of the Nativity Play that had so captivated the staff when it was produced at Christmas.

The next morning, virtually the entire hospital turned out to wave goodbye to Maria as she left by pirogue. I saw Trudi, holding a small leper child by the hand, standing not far from Dr. Schweitzer, on a bank overlooking the dock. Dr. Schweitzer was standing in his most characteristic manner—his head forward and his hands folded behind his back. Dr. Friedmann, standing close to Dr. Schweitzer, was waving his helmet as the pirogue carrying Maria slid away from the dock. Perhaps a dozen others rounded out the tableau, as the pirogue, aided by the swift current, eased downstream. I remembered thinking that the group on the bank would have made the ideal subject for a mural symbolizing the Schweitzer Hospital.

On the way back from the dock, Clara spoke to Trudi about the possibility of having the lepers do another performance of the Nativ-

ity Play. Trudi was delighted by the suggestion and said she was certain that the members of the cast all remembered their parts and would welcome the opportunity to play before the people who hadn't been at the hospital during Christmas.

Trudi herself was clearly excited about the prospect. Her large gray-blue eyes sparkled as she anticipated the joy that the idea of a repeat performance would bring to the lepers. It would take no time at all, she said, to prepare the production. Perhaps it could be done as early as the following afternoon. Since our next meeting with the Doctor was to be in the evening, the suggestion seemed ideal.

As I got to know Trudi, I was to learn that nothing was more characteristic of her than her spontaneous enthusiasm and sense of immediacy for things that were worth doing. She was open and direct in her dealings with people; no one who knew her entertained any doubts about her intentions or purposes. Nor did she hesitate for a single second to put up a battle for her point of view concerning the operation of the leper village.

Two years earlier Trudi had had a disagreement with Dr. Schweitzer on an administrative matter regarding the leper village. Unable to persuade the Doctor, she left the hospital and returned to her native Switzerland. For the next six months, neither Trudi nor Dr. Schweitzer rested easily about her departure. Then she wrote to him, asking whether she could return. Though Dr. Schweitzer had strongly espoused his own viewpoint, he was big enough to tell Trudi he was glad she would return and that she could administer the village in accordance with her own ideas.

Trudi returned to Lambaréné at once. While she had been away, she had put each minute to good use, studying every book she could find on the subject of leper colonies. In fact, there was very little that had been published on lepers—whether with respect to medical treatment or their social problems—that Trudi had not read. Her nurse's training had been of a general nature. When she had come to the hospital for the first time, and she had started to work with the lepers, she went at it as though it would become her life's work. This combination of day-by-day experience and observation and her

constant study had now made her, as Dr. Friedmann had remarked, one of the best-informed and most competent persons on the subject in the world.

When Trudi returned to the hospital she resumed her work with the enthusiastic devotion that is basic in her personality. Increasingly, Dr. Schweitzer tended to give her autonomy in the administration of the village. She became general manager, nurse, intern, teacher, confidante, minister, and family head. And she was getting good results. It was fascinating to see Trudi at work. The lepers worshipped her as though she were their queen, which in many ways she was. She was directly concerned not only about their physical but their emotional well-being. Their trust in her was absolute. When she prescribed a certain routine of medical treatment at the leper clinic, they would accept it without question.

Trudi's only real difficulties were with the witch doctors who hovered just outside the village. Once, when Trudi discovered that some of the patients were not taking their medicines because of omens cast by a witch doctor, she tracked down the fetisher and threatened right then and there to wreak all sorts of havoc on him if he didn't remove his hex at once. The fetisher lost no time in notifying the patients that it was proper and necessary for them to resume their medication.

This young white goddess looked the part. She was twenty-four or twenty-five, flaxen-haired, slender, attractive, intense, inexhaustible. It was clear that her work was giving her the kind of fulfillment she sought in life. She was responsible for the education of the leper youngsters, and each morning she conducted classes and arranged for the purposeful use of the children's time during the afternoon when she had to attend to her medical duties.

When Trudi proposed to her lepers that they put on a performance of the Nativity Play for the visitors at the hospital, they responded with gleeful anticipation, as she knew they would. Getting up the production for the following day was not an easy undertaking—the costumes had to be located and repaired; the stage props had to be put in order; each person had to brush up on his or her

part; and there had to be a complete rehearsal. But Trudi's certainty that the project was well within their reach was shared by all those who had a part in the play.

The next afternoon, I joined Clara, Dr. Catchpool, and the staff members who were eager to see the play again. We walked down to the leper village. The compound in front of the leper clinic had been transformed into an open-air theater. There were several rows of benches, one of which was already filled with visitors from the Catholic Mission across the river. Behind the benches were perhaps two dozen young African girls from the Mission who had come to pay their respects. They comprised a choir and were to sing during the intermission and at the end of the play.

At the sides of the compound, sitting on benches or on chairs or on the ground, were the lepers. Some of them had bulky bandages on their feet. Others had crutches stretched out alongside them. Even without the bandages and the crutches, the effects of the disease were clearly visible. Toes or fingers were missing, or the feet would be stubbed. A little boy of about ten whose foot had been amputated several weeks earlier went hopping around as he helped put the props into place.

Within five minutes after the play began, a spell of magic settled over the compound. The singing of the actors was full of life and conviction. Two or three of the leper voices had excellent depth and tone. The costumes were crude, very crude, but they helped to create the necessary illusion. The baby Jesus was beautifully behaved, and did not cry until the intermission, and then only briefly. The Three Wise Men were very deliberate in the roles. The leper who took the part of Joseph was compassionate and gentle in his interpretation. Mary obviously relished her role and sang with vigor.

And all the time the play was unfolding Trudi sat off to one side, her hands clasped and held close to her chest. Her mouth moved in the manner so well known to prompters.

If I say that the entire experience was almost beyond awareness or comprehension, what do those words suggest? Can they possibly indicate the range of emotion or the stretches of thought produced

by watching condemned people give life to a spiritual concept? The play was concerned, essentially, with the triumph of hope through faith; but the brief moment of the lepers in a glittering spiritual universe was surrounded on all sides by the evidence of a closed-in world. Yet in that brief moment, they were connected to the things that meant life for most people.

There was something else. The play, in a sense, was almost a symbol of forgiveness. For the white man in Africa had not, in the main, been a friend. Historically, he had not been a liberator or a benefactor. He had used his superior knowledge and power to capture the Africans and impress them into slavery. He had brought with him venereal disease. He had caused the African women to bear children and then he had discarded the mothers and their young. He had advertised a religion of mercy and compassion but there had been little of either in his manner. While I watched the lepers at Trudi's village in the Nativity Play, I became conscious of the fact that the play was saying something about a world large enough to hold both black and white. This was close to the original purpose of the play, but original purpose in religion is not too often a remembered part of life. The actors, however, clearly seemed to reflect this original purpose, to which forgiveness belonged.

All this was possible because we were in a segment of Africa where there was a Trudi Bochsler and an Albert Schweitzer and a Dr. Margaret van der Kreek and an Albertina van Beek Vollenhoven and a Dr. Jan van Stolk and a Dr. Richard Friedmann and all the others who rescued their whiteness from the evil that the others had spawned.

To the lepers who were on the sidelines, the spotlight for them frequently moved from the actors to the white audience. Comparatively, the poorest among us were rich as kings alongside an African, for we were in a place where wealth was measured by a pair of shoes or an extra pair of pants or an unfrayed blanket. And the lepers heard that we had come from an unbelievable world where people lived in beautiful dwellings of more than one room and could turn a knob that would produce water right in the house, and another knob that would control several fires for cooking. And, miracle of mira-

cles, they saw that education for everyone in the white world was free. There were schools for the blacks in French Equatorial Africa, of course, but these were mainly in the large cities. And the schools didn't go as far or teach as much as every white child was able to get.

There was nothing resentful in the gazes of the African lepers as they watched us. From their vantage point, we were the main show. The imaginative play of their minds was directed to us rather than to the actors. We probably touched off all sorts of wonderment and speculation, especially for the children. Nothing is stranger to the eye of an African child than a white person when seen for the first time. The lack of color creates an aspect of ghastly pallor. It is as though layer after layer of skin had been stripped away, producing what Africans generally refer to as a "peeled" look. The thinness of the facial features of a white person gives him a pinched, closed appearance. I could almost feel the scrutiny of the African children near me.

After the play ended, we sat still for a few minutes. I had no way of knowing whether the same thoughts that had preoccupied my mind were being shared by the others; in any case, the other white visitors sat quietly. They seemed far away in their thoughts. Then the children's choir from the Catholic Mission sang for a few minutes.

We got up to leave. Trudi announced that the leper children had a surprise for us. They had made gifts for each of us—hand-carved letter openers or ship models for the men and beads or pendants or necklaces for the women. Each child had a little presentation speech to make in French; he said he hoped we had enjoyed the play and that we would come to visit the village again.

Let me digress a moment.

I suppose people will ask: Is it safe to touch things handled or made by lepers? Is it safe to shake their hands or get close to them?

I have heard much conflicting medical testimony on the subject. Modern theory tends to support the view that leprosy is somewhat akin to tuberculosis and that there are varying stages and degrees of

contagion. If the leprosy involves the muscles or nerves, it is not believed to be infectious. If it involves the skin, however, especially where open sores are concerned, then there is the possibility of contagion. Lepers who have lost fingers or toes are in this category. Inflammation of the nasal mucosa with consequent discharge can be a source of infection. Children contract the disease through constant intimacy with leprous members of their families.

Generally speaking, however, outsiders who are in good health are not considered to be in any danger as the result of casual contact with lepers.

It goes without saying the Dr. Schweitzer and his staff exposed themselves constantly, regardless of the virulent condition of some lepers. But Dr. Schweitzer was careful to the point of seeming over-cautious in his policy about visitors. He advised them not to get too close to the leper patients and not to shake their hands or touch them. The reason, of course, was that he felt a total responsibility where any risk, however small, to outsiders was involved.

It wasn't always easy, however, to follow the Doctor's admonitions. When the little leper boy who handed me the hand-carved letter opener also offered me his hand, I did not see how I could turn away.

On the occasion of another visit to the leper village, a leper introduced me to his wife who was carrying a baby boy of perhaps twenty months or two years. The father told me his child was leprous, too. The baby's nose was running and he had sores all over his face. As I chattted with the parents, the baby twisted in his mother's arms and reached out for me to take him, which I did. To do otherwise, under the circumstances, would have been awkward and indeed impossible.

In general, if you want to see something of Asia or Africa—which is to say, if you want to get close to the people—you would do well to leave your apprehensions behind and take the plunge. If you are in good health, you will have little to fear. Now and then, of course, you are apt to find yourself in delicate situations where a few uneasy thoughts may cross your mind. Once, in a grove not far from Cal-

cutta, I came across a crying child of three or four who was obviously feverish. I carried the child to the nearest village compound. There I learned that the child's parents had died several days earlier, the victims of a smallpox epidemic still raging that had decimated the population of the village. I turned the child over to one of the older women. Certainly it occurred to me that I was in an exposed situation; but I tried to take some comfort at least in the fact that I had been inoculated against the disease.

This is not to say that I have been totally immune to infection or illness while abroad. I think I have sampled every species of dysentery recorded in the annals of medicine. I have had to make numberless, unscheduled, and speedy departures from receptions or social functions or public platforms all the way from Djakarta to Mexico City. There were times on the lecture platform in universities in Asia when I was certain I was capable of setting new records for the short sprint and I desperately longed for nothing so much as the chance to prove it. At such times, philosophical calm seems only vaguely attainable and, in fact, quite academic.

This digression, of course, is touched off by a consideration of the inevitable questions generally asked by prospective travelers about the personal health factor. Generally speaking, the risk while traveling is extremely small. Such deviations as occur are more the result of sudden changes in one's living routine than of basically unhealthy situations. Just the business of adjusting to severe time changes can be constitutionally unsettling. The pursuit of new foods is a delightful adventure; when carried to unreasonable lengths, it can produce deceptively intense but fortunately temporary discomforts.

Experiences such as these, of course, are not peculiar to Americans abroad. They apply equally to visitors to our own shores. The foreign visitor also has to adjust himself to exhaust gases from buses, trucks, and cars on a scale far beyond anything he would experience in his own city, wherever it may be. The heavy monoxide fumes added to the industrial smoke of American cities, to a person unaccustomed to them, can produce severe headaches and nausea.

There is also the matter of crowds. When Americans think of

dense population masses, they are apt to think of cities in India or Japan. But nowhere in the world are more people crowded into a smaller space than in New York City. I have seen the teeming millions in Asian cities, but never have I seen greater human congestion than in the Grand Central section of New York City during the lunch hour. The business of navigating even a short distance through the crowded sidewalks calls for a special knowledge and a certain conditioning. Little wonder that people from abroad who see New York City for the first time have the feeling of being overwhelmed and exhausted—almost to the point of illness.

I have had the good fortune to be the host in the United States to visitors from Asia. And I could tell that the noonday crowds charging through New York streets produced an effect on some of them akin to panic. They had never seen so many people under such compressed conditions before. All this, combined with the new rich diet and the accelerated American pace, caused more than a few of them to long for the comparative openness of Calcutta or Tokyo.

In any event, Americans need not fear that they are in mortal jeopardy every time they leave their own country. Nor need they believe that such minor discomforts as they may encounter are the exclusive products of foreign places.

This disgression out of the way, I should like to revert to the people at Lambaréné.

Like the Schweitzer Hospital itself, the leper village was understaffed. Trudi received some assistance from the regular staff members and she had considerable assistance from the lepers themselves. But her personal workload was very heavy indeed. One of the newcomers to the hospital, Olga Deterding, was aware of this and volunteered to work full time as her assistant. In particular, she wanted to accept responsibility for the education of the youngsters. But Olga had been at the Schweitzer Hospital only two months at the time of our visit. Her apprenticeship was not yet complete. It was necessary for her to spend a few more additional weeks on kitchen duty and mop-up detail before she would feel justified in asking Dr. Schweitzer to assign her to the leper village.

Olga Deterding came to Lambaréné almost by accident. She had

started out across the African desert in a large jeep with some friends. The jeep had broken down several times and the expedition finally broke up. Olga decided to press on by herself and see something of Africa. That was how she happened to arrive at the Schweitzer Hospital. What she saw she liked and she decided to stay on and work for Dr. Schweitzer for as long as he would have her.

Olga arrived with a secret and did her best to keep it. She was the daughter of an English multimillionaire. She said nothing about her economic and social station because it might appear to others on the staff that she was staying on at Lambaréné for a lark. Also, she didn't want the staff people to feel any disparity in their relations with her.

Unfortunately for Olga there were factors beyond her control that made it impossible for her to keep her secret. Word slipped out in London, with the inevitable result that stories began to appear in the press, some of which filtered back to Lambaréné. Olga began to get cables from magazines or news services asking for permission to send writers and photographers to the hospital to do feature stories.

All these Olga ignored. But one day Dr. Schweitzer received a cable from a Paris picture magazine saying it wanted to send staff members to the hospital for a story built around Olga. Dr. Schweitzer, after talking to Olga, politely declined. Despite this, two days later there arrived at the hospital, unheralded, a French photographer-writer and his wife and a Japanese correspondent (also carrying a camera).

Dr. Schweitzer was informed by the French correspondent that his editor had discovered that his magazine's files were somewhat out of date and he wanted some fresh material about the hospital. Dr. Schweitzer was aware that the correspondents had made a long trip and did not want to send them away empty-handed. He said he would be glad to escort them around the hospital grounds. Then he put a direct question to them: was there anything they wished?

Yes, there was. They said they would like to meet the members of the staff and do some stories about them, too.

Was there anyone in particular they would like to meet, the Doctor asked.

Why, yes: they would like to see Miss Deterding.

Well, then, said the Doctor, this was something only Miss Deterding could decide. He would put the question to her.

The reporters waited in the dining room while Dr. Schweitzer sought out Olga. Her reply was given without hesitation. She did not under any circumstances wish to see the journalists. She felt that any publicity would be inconsistent with the character of the hospital and that of the people who worked there. She felt, too, that her purpose in staying on at Lambaréné would be defeated if she were placed in the spotlight. Besides, she was a comparative newcomer and wanted to prove herself.

Dr. Schweitzer relayed this message to the waiting reporters. They tried to convince Dr. Schweitzer that he could persuade Olga to change her mind.

The Doctor said he did not feel free to do this. Was there anything else he might do for them?

The reporters consulted among themselves and then said they were eager to accept Dr. Schweitzer's offer to escort them around the hospital grounds.

Dr. Schweitzer replied that he would be happy to do this on condition that they would agree not to pursue Miss Deterding.

They agreed.

The tour of the hospital began, but every now and then one of the reporters would quietly detach himself from the party and go searching for his quarry. It was apparent that they had no idea what Miss Deterding looked like, for they confronted Dr. Margaret, Albertina, Trudi, and at least three nurses and proceeded to act as if they knew the person was Olga.

They did see Olga but failed to make the identification. Olga's assignment that week happened to be kitchen detail. The reporters peered into the kitchen. It didn't occur to them that the girl with the soiled apron involved in the messy job of cleaning the innards from fish and peeling vegetables could possibly be the glamorous multi-millionairess they were looking for.

It was hot in the skullery. Olga was drenched with perspiration. Her hair clung to the sides of her face. When the reporters looked at

her she smiled politely. They smiled back and passed on.

Finally, the party gave up the chase and left the hospital. When Dr. Schweitzer met us that evening in Clara's room, he sat down hard and breathed deeply.

Well, now, he said, maybe we could see the way it was. Another day very largely lost. One day is given over to filling out elaborate forms for the government. No sooner is that finished than another day has to be devoted to parrying with the fourth estate.

Then, characteristically, the Doctor's sense of humor lifted him out of his despairing mood.

"The tour of the hospital was most thoroughly done," he said. "Even if it wasn't what they really wanted, they saw all that there was to see. Finally"—and here he grinned widely—"just to keep them occupied, I gave them a lecture on philosophy. It was a good lecture, but I'm not sure they were in a philosophical mood. Anyway, they have now gone and we can get back to our various projects."

"Which of your two purposes do you consider more important?" Dr. Schweitzer asked. "My unpublished manuscripts, or the general question of world peace?"

I told the Doctor that we felt the purposes were related, but that we were perfectly willing to have him decide which one was to be taken up first.

"But you are leaving in a few days," he said. "We may not have enough time to do both. Therefore, I ask you again: which one of your two purposes are you most bent on achieving before you leave?"

I said Clara and I had hoped to leave with some statement by him having to do with world peace. We also wanted to photograph such unpublished material as he had with him at Lambaréné.

Let us revert, however, he said, to the matter of the peace. Over the years he had been collecting materials on the question of nuclear energy, military and non-military. When he had visited Europe some months earlier, his concern had been considerably increased as a

result of a meeting of Nobel Prize winners in Lindau, Germany. Many of the scientists there spoke with the utmost sense of urgency and gravity about the growing problem. Alongside the problem of peace, everything else seemed small.

Nothing to me was more striking than Dr. Schweitzer's face as he contemplated and spoke about the situation that confronted people in the world today. There seemed to be an infinity of detail in that face; it seemed as though every event in human history were clearly recorded there. Most of the time he sat forward in his straight chair, his eyes seemingly fixed on a distant object.

Only a few years ago, he added, the statement that this planet could be made unfit for life seemed absurdly melodramatic. But there was no longer any question that such power now existed. And even without a war, the atmosphere could become dangerously contaminated.

"After our earlier talk," he said, "I reflected that danger of this magnitude is not easily grasped by the human mind. As day after day passes, and as the sun continues to rise and set, the sheer regularity of nature seems to rule out such terrible thoughts. But what we seem to forget is that, yes, the sun will continue to rise and set and the moon will continue to move across the skies, but mankind can create a situation in which the sun and moon can look down upon an earth that has been stripped of all life.

"We must find some way of bringing about an increased awareness of the danger," he continued. "It is a serious thing that the governments have supplied so little information to their people on this subject. There is no reason why people should not know exactly where they stand. Every once in a while, the governments will reassure the people but this comes only after there has been a serious alarm. What is needed is genuine information. Nothing that a government knows about the nature of this new force is improper for its people to know."

Dr. Schweitzer asked me if I had brought any documentary data on the matter we were discussing.

I took out from my bag a number of papers, among them an abstract

of a report, of which Dr. Willard F. Libby was a co-author, that had been prepared for the United States Atomic Energy Commission in August 1954. The report was concerned with the effect of fallout of radioactive strontium on milk resulting from the uranium and plutonium nuclear explosions that had taken place up to that date.

Samples of milk taken from various places showed evidence of some contamination. The quantities of this radioactive strontium were found at the time to be well under dangerous levels. Even so, Dr. Libby's report showed evidence of growing apprehension, especially in his recommendation that the federal government undertake estimates on the cost of decontaminating milk. The decontamination would be effected by removing the calcium from the milk. Calcium has an affinity for radioactive strontium.

Three things were significant about that report. The first was that most of the radioactive fallout resulting from previous nuclear explosions had yet to come to earth at the time the survey was made. The second was that the biggest nuclear explosions were to occur after the report was published in August 1954. The third was that no precise data are available on the tolerance limits of human beings to radioactive strontium.

In other forms of radiation, it is definitely known that there is far less safety than had earlier been supposed. Only ten or fifteen years before, for example, the public had been assured that it had nothing to fear from regular X-ray examinations. More recently, however, it was disclosed that the tolerances were astoundingly lower than once had been so confidently claimed. Scientists had yet to perform the same kind of exhaustive researches into the tolerance limits of radioactive strontium that had been made on X-ray radiation. If, through additional research, it developed that the effects of radioactive strontium had been underestimated, as in the case of X rays, then colossal damage to all living creatures would have been done. And this is the kind of damage that cannot be undone.

The discussion with Dr. Schweitzer then turned to the power of the new bombs. One way of visualizing this new power would be to imagine a procession of one million trucks, each of which contained

ten tons of TNT. The total tonnage would form a man-made mountain of dynamite several times the height of the Empire State Building. If this mountain were to be detonated it would represent the approximate power in a single twenty-megaton hydrogen bomb that can be carried by a single plane.

Dr. Schweitzer said that a very high order of public understanding throughout the world was necessary in order to deal with this problem.

I then told him that this was precisely what he was in a position to do. He was among the few individuals in the world who would have an almost universal audience for anything he might say.

His eyes turned from a distant object and he looked at me directly.

"All my life," he said, "I have carefully stayed away from making pronouncements on public matters. Groups would come to me for statements or I would be asked to sign joint letters or the press would ask for my views on certain political questions. And always I would feel forced to say no.

"It was not because I had no interest in world affairs or politics. My interest and my concerns in these things are great. It was just that I felt that my connection with the outside world should grow out of my work or thought in the fields of theology or philosophy or music. I have tried to relate myself to the problems of all humankind rather then to become involved in disputes between this or that group. I wanted to be one man speaking to another man."

I asked whether the Doctor felt that the matter we had been discussing was as much moral as it was scientific or political. I told him I believed there was no living person whose voice on such an issue would be more widely heard or respected.

Dr. Schweitzer thanked me for the compliment, but said that this was a problem for scientists. He believed that it would be too easy to attempt to discredit any non-scientist who spoke out on these matters.

I told him that I thought it inconceivable that this would be true in his case. Moreover, this was not solely a laboratory question. If nuclear power could have the effect of damaging the genes of human

beings, then the nature of man himself was involved. Sovereign nations were now in a position to make decisions that were not properly theirs to make.

In saying this, I told him I recognized that the problem could not be considered apart from the larger uncertainty in the world today. Nuclear experimentation did not exist in an otherwise placid world. This, of course, added to the peril of mankind. For what we had most to fear was not merely the tests themselves, hazardous though they might be, but a saturation of tensions resulting in all-out nuclear war.

Dr. Schweitzer agreed, saying that anything that would be done against nuclear experimentation should not have the effect of putting the West at a disadvantage with respect to Soviet Russia.

He said, however, that the very real challenge of world communism should not be used as the reason for withholding vital information from the human race concerning the dangers of unlimited nuclear testing. It was possible that an informed and determined world public opinion could serve as a powerful force in bringing about enforceable agreements with respect to arms control and in leading to other long-range measures for peace.

In view of all this, I asked the Doctor whether he felt justified in putting aside his reticence about making a public statement.

He said that he would continue to give careful thought to the matter. He was still troubled, he said, about the form a constructive statement might take. How would it be issued? How would one go about drafting a statement that would be outside the context of the ideological struggle in the world today? He re-emphasized that he didn't want people to think that he was admonishing the United States or trying to intrude into domestic concerns. He wanted more time to think about these things.

When we resumed our discussion the next day he said he was still uncertain about the form of a statement or the method of its release.

Meanwhile, he was eager to consider an aspect of the problem that was highly significant. This was the fact that nations which were setting off nuclear explosions in the pursuit of their own security

were possibly jeopardizing the health of other peoples.

On the basis of recent visits to Japan, it became apparent to me that the Japanese government was confronted with a profound dilemma. It did not wish to oppose the American government, nor did it see any way of condemning Soviet Russia at the United Nations without including the United States. But Japan had increasing evidence of soil contamination as the result of the Russian tests and fish contamination as the result of the American tests. Autopsies had indicated the presence of radioactive strontium in a number of corpses. The American hydrogen bomb explosion called "Operation Castle" had not been under complete control. Japanese fishermen outside the prohibited area had been hit by radioactive ashes. The Japanese government had just issued instructions to its people about precautionary measures in the preparation of leafy vegetables and fish. But decontamination of food was a complicated laboratory process; it was doubtful whether even the most careful washing and boiling would be adequate.

As a result, Japanese public opinion was sensitive on the subject and was now becoming articulate and potent. Meanwhile, some Japanese were exploiting the issue of testing against the United States, making it appear that America was responsible for the failure to arrive at cessation agreements, and saying little about the fact of Soviet nuclear testing.

As we discussed the role of the bystanders with respect to nuclear testing, I could see that Dr. Schweitzer felt that this was a vital issue. As a citizen of a democratic nation, I did not feel that we had any right to take measures that were of possible danger to others without their consent. Indeed, one of the main arguments against Nazism and more recently against the USSR was that they were scornful of the rights of others and did harm to innocent people in their pursuit of military advantage. Is it any less immoral for any nation to jeopardize the health and safety of other peoples through uncontrolled air dispersal of radioactive poisons? If other peoples are involved, then they have a right to participate in the basic decisions involved in testing. There is no more basic tenent in democratic

government than that people who are affected by the acts of government have a right to participate in the affairs of that government.

If it is wrong to impose a tax on a man without giving him a voice in government, is it any less wrong to deprive his soil or water of their purity without giving him a chance to be represented and heard?

There was no argument about any of this, the Doctor said. What concerned him was the propriety of his making any statement. It was something he wanted to think about carefully. Meanwhile, he asked me if I would put down in writing a summary of such facts on the question of nuclear fallout as I happened to have with me.

Then he got up to leave. He opened the door, then said, as though by afterthought, that he would put together the manuscript of *The Kingdom of God* and would turn it over to us in the next day or so.

When Dr. Schweitzer came for our meeting the next afternoon, he was carrying a small bundle. It was neatly wrapped in a large napkin. He handed it to me. "This is the manuscript of *The Kingdom of God*," he said simply. "It is practically complete."

I opened the bundle. Here, for all I knew, was one of the most important books of our time. The sheets had been perforated at the top and were tied together by a string. But I gasped when I saw the kind of paper that had been used for the manuscript. There were sheets of every size and description. Dr. Schweitzer had written his book in longhand on the reverse side of miscellaneous papers. Some of them were outdated tax forms that had been donated to Lambaréné by the French colonial administration. Some were lumber requisition forms used by a lumber mill not far away on the Ogowe River. Some came from old calendars. I couldn't even begin to count the number of manuscript pages which were written on the reverse sides of letters sent to him many years earlier.

In any other man, this would have seemed quixotic and inexplicable. In Schweitzer, however, it represented a complete consistency with everything else in his life. There was the crude piano in

the dining room he wouldn't replace or repair because the money could better be used elsewhere. There was the fact that he shaved without soap or lather because he considered it a luxury. There was the fact that he traveled third class only because "there was no fourth class." He could no more think of buying paper for his own literary use than he could buy an easy chair.

This, then, was *The Kingdom of God*. It was written in German longhand. The interlinear editing was prodigious. To conserve space, he had written in a very small hand. Down the right-hand margin, in even smaller longhand, were penciled notes.

Thrilled though I was with the manuscript, I was severely apprehensive over the ability of the camera to deal with such close and faded written material. I feared, in fact, that the penciled notations might be substantially lost and said so to the Doctor.

"That is nothing to worry about," he replied. "The penciled notes are for me alone. That is the way I like to write. When I sit down to my work, the first thing I do is write my outline down the right-hand margin of each page. Then I use the main part of each sheet for the actual writing by pen."

Dr. Schweitzer said that he had started the previous evening to assemble the manuscript. All the pages were in a trunk, but they had not been in the proper order. It had taken him several hours to get all the pages together and put them in sequence. I shuddered at the invasion of his time represented by this special effort.

As for *The Philosophy of Civilization*, Dr. Schweitzer feared that getting this manuscript together would take several days of uninterrupted work, at least. There were more than four hundred thousand words in the *Philosophy*, which made it several times longer than the *Kingdom*. It was doubtful, he said, that he would be able to get to this for several months. But he promised that he would make a special effort in this direction.

Then the Doctor said that if there was nothing further to discuss about the manuscript, he would like to revert to the matter of the statement about peace.

"Even while I was sorting the manuscript papers last night and

this morning I have been thinking about the declaration or statement or whatever it is you want to call it," he said. "I have no reason to believe that anything I might do or say would or should have any substantial effect. Even so, if there would be even the smallest usefulness that I or anyone else might have on this question, it would seem almost mandatory that the effort be made.

"This crisis intimately concerns the individual," he continued. "The individual must therefore establish a connection with it. The leaders of the world today have to act in an unprecedented way if the crisis is to be met. Therefore they must be strengthened in their determination to do the new and bold things that must be done. That means that the individual has a greater role to play than before. The leaders will act only as they become aware of a higher responsibility that has behind it a wall of insistence from the people themselves. I have no way of knowing whether I can help in this. Perhaps I may be justified in trying."

This was the first intimation Clara and I had had that he was giving favorable consideration to the issuing of a statement. We exchanged glances that revealed clearly how heartened each of us was by what the Doctor had said.

"I am still worried, however, about some of the special problems involved in this declaration," Dr. Schweitzer resumed. "I am not sure that I agree with you that a broad statement addressing itself to the danger of war and the consequences of war would be the most effective way of approaching it. Yes, the world needs a system of enforceable law to prevent aggression and deal with the threats to the peace, but the important thing to do is to make a start somewhere before we get into the broader questions."

He paused for a moment. Some baby goats were bleating just outside the rear of the bungalow and he went to the screen to see what was happening. The bleating stopped and he returned to his seat at the end of the bed.

"I think maybe the place to take hold is with the matter of nuclear testing," he said. "The scientific aspects of testing may be complicated but the issues involved in testing are not. A ban on testing

requires no intricate system of enforcement. All peoples are involved, therefore the matter transcends the military interests of the testing nations. It is clearly in the human interest that the tests be stopped. Even if there is a small chance that the tests are harmful, it is important that the nations set aside the tests until they are absolutely certain what this chance involves.

"If a ban on nuclear testing can be put into effect, then perhaps the stage can be set for other and broader measures related to the peace. That is why I am inclined to a fairly limited objective. Later we will be in a better position to do the bigger things you have been talking about."

I told the Doctor that I agreed it might be easier to rally world public opinion around the need to suspend nuclear testing by all nations than it would be to deal with the basic structure of a workable peace. The main problem was war itself. But if he felt that it might be wise to confine his initial efforts to the matter of nuclear testing, I would of course respect his decision.

Dr. Schweitzer said his mind had not been finally made up on this question; he had been thinking out loud. He would continue to study the alternatives. Meanwhile, he said, there was yet another important question: What form would the statement or declaration take? How would it be issued?

Had I given any thought to these questions, he asked.

I said that I felt a direct statement, released to all the news agencies, might be effective.

He shook his head at this, saying that he had serious doubts about the news release type of story. What it gains in immediate attention it tends to lose in long-term impact. Besides, he said, one runs the risk of competing with all the other news that may be breaking on a certain day. Here he reverted to one of his favorite themes.

"I am worried about present-day journalism," he said. "The emphasis on negative happenings is much too strong. Not infrequently, news about events marking great progress is overlooked or minimized. It tends to make for a negative and discouraging atmosphere. There is a danger that people may lose faith in the forward

direction of humanity if they feel that very little happens to support that faith. And real progress is related to the belief by people that it is possible.

"Well," he continued, "maybe this is the wrong time to worry how the statement is to be issued. Our first job is to bring the baby into the world. Then we can decide what to do with it. We will therefore worry first about what the statement should be; then we will study it and determine how it might be used."

Mathilde Kottman came to the room and reminded us that it was getting late. I could see she was concerned about the Doctor. I stood up but the Doctor put me at my ease.

"In a way," he said, "the two of you in coming here have broken down my resolve not to involve myself in anything remotely concerned with political matters. But as I said the other day, the problem goes beyond politics. It affects all men. All men must speak. Some way must be found to bring about an increased awareness of the danger. Anything that is done should above all be simple and direct. It should not be ponderous or academic."

Once again, as he spoke, he leaned forward in an aspect of intense concentration. His eyes were closed and he seemed to measure every word. As Clara interpreted, I could see that he listened to her carefully in order to make sure that the precise nuance or emphasis would be given to what he was saying.

It was clear, from both his words and his manner, that this subject was now preoccupying most of his thoughts. He looked out through the latticed window at the scudding clouds in the late afternoon sky.

"I know the weather in this part of the world like the back of my own hand," he said. "For forty-three years I have observed its habits and variations. And this is the time of the year when unfailingly there is hardly a breeze. And yet now there are winds that I have never known before. One must always be prepared, of course, for sharp changes in natural phenomena. But it is important at the same time not to ignore new factors which may not be of nature's making. Some scientific reports I have seen raise serious questions concerning the effect on weather caused by nuclear explosions. Obviously

much more study is required. But at least the question exists. If there is the slightest chance that man's crops are being jeopardized, it is the duty of the nations to find out definitely before they proceed blindly."

I told the Doctor of the report *The Saturday Review* had carried by Dr. Irving Bengelsdorf of the General Electric Company in the United States. Dr. Bengelsdorf had correlated freak weather occurring in various parts of the world with hydrogen explosions and the patterns of weather movements.

"All things are now possible," Dr. Schweitzer said. "Man can hardly even recognize the devils of his own creation."

Mathilde Kottman was still waiting in the doorway. The Doctor rose to leave.

"If you are not too tired tomorrow, we can think and talk further," he said. "Meanwhile, you now have the manuscript of the *Kingdom* for such use as you wish to make of it."

Late that evening, after most of the oil lamps at the hospital had been turned out, I walked down toward the compound. From the direction of Dr. Schweitzer's quarters I could hear the stately progression of a Bach toccata. The Doctor was playing on the piano in his small workroom. I had heard that this piano had an organ footboard attachment so that the Doctor could keep his feet in playing condition.

I went up on the porch and stood for perhaps five minutes near the latticed window, through which I could see Dr. Schweitzer's silhouette in the dim-lighted room. Then there was a pause in the music and the Doctor called out to me. It surprised me that he should have known I was standing outside in the dark. I entered his room and he bid me sit on the piano bench next to him while he continued the fugue. His feet moved over the organ footboard with speed and precision. His powerful hands were in total control of the piano as he met Bach's demands for complete definition of each note—each with its own weight and value, yet all of them intimately laced together to create an ordered whole.

Sitting there in the dim light with the vibrations of the toccata

racing through me, I had a stronger sense of listening to a great
console than if I had been in the world's largest cathedral. I knew
there might be things about Albert Schweitzer I would never com-
prehend or reconcile; but this particular Albert Schweitzer I felt I
knew and had complete access to. The yearning for an ordered beauty;
the search for a creative abandonment—yet an abandonment inside
a disciplined artistry; the desire to re-create a meaningful past; the
need for outpouring, the release, catharsis—all these things inside
Albert Schweitzer spoke in his playing. And when he was through,
he sat with his hands resting lightly on the keys, his great head bent
forward as though to catch any still-lingering echoes.

He was now freed of the pressures and tensions of the hospital,
with its forms to fill out in triplicate and the mounting demands of
officialdom; freed of the mounds of unanswered mail on his desk;
freed of the heat and the saturating moisture and the fetishers and
the ants that get into the medicines. Johann Sebastian Bach had helped
make it possible for Schweitzer to come to Lambaréné in the first
place, through book royalties. Now Bach was restoring him to a
world of creative and ordered splendor. For perhaps half an hour we
chatted on that piano bench in the thin light from the flickering oil
lamp at the far side of the room. He was speaking personally now—
about his hopes mostly, like a young man just starting out in a career
and musing about what he would like to accomplish. First, he would
like to see his hospital in tip top running order. Second, he would
like to be able to train others to run the hospital after he was gone.
Third, he would like to have just a little time to himself—to work
quietly and finish his writings.

He did not wish these longings of his to give the impression that
he was unhappy in his work. Actually, he never thought much about
happiness or unhappiness in terms of his own life. Generally, he
thought in terms of what had to be done and the time required for
doing it. Now and then something would happen that would give
him a sense of fulfillment and deep reward. Only a few days earlier,
for example, he received word from a professorial colleague in France
about an examination paper turned in by a nineteen-year-old boy.

The question that had been put was: "How would you define the best hope for the culture of Western Europe?" The answer given by the student was: "It is not in any part of Europe. It is in a small African village and it can be identified with an eighty-two-year-old man."

Dr. Schweitzer paused. He held in his hand the letter that had told of the student's conception of his role in the modern world. He was profoundly moved.

"In the morning," he said, "when the sun is up and I hear the cries of the hospital, I do not think of these lofty ideas. But at a moment like this, when the hospital is asleep, it means much to me that the student should believe these things, whether they are true or not."

As we had anticipated, the photographing of the *Kingdom* took about six hours, spread over two sessions. During the rest of the time I worked on a memorandum covering the nuclear situation as Dr. Schweitzer had requested. This memorandum was based on various documents I had brought with me to Lambaréné, including the Libby report on radioactive strontium in milk, the report of the National Academy of Sciences in the United States, the report of the British Academy, and the official findings of the Indian government.

The following morning at breakfast, Dr. Schweitzer told Clara that he wished to spend most of the day with us and asked if we might be available. He would come to us at 11:00 A.M. and stay with us until lunch; he would meet us again at four in the afternoon; then we would spend the evening together.

The morning meeting was devoted to a discussion of the nuclear situation. The Doctor had been giving his constant thought to it. Concerning the matter of a possible news release, of one thing he now seemed certain: a direct press statement would be unwise. It was too pretentious, smacking of publicity-seeking. Perhaps a small journal would be best. If the statement were of any value, it might be reprinted in various ways. It might stay in circulation for a period of time and have a cumulative value.

I recognized that such an approach would be entirely in character, I said. At the same time, it was important to face the likelihood that anything the Doctor said on this subject, even in a small journal, would be picked up instantly and made into headline news.

In any event, I added, it seemed clear that the best way for the Doctor to proceed would be in a manner that he felt was natural to him.

We come now to the statement itself, he said. He felt that he should not aim at any arbitrarily chosen length as being especially desirable but rather should concentrate on making the statement as clear and as complete as was humanly possible regardless of length.

"I must be careful to develop the facts very fully," he said. "I don't want to be criticized for leaving large gaps in the argument."

The Doctor then recalled an experience in Oslo in connection with the Nobel Prize. It was an experience from which he had learned a great deal.

"I was told I was expected to give an acceptance talk. I worked on the talk for several months, developing my theme with great care. When the message was completed, I estimated that it would take from seventy to eighty minutes in the reading.

"But when I arrived in Oslo I learned that I would be given thirty-five minutes for the talk. That meant cutting the message in half. I was most unhappy but I proceeded according to the limitations. The original message had been as closely knit as I knew how to make it; the shortened version was uneven and the main points inadequately developed.

"For a moment, just before I got up to speak, I was tempted to reach for the full message even at the risk of being stopped halfway through my speech. But I downed the temptation out of courtesy to my hosts. After all, it was up to them to decide what kind of program they wanted.

"The printed version, of course, was of the short talk as delivered. I didn't like it and had no interest in seeing it or acknowledging its existence. Even so, I was surprised to see how it kept being reprinted

by various journals throughout the world and how long it seemed to stay alive."

He leaned back and drew a deep breath. Then he said the reason he brought up the matter was that he felt the question of length in the new statement should be put to one side; the only thing that should concern him was the accuracy and the relevance of what it was he had to say. I agreed.

What should be of most concern to him now and in the weeks ahead, he said, was to complete his study of the materials I had turned over to him. He would also correspond with some of the names I had given him and with various scientists in Europe who had expressed concern to him about these matters the last time he had seen them in Europe, at the meeting of the Nobel laureates in Lindau, Germany.

At the afternoon meeting, he did not sit down on the edge of the bed, as was his usual manner. Instead he cleared the small table and arranged three chairs around it. He had brought with him his regular stub pen and a bottle of ink.

"We must clear up our remaining business," he said. "Are there any new matters you would like to discuss?"

I broached a subject that had been very much on my mind but that was awkward to bring up in direct discussion with him.

He said that if this had anything to do with his affairs in the event of his death, it would please him if I felt free to proceed.

What about the manuscripts? I asked. If anything should happen, who would have the authorization to edit them and approve them for possible publication?

Did I have a suggestion to make on that score? he asked.

I replied that I felt a small group, consisting perhaps of Emory Ross, J. D. Newth, his English publisher, and Clara might be in a good position to superintend the publication of the books.

"Yes, that would be a good idea," he said. "If anything happens to me, you have the authorization to bring such a group together and make the essential decisions about my unpublished work. I ask only that you observe the following conditions:

"1. That you consider carefully whether the material is actually worth publication, and, if so, what form it is to take.

"2. That nothing be added to my work of any nature.

"3. That no one be permitted to write anything in my name."

I gave him my assurance that I would convey these conditions to the other members of this literary trustee group. As I did so, however, I could not help thinking that the Doctor would probably outlive all of us. His skin had the color and texture of a man at least forty years younger. His eyes were clear and sharply focused. His hands—perhaps the most impressive hands I have ever seen on a human being, combining strength with sensitivity—were without the slightest trace of any tremor. I could recall, too, that three days earlier I had accompanied him on his "rounds," which included everything from moving large boxes of medical supplies in a hot sun and carpentry work to an inspection tour of the hospital, walking uphill and down. He was less fatigued at the end of four hours than I was at the end of one. In fact, I found it difficult to think of any middle-aged man who could have kept up with him.

This matter disposed of, the Doctor inquired about other items of business.

I referred to the fifteen-year-old boy, Marc Chalufour, and his fight to save the old organ in his church from being replaced with a new electronic machine. Marc, who knew something about the subject, felt that the church was giving up a superior instrument, and had given me a letter for Dr. Schweitzer. The letter identified the old organ according to make and year, and reported on its condition. Marc felt that if he could have a note of support from Dr. Schweitzer, he might win over the elders.

Twenty-five years earlier, as a youth deeply interested in the organ, I had dreamed that it might some day be possible to talk to Albert Schweitzer about the art of organ building. No man alive knew more about the Silbermann organ—the finest church organ up through the nineteenth century. And now, a letter from a fifteen-year-old boy was the open sesame. To my great delight, he spoke at length about the wonders of the Silbermann organ—about the

knowledge and craftmanship that went into it, about its tone and its unique features, about methods for keeping it in good working condition.

Then, with obvious relish, he reached for paper and pen, and wrote a letter to Master Chalufour:

Dear Marc:

If the organ was made in 1858, it is a good one. That was an age of fine organ building in Germany, France, England, and the United States. The period of good organ construction lasted from 1850 to 1885. After that, organs were built in factories. The organs built in the 1850s had an excellent tone—sweet, not too strong, but noble. If your church organ is still in reasonably good physical condition, it is certainly worth conserving and restoring, for it is most valuable.

In Alsace, there are organs dating from 1730 that are still in use in the churches; and if your church does not want the organ, perhaps you may be able to find a place for it yourself. One day its value will be realized. The old organs are better because they were built by artisans. In those days there was not the competition in price that there is today. The organ builder was able to use the finest material and did not have to count the hours necessary to put into it, as one has to do today. He could deliver an instrument of the highest quality.

Good luck from my heart to the courageous and intelligent young man who wants to save an organ.

ALBERT SCHWEITZER

The Doctor put down his pen; the conversation about the organ and the letter had taken the better part of an hour. Despite the expenditure, I had no regrets for having opened up the subject; he had enjoyed himself thoroughly.

We went off to dinner, at the end of which several members of the staff remarked that they had seldom seen the Doctor in such a joyous mood.

After dinner, Dr. Schweitzer came to Clara's room again. The first thing that had to be done, he said, was to write a letter to President Eisenhower. In this letter, he wanted to thank the President for the cordial birthday greetings. He was also eager to express his concern about the world situation, especially with reference to the armaments race. After about twenty minutes, he showed us the draft:

Lambaréné
January 10, 1957

The Hon. Dwight D. Eisenhower
The White House
Washington, D. C.

Dear Mr. President:

I send you my heartfelt thanks for your friendly letter in which you send me your good wishes and those of Mrs. Eisenhower on the occasion of my eighty-second birthday. This expression of your good wishes was the first birthday greeting I received. Your generous and kind thoughts touch me deeply.

In my heart I carry the hope I may somehow be able to contribute to the peace of the world. This I know has always been your own deepest wish. We both share the conviction that humanity must find a way to control the weapons which now menace the very existence of life on earth. May it be given to us both to see the day when the world's peoples will realize that the fate of all humanity is now at stake, and that it is urgently necessary to make the bold decisions that can deal adequately with the agonizing situation in which the world now finds itself.

I was very happy to have Mr. Cousins, who will take this letter to you, here with me in Lambaréné. It was rewarding to spend time together and to see how many ideas and opinions we shared.

With assurance of my highest esteem, I am,

Yours devotedly,
ALBERT SCHWEITZER

He then wrote a final copy on thin white paper, put it into an unsealed envelope, and handed it to me to transmit to the President. He leaned back in his chair and asked whether I was glad I had come to Lambaréné.

Most certainly, I replied. I hoped he didn't think it presumptuous of me if I asked whether *he* was glad he had come to Lambaréné.

He said he had had some forty years in which to reflect on the answer to that question, so that there need be no hesitation in his reply. Yes; he was glad he had come to Lambaréné, very glad. It was while he was coming up the river Ogowe one day many years ago, passing one of the luxurient islands in the river and looking up at the scudding clouds, that the idea of reverence for life occurred to him.

Lambaréné had also made it possible for him to make his life his argument, he said.

This puzzled me and I looked up quizzically.

"As a young man, my main ambition was to be a good minister," he explained. "I completed my studies; then, after a while I started to teach. I became the principal of the seminary. All this while I had been studying and thinking about the life of Jesus and the meaning of Jesus. And the more I studied and thought, the more convinced I became that Christian theology had become over-complicated. In the early centuries after Christ, the beautiful simplicities relating to Jesus became somewhat obscured by the conflicting interpretations and the incredibly involved dogma growing out of the theological debates. For example, more than a century after Christ, there was a theological dispute growing out of questions such as these:

"Is Jesus actually God or the son of God?

"If he is God, why did he suffer? If he was the son of God, why was he made to suffer?

"What is meant by the spirit of Jesus?

"What is the true position of Mary in Christian theology?

"Elaborate theology dealing with such questions disturbed me, for it tended to lead away from the great and simple truths revealed in Jesus' own words and life. Jesus Christ did not proclaim himself to

be God or the son of God; his mission was to awaken people to the Kingdom of God which he felt to be imminent.

"In my effort to get away from intricate Christian theology based on later interpretations, I developed some ideas of my own. These ideas were at variance with the ideas that had been taught me. Now, what was I to do? Was I to teach that which I myself had been taught but that I now did not believe? How could I, as the principal of a seminary, accept the responsibility for teaching young men that which I did not believe?

"But was I to teach that which I did believe? If I did so, would this not bring pain to those who had taught me?

"Faced with these two questions, I decided that I would do neither. I decided that I would leave the seminary. Instead of trying to get acceptance for my ideas, involving painful controversy, I decided I would make my life my argument. I would advocate the things I believed in terms of the life I lived and what I did. Instead of vocalizing my belief in the existence of God within each of us, I would attempt to have my life and work say what I believed."

I recalled a discussion I had had several nights earlier with Dr. Friedmann and Dr. Margaret. We agreed that it was necessary only to see Dr. Schweitzer working with his hammer or making the rounds of the hospital to recognize a profound symbol. The symbol, of course, had to do with the carpenter and the healer.

And so I asked Dr. Schweitzer if this symbol to him was a conscious one; in short, whether he had come to Lambaréné in imitation of Christ.

When I asked the question, I couldn't be sure whether I had asked the most obvious question in the world, or whether I was pushing at a door that was meant to be kept closed.

Dr. Schweitzer looked up and said simply that the pursuit of the Christian ideal was a worthwhile aim for any man.

Then, after a moment, he said that he did not want anyone to believe what he had done was the result of hearing the voice of God or anything like that. The decision he had made was a completely rational one, consistent with everything else in his own life.

Indeed, he said, some theologians had told him that they had had direct word from God. He didn't argue. All he could say about that was that their ears were sharper than his.

He said, however, that he believed in the evolution of human spirituality, and that the higher this development in the individual, the greater his awareness of God. Therefore, if by the expression, "hearing the voice of God," one means a pure and lively and advanced development of spirituality, then the expression was correct. This is what is meant by the "dictates of the spirit."

By an advanced spiritual evolution, he emphasized that he was not thinking so much in theological terms as in ethical and moral terms. Thus he disagreed with the impression created by some of the Psalms that if people were good they would receive their reward. Goodness need not depend on rewards, or on the absence of punishments. True spiritual evolution means that there is an awareness by the individual of the natural goodness inside him; therefore he is not reaching out but actually discovering his true self when he brings the goodness to life. There is the need to do good. If one does it because he expects tangible rewards he will be mistaken.

This led to a discussion of man's expectations with respect to the deity. If man conceived of the deity as an omnipresent guarantor of the good, he was stretching the concept of the deity to suit his own needs and therefore he was mistaken. There is no point in expecting God to prevent injustice by man. He said that after the last great war, with all its killing and injustice, with its persecution of religious minorities and the concentration camps and gas chambers and soap made from the remains of slaughtered Jews—after all this, he did not see how it was possible to hold to the concept of a God who would intervene on the side of justice.

This, he felt, is not how God manifests himself. God manifests himself through the spiritual evolution of man and through the struggle of man to become aware of the spiritual nature of his being and then to nurture it and give it scope. The existence of evil—or the occasional triumph of the evil over the good, as in the case of persecution and concentration camps—did not mean that God was oblivious of

evil or indifferent to it. It means that man has the responsibility to deal with the evil and should not sit back and expect divine intervention.

Not infrequently in history, he said, religious leaders themselves would invoke the name of God for acts that were unjust. Calvin killed his enemies; Luther failed to speak out against the persecution of Jews; the early Israelites believed at times that it was their divine mission to kill; the Crusaders used the sword freely in the name of God. Modern instances were many. One example was furnished by religious Spaniards who went to mass and then went to see creatures slaughtered in the bull ring.

To talk of the "will of God" was a presumption and often a profanation, especially when one used the term to purify ungodlike acts. Moreover, to speak of the "will of God" is to use illusion. We must accept reality. And the dominant reality, to repeat, is that God manifests himself through the human spirit. Insofar as the individual is able to discover and develop his spiritual awareness, he is at one with the deity. Nothing is more wonderful or mysterious than the workings of the inner awareness by which man discovers his true spirituality.

I asked Dr. Schweitzer whether I detected an echo of Hegel's "only the spiritual principle, which is synonymous with God, is real." Hadn't Kant made a similar distinction—between believing God and believing in God?

He replied that he had always regarded Hegel as one of his most important teachers; he also reminded me of his debt to the Stoics and the early Chinese. As for Kant, he agreed with the distinction but said that so far as Kant's ideas in general were concerned, he could be impressed by them without being moved by them.

There is no reason why religion should not grow and evolve, as man himself must grow and evolve, he continued. When, for example, Apostolic belief is used as final authority for theological positions, it should be remembered that the Apostolic doctrine was not developed by the Apostles but was created by interpretation in the middle of the second century after Christ.

Theological rigidity, he feared, was hurting religion. Young people, especially, were looking to religion as a great spiritual adventure but were being disappointed because it was not searching and probing for expanding truths. Instead it was holding to fixed ideas which young people could not fully accept. There is nothing irreligious in the search for true religiosity. The more we think and the more we are aware, the greater our concentration on the development of human spirituality and the more religious we become.

A great cathedral may help to awaken the human spirit, but it cannot create it.

Each man, in a very real sense, carries his cathedral inside him.

St. Paul preached out in the open, so that all could hear. At the hospital in Lambaréné, there was no chapel. The preaching followed the pattern of St. Paul; it was in the open.

In all these respects, the Reformation is not yet complete. It has not given adequate weight to the Christianity of the spirit. Reformation means change; Christianity must not be afraid of change; it must not be afraid to examine and re-examine and grow. Jesus symbolized change and growth.

The ideas contained in "reverence for life" are consistent, he said, with an evolving Christianity. The door is open but Christian theology has not gone in.

To the extent that his thinking on Christian theology and religion in general have created differences of opinion, Dr. Schweitzer said that this was a matter that affected him deeply.

"I have not wished to create problems for Christianity," he said. "I have suffered deeply because some of my ideas have become problems for Christianity."

"Wasn't this what happened to Ernest Renan?" I asked. "Didn't Renan suffer because his own thinking caused him to veer away from the tradition in which he had been brought up?"

Dr. Schweitzer replied, "It is true that Renan, who was concerned with the life and meaning of Jesus, found himself at odds with the Christian theology he himself had been taught. This caused Renan great pain. In the end it tore him to pieces because he failed

to find an outlet by which he could make his own new ideas come to life. New ideas in this field of thought are powerful things. One cannot just conceive of them as mere intellectual properties and then take leave of them. My own ideas do not happen to coincide with Renan's. I am much more concerned with the actual shape of history in the life of Jesus. But I think I can understand how Renan's work affected him when he didn't allow it to redefine his life for him. This is what I mean when I say I came to Lambaréné because I wanted my life to be my argument. I didn't want my ideas to become an end in themselves. The ideas took hold of me and changed my life. Resistance to those ideas would have been impossible."

The Doctor got up to leave. It was now close to 11 P.M. After his earlier admonition on this score, I had avoided any mention of the hour or the need to conserve his energies. I consoled myself with the thought that even St. Paul recognized that there were limits beyond which it was unreasonable to berate a weak conscience.

I looked over at Clara. She was tranquil and content. But she had been scrutinizing me and could read my concern.

"You mustn't worry about the Doctor," she said after he left. "He does exactly what he want to do. That is one thing no one can take from him. Besides, he feels cut off from the world and relishes the chance to talk to people from the outside.

"We should be proud and happy," she continued. "Everything we wanted to accomplish has been done. The Doctor will do the statement and it will be a good one, a very good one, and he has promised to work on his manuscripts, and I believe this time he will do it.

"You know, for the past week or so I've been watching you closely and I have the feeling that this place had no strangeness for you from the start. I don't know how to explain it except to say that you made me think you had once lived here or a place like it and knew the kind of thing to expect."

She was right about one thing: I did have a special feeling about

Lambaréné long before I came. This grew not only out of Schweitzer's own descriptions of life in the jungle, but out of some experiences I had had as a child. For when I read his account of the hospital, it made a connection with part of my boyhood.

His books had been for me, as they have been for countless others, an intense reading experience. What he wrote had the effect of reawakening incidents and ideas in one's own life. The ideas may be only half-formed in your mind, and the incidents may be part of long-slumbering memories; but they spring to life full-size under the stimulation of his descriptions. When, for example, I came across a passage in Schweitzer's *On the Edge of the Primeval Forest* I had a burst of recognition.

This particular passage was concerned with the effect of illness on Dr. Schweitzer in his early forties. His future seemed uncertain. Two operations were necessary. They were a success and the recovery was complete. After it he could write: "The misery I have seen gives me strength, and faith in my fellow man supports my confidence in the future. I do hope I shall find a sufficient number of people who, because they themselves have been saved from physical suffering, will respond to those in need."

He had coined a striking phrase: "The Fellowship of those who bear the Mark of Pain." He identified the members of this Fellowship as "those who have learned by experience what physical pain and bodily anguish mean. They belong together, all the world over; they are united by a secret bond."

It was at this point that the magic junction of Schweitzer's ideas with my own experience took place. Years earlier, as a boy of ten, I had been sent to a public sanatorium for tuberculosis. The pain I felt was not one of sickness but of loneliness. It was the pain of being detached from everything warm and meaningful and joyous in life.

There was also the pain of being separated from hope. On Sundays I would find my perch on the wall near the entrance gate to the sanatorium and would watch the healthy people, many of them young married couples, as they walked up the hill from the bus station. They had come to visit relatives and friends but they owned the

miracle of being able to leave when they wanted to. I wondered about their world of health and total option and whether they rejoiced in it. I had no reason to believe I might ever be able to join that world. The boys in my age group in the ward seldom spoke about a life beyond the sanatorium. We knew that cures took place but we also knew that although people who left the sanatorium lived a careful, disciplined life, many of them came back.

In those days, antibiotics had not yet been born and tuberculosis sanatoriums existed as much for the purpose of keeping infectious people out of society as for treating them. As a result, the outside world was something of an unreality. We longed for it but it was like pressing our noses against the windowpane of a non-existent tomorrow.

The physical suffering was not severe. There would be some dizziness, a slight fever in the evenings, but we were used to it. Most of the discomfort, I suppose, came during the winter nights. Cold was considered useful therapy at that time and the ward would be converted into open-air shelters at night. Each patient had two blankets, ample for most weather, but there were a dozen or more sub-zero nights during the winter when it was too cold to sleep and we shivered violently until daybreak.

There was also the pain of human relationships. As in most dependent or disciplined groups, whether in a sanatorium, school, or penitentiary, there was a sharp division between the strong and the weak. Weakness was not necessarily a biological trait but was assigned to the newcomers, who were treated as outcasts. They served the old-timers and took orders; and they marked time until the shine of their newness wore off, when they were relieved of much of their underprivileged status. It had never occurred to me until then that individuals who were in the midst of suffering themselves could be cruel, but I soon realized that when people are thrown together, whether ill or healthy, some of them assert power by being bullies, just as there are some who have positive qualities of leadership. We had our share of both, especially the former.

On occasions, there would be something of a dissolution of the

animosities within the sanatorium; indeed, the dissolution would extend to the barriers that separated us from the outside world. One such occasion, of course, was at Christmas, when we put on the Nativity Play for the visitors. Even the bullies became just so many good voices in the choir. The feeling we had then of being able to join the world of the healthy and the warmth of being in their favor was a feeling I have never been able to forget. And when, years later, I sat in the section for the healthy outsiders at Trudi's leper village at the Schweitzer Hospital and watched the leper children perform in the Nativity Play, I could sense their emotions in this hour of glorious connection with the rest of the world. I could also sense their emotions when, after many rounds of applause, the connection ceased and the outsiders returned to the universe of unlimited options. The feeling the youngsters had, I was certain, was that only a miracle would enable them to become whole again.

The miracle had happened for me at the sanatorium. Six months after being admitted, I was discharged and went back to family and school. It took many years before I could comprehend the fact that I was fully cured. I didn't quite know how to go about establishing my membership in the world of the healthy. I hesitated to ask other boys whether I could play ball with them for fear they would laugh at me. And well they might: on my fourteenth birthday I weighed seventy-eight pounds. But we lived near a public park and I invested my weekly allowance of twenty-five cents in baseball practice. I hired a boy of ten to throw grounders to me and retrieve my throws from. the outfield. Within two years—some six inches taller and forty pounds heavier—I became the captain of the neighborhood baseball team, alternating between first base and shortstop. Sometimes, after league games, I would stay on the field, practicing running bases and sliding, so that I would know automatically where my feet should leave the ground without taking my eye off the ball in order to hook my slide away from the bag.

My debt to baseball was great. Even when, at college, I had a head-on collision in attempting to catch a fly ball, resulting in a serious concussion and temporary loss of memory, I almost rejoiced in the

fact that this was the sort of thing that sometimes happened to healthy people in the fullest use of their physical resources. What was happening, of course, was that I was enchanted with the idea of being alive. The magic of being able to run swiftly was worth almost any price. I gloried in the fatigue and perspiration that came from muscular activity, for earlier in my life the only perspiration I had known came from fever.

Even after I was able to accept fully the fact that I could live a normal life, I carried with me the feeling that I had the obligation somehow to pay back. The sense of debt was much more than an intellectual one. It lay deep in my bones and I had no way of ignoring it. Indeed, from the moment I walked out of the sanatorium and looked back at my Sunday perch on the old wall near the entrance, I knew that my life would be unbearable unless I could find some way of making good a debt I couldn't quite define but that I knew would be with me as long as I lived.

Albert Schweitzer expressed this feeling for me in *On the Edge of the Primeval Forest* when he wrote that "he who has been delivered from pain must not think he is now free again, and at liberty to take life up as it was before, entirely forgetful of the past. He is now a man whose eyes are open with regard to pain and anguish, and he must help to overcome these two enemies and bring to others the deliverance which he has himself enjoyed."

If I felt "at home" in Lambaréné, as Clara put it, perhaps it was because there had been something in my own life years earlier that enabled me to recognize the chemistry of human emotions that existed in a place like this. I could also recognize what Schweitzer meant when he spoke about the sense of summons he felt. He was not tormented by the tragic question that has stunted the growth of civilizations—the inevitable question asked by the individual: "What can one man do?" If the purpose were strong enough, the question answered itself. The fact that thousands of doctors were required to take care of the millions of people who were in need of them in Africa did not produce in Schweitzer either awe or surrender. A single doctor, he knew, could show that was possible. In the very

act of accepting a responsibility, he could make it visible to others. Besides, to deprive one man of help because many more also needed help was to design the moral paralysis of society.

"A single doctor in Africa," Dr. Schweitzer has said, "even with the most modest equipment, can mean very much for very many. The good which he can accomplish surpasses a hundredfold what he gives of his own life and the cost of material support he must have. Just with quinine and arsenic for malaria, with novarsenobenzol for the various diseases which spread through ulcerating sores, and with emetine for dysentery, and with sufficient skill and apparatus for the most necessary operations, he can in a single year free hundreds of men from the grip of suffering and death."

Albert Schweitzer had always been troubled by the fact that the white man, carrying with him the cross of Jesus, not infrequently also carried the means of cheapening the lives of people he sought to change or dominate.

"Ever since the world's far-off lands were discovered, what has been the relationship of the white people to the colored?" he has asked. "What is the meaning of the simple fact that this and that people have died out, and that the condition of others is getting worse because they were 'discovered' by men who professed to be followers of Jesus? Who can measure the misery produced by the fiery liquids and hideous diseases we have brought them?"

Dr. Schweitzer had given me some thoughts to carry to bed with me in the bungalow overlooking the wards on my last night in Lambaréné.

The plane made a half circle as it rose from the jungle clearing. Looking out the right side I could see the fast-shrinking figure of Dr. Schweitzer slowly waving his white helmet. In a few seconds the airstrip was obscured by the jungle hills.

I observed my fellow passengers in the plane. Their faces were close to the windows. This was Lambaréné country. It had some-

thing to say to the moral imagination; its images and symbols filled the mind. I looked down at the Ogowe River and thought of the thousand-year gap between the pirogue paddled by the lepers and the man-made metal bird that had lifted us out of the jungle and into the clouds.

I thought, too, of the gap between the hospital at Lambaréné and science in modern dress; but that was not what was important. Nor was it important that the Schweitzer Hospital should be at odds with advanced hospital design and practice. What was important was the timelessness of the Lambaréné message and the enduring nature of the teachings and the commitment and the symbol that belonged to it. The lesson was not new; in fact, it was one of the oldest lessons in the world, but it had yet to be fully understood. The lesson was concerned with the nature of human connection and obligation, with the reality of pain, the chemistry of human response, and the reach of the moral man.

I thought back to the long discussions I had had before coming to Lambaréné—of Clara's compassionate cautions and her concern lest I leave Lambaréné under a burden of disenchantment and hurt. I thought, too, of the talk with Frank Catchpool in the plane just before arriving at Lambaréné. And now I could dwell on these earlier cautions and anticipations in the full play of retrospect.

The biggest impression I had in leaving Lambaréné was of the enormous reach of a single human being. Yet such a life was not without the punishment of fatigue. Albert Schweitzer was supposed to be severe in his demands on the people who worked with him. Yet any demands he made on others were as nothing compared to the demands he made on himself. He was not concerned about the attainability of perfection; he was concerned, however, about the pursuit of perfection. He considered the desire to seek the best and work for the best as a vital part of the nature of man. When he sat down to play the piano or organ, and he was alone, he might stay with it for hours at a time. He might practice a single phrase for two hours or more. The difference between the phrase when he first played it and when he himself was satisfied with it might have been

imperceptible even to a trained musical ear. But he had a stern idea of his own capacity for interpreting Bach, for example, and he felt he must stretch himself to whatever extent was necessary to achieve it. This was no mere obsession. He sought his own outermost limits as a natural part of purposeful living. If he seemed to prod and push others, it was an almost automatic carryover of his own work habits.

There were other thoughts that occurred to me as we flew over the jungle hills of French Equatorial Africa. I considered the matter of Dr. Schweitzer's relationship with the Africans, and the many misconceptions about it that had found their way into print. When the Doctor first came to Lambaréné the life of the African had barely been touched by industrial civilization. It was difficult to get Africans to work steadily in putting up the buildings and in doing hard jobs for the hospital.

There was the temptation at first to think that the Africans were naturally lazy. But Dr. Schweitzer very early realized that it made a difference when one lives in a climate and in an environment where the needs are few. Living close to nature, the African saw no need to work beyond that which was necessary to the immediate well-being and the minimal needs of his family. The idea of putting up extensive buildings, making concrete piles, sawing and storing woods—all this seemed to have little connection with reality as the African lived it. But the lack of incentive did not mean, as Dr. Schweitzer soon came to realize, that the Africans would not work hard under any circumstances. When they understood the reason for making a special effort, they were more than equal to the challenge.

"Watching them one day as we made an emergency trip in the canoe to save the life of a woman who was seriously ill," Dr. Schweitzer had said, "I marveled at their stamina and their determination and I resolved never to fall into the careless habit of regarding them as shiftless."

Yet he was aware that he had been heavily criticized precisely on these counts. He had been accused of being patronizing and autocratic towards the blacks. He had even been accused of exploiting them.

"I must forgive the lies directed against myself," he had written, "because my own life has been so many times blotted by lies. . . . I am obliged to exercise unlimited forgiveness because, if I did not, I should be untrue to myself in that I should thus act as if I were not guilty in the same way as the other has been guilty with regard to me."

Albert Schweitzer is not above criticism. Few men of our century have come closer to attaining the Greek idea of the whole man—the thinker, the leader, the man of action, the scientist, the artist. But like all great figures in history, he becomes real not despite his frailties but because of them.

Men, like history, come to life in their paradoxes. Gandhi welded a nation of four hundred million people but he couldn't hold his own family together. The cause he defined required a Congress party to fight for it, but Gandhi never gave it the power of his own name. He was the apostle of non-violence in the attainment of national freedom, but once the freedom was won he did not object to the use of military force in the Kashmir.

No man was more effective in defining and working for the liberties of the American people than Thomas Jefferson. He was permeated with the cause of human rights; he saw it in all its aspects—historically, philosophically, spiritually. His great subject in life was the anatomy of freedom. Yet he owned slaves. Like Solon and Pericles centuries before him, he made prodigious contributions to the democratic design of his nation. But, also like the Greek leaders, he did not become passionately involved in the fight against human slavery. All this is now seen in perspective. It is what Jefferson did rather than what he failed to do that inspired his generation and has given him his place in history. Moreover, the principles defined by Jefferson later became the philosophical structure for the victorious fight against slavery.

The American name most associated with the uprooting of slavery, of course, is Abraham Lincoln. Yet only a few days before he became president, Abraham Lincoln said that he did not argue against slavery where slavery existed; he would argue only against its extension to new states. He said he would not eliminate slavery in the

South even if he had the power to do so. He appalled those who did not want to compromise on the issue. But when the moral summons was presented by history in its final form, Lincoln accepted magnificently.

The story of Lincoln in his relations with the blacks would be incomplete if told only in terms of his attitudes during the early days of the presidency. The inconsistencies and the paradoxes are neither ignored nor set aside by history; they merely yield to the consequential and to the main impact made by the man on the lives of others.

The sublimest paradox of all, of course, is represented by the fact that the most important prophecy of Jesus was proved to be historically false, yet this did not interfere with the establishment of a religion based on the total truth of his mission. Jesus prophesied the imminent end of the world. By imminent he did not mean a matter of several generations; he meant a few years. The fact that this did not eventuate was no obstacle to the creation or the growth of Christianity, based on the divinity and omniscience of Jesus. What was central and what made its impact on the spiritual nature of man were the godlike qualities of Jesus. His example and moral teachings awakened the natural spiritual responses of people; the rest was subordinated or forgotten.

History is willing to overlook almost anything—errors, paradoxes, personal weaknesses or faults—if only a man will give enough of himself to others. The greater the ability to identify and serve, the more genuine the response. In the case of Schweitzer, later generations will not clutter their minds with petty reflections about his possible faults or inconsistencies. In his life and work will be found energy for moral imagination. This is all that will matter.

Albert Schweitzer has not been immune from attack. There was a period of carping and exposure, much of it with an air of fresh discovery and all of it in a mood of disillusion. But in the long run the inconsistencies and paradoxes were as nothing alongside the real meaning of Albert Schweitzer and his place in history. For Albert Schweitzer has done more to dramatize the reach of the moral man than anyone in contemporary Western civilization. No one in our

times has taught us more about the potentiality of a human being. No one in our times has done more to liberate men of darkened skin. No one in our times has provided more inspiration.

If Albert Schweitzer is a myth, the myth is more important than the reality. For mankind needs such an image in order to exist. People need to believe that man will sacrifice for man, that he is willing to walk the wide earth in the service of man. Long after the hospital at Lambaréné is forgotten, the symbol of Albert Schweitzer will be known and held high. It would simplify matters if Albert Schweitzer were totally without blemish, if his sense of duty toward all men carried with it an equally high sense of forbearance. But we cannot insist on the morally symmetrical. In the presence of renunciation and dedicated service such as few men are able to achieve, we can at least attempt responsible judgments and we can derive spiritual nourishment from the larger significance of his life as distinct from the fragmented reality.

There is something else we can respect: we can respect the image of Schweitzer that exists in the souls of people. This image gives them strength and purpose; it brings them closer to other people and establishes connections beyond the power of machines and explosives to alter or sever. This is what men most need for today and tomorrow but especially for today. For the making of tomorrow requires most of all a sense of connection beyond reward or compulsion. Also a sense of service that has something to do with reverence and compassion for life. This is more meaningful to man than the things he makes or the conveniences he acquires or the ornamental props of his personal kingdoms. For he reaches his full growth only as he believes in the essential beauty of the human soul. It is this that Albert Schweitzer gives him.

Albert Schweitzer is a spiritual immortal. We can be glad that this is so. Each age has need of its saints. A saint becomes a saint when he is claimed by many men as their own, when he awakens in them a desire to know the best that is in them, and the desire to soar morally.

"Anyone who proposes to do good," he wrote, "must not expect

people to roll stones out of his way, but must accept his lot calmly if they even roll a few more upon it."

If there is a need in America today, it is for Schweitzers among us. We are swollen with meaningless satisfactions and dulled by petty immediacies—but the threat to this nation and its freedoms and to human life in general has never been greater. To the extent that part of this threat is recognized, it is assumed it can be adequately met by a posture of military and material strength. But the crisis is basically moral and demands moral strength.

We can't save the nation by acting as though only the nation is in jeopardy, nor by acting as though the highest value is the nation. The highest value is the human being and the human potential. In order to safeguard this human potential we have to do more than to surround ourselves with high explosives. We have to make the supreme identification with other people, including those who are different from us or who have less than we. If sacrifice is required, we shall have to sacrifice. If we are to lead, what we say and what we do must become more important in our own minds than what we sell or what we use. At a time when men possess the means for demolishing a planet the only business that makes sense is the business of inspired purpose.

We live in eternal dread of hunger; but we shall never escape the hunger inside us if we are starved for inspiration or are empty of vital purpose. And if we see not at all into these things, the things that make for a single body of all those who now live or who have ever lived, then we shall have lived only half a life. It is in this sense that Albert Schweitzer has helped to make men whole.

We can rejoice in this, for Schweitzer has given an infusion of spiritual energy to our age that is real and that will persist.

Returning home, I felt happy that my two specific purposes in going to Lambaréné had been met. But even more important was the fact that the image of Albert Schweitzer I carried away with me was intact—fortified, if anything, by a direct view. For at Lambaréné I learned that a man does not have to be an angel to be a saint.

Part II

The Correspondence

Introduction

*T*he correspondence with Dr. Schweitzer began several years before my visit to his jungle hospital described in the first part of this book. As is well known, some visitors to Lambaréné returned with complaints about lack of sanitation and modern medical equipment. The debunking of Albert Schweitzer had started. Much of it was to be expected. Few world figures escape the assaults of critics who seize upon little-known flaws or faults which are raised to monopoly status. In this case, Schweitzer's claim on history rested on something far more substantial than the appearance of his hospital. Schweitzer supplied a working demonstration of reverence for life.

My feelings along these lines took the form of an editorial in The Saturday Review. Several months after the editorial appeared, I received a letter from Dr. Schweitzer saying that he was grateful that I had perceived the essence of his purpose.

Thus began a correspondence with him which continued for ten years until his death in 1965. His letters were written in French or German, usually accompanied by an English translation from one of the two nurses who assisted him with correspondence. The letters reproduced here reflect to some degree the nuances and styles of his translators. Most of the correspondence was on the key issues of the times—the deterioration of international relations, the hazards of the nuclear arms race (including dangers to the environment caused by testing), and the pervasive sense of uncontrolled drift toward a nuclear holocaust. Yet, as Schweitzer's letters reveal, he did not feel that the human race was locked into a tragic inevitability. What these letters tell us is that, although human beings have no jurisdiction over the fact of their existence, they hold supreme command over its meaning.

1957

Air France

en plein ciel, le
January 12, 1957

My dear Dr. Schweitzer,

This letter, written in flight, can at best be an inadequate expression of my gratitude for the privilege of being with you in Lambaréné. You gave freely to me of the most valuable thing you have to give—your time. You gave me an opportunity to share directly and intimately in your thoughts and work. For this, I am profoundly grateful.

In anything I write concerning my visit and our conversations, I shall respect your request to say nothing about matters you wish to remain confidential. Concerning your philosophical and religious ideas, I shall put these down in approximately the form that I would plan to use them and send them on to Clara for her advice. If there is any question in her mind, I will of course make the appropriate omissions or corrections.

Apart from this, I should like to feel free to write with as much depth and range as I may be able to command. In this connection, I told Clara yesterday that I was still attempting to achieve a necessary

perspective about my visit. In fact, I feel somewhat inhibited because of three factors that now condition anything I might write:

1. What I have learned at Lambaréné that I have been asked not to write about

2. What I have learned at Lambaréné that my own discretion tells me I ought not write about

3. What I have learned at Lambaréné that everyone knows about and therefore need not be written about

Perhaps Clara can create in me a feeling of greater scope and margin for insight than the three conditions above now seem to allow. This is important for I have a great deal I feel I must share.

In connection with a possible letter you might write to Premier Khrushchev accompanying the text of your appeal: In view of the fact that almost anything you might write to Khrushchev may be distorted, it might be advisable to stress the fact that your statement emphasizes the need for *enforceable* controls of weapons adapted to mass destruction under fully functioning world law. Otherwise, it might be too easy for the Soviet leaders to agree to abandon nuclear weapons under treaty without enforceable controls, which would be hazardous and possibly meaningless.

In thinking carefully about the method by which your "Appeal" would be released, it occurs to me that we have a problem in timing. If the Zurich newspaper has an absolute exclusive in terms of the first release, what is likely to happen is that the news wire services will pick it up and flash the story everywhere the first day. This may have the effect of eliminating full publication in other influential journals later. My suggestion, therefore, is that we attempt, so far as it is possible, to release the statement in at least three places at approximately the same time. I would hope that the United States might be one of the three.

<div style="text-align:right">

Faithfully,
Norman Cousins

</div>

Dr. Schweitzer decided against writing to Premier Khrushchev, feeling perhaps that the groundwork for direct communications with the Soviet leader had not been laid. He did, however, write a letter to President Eisenhower about a quite different matter from the nuclear arms race—Algeria. This entire incident served to dramatize for me the political context in which his hospital had to exist.

Life for Dr. Schweitzer at his jungle hospital was not just a matter of ministering to the health of the Africans, or running a staff, or sheltering medical supplies, or looking after a constant stream of visitors and curiosity seekers. To a far greater extent than was generally realized, he had to do a political balancing-act. The Gabon was still a French colony, and the Doctor had to assess the effect of anything he might do or say on the political sensitivities of officials who held the power of life or death over the hospital.

Very early in our correspondence, I had a strong sense of the difficulties confronting Dr. Schweitzer in his dealings with government authorities. A trio of officials arrived from Paris for the purpose of exploiting Dr. Schweitzer's prestige in favor of the French position on Algeria before the United Nations. Dr. Schweitzer had no intention of issuing a statement on Algeria to the world press, as they requested, but neither did he wish to rebuff his powerful visitors altogether. His formula, as the correspondence makes clear, was to say to the officials that he would write to President Eisenhower about the Algerian situation; but he would send the letter to me for transmittal. What he didn't say to the French officials was that he was counting on me to explain to the President the circumstances of the letter. The Doctor had no way of foreseeing that the French officials, who were given a copy of the letter, would release it to the world press on their return to Paris.*

* In an effort to gain independence from France, guerrilla warfare was launched in 1954 by Algerian rebels. A revolutionary war involving at least 450,000 French troops continued for seven years at a high cost in lives and property. On July 3, 1962, France formally declared Algeria's independence.

Albert Schweitzer
Lambaréné
January 27, 1957

President Dwight D. Eisenhower
The White House

Dear Mr. President:

My friends in governmental circles in Paris have apprised me of the anxiety with which they view the fate of Algeria at the United Nations. I share their anxiety. This is what gives me the courage to write to you. Please forgive me for approaching you about the serious consequences that this could have for the French government on suffering a defeat at the United Nations through not having the support of the United States. The situation would be so compromising that it would hardly seem possible they could remain in power. This could even bring danger for French institutions, which would have its serious repercussions on Europe in the making for which M. Guy Mollet is one of the most outstanding protagonists. The defeat of France at the United Nations in the upcoming vote would seriously compromise the cause of Europe.

My anguish is dictating these lines to me. Be good enough to forgive me for daring to transmit them to you.

With respectful devotion,
Albert Schweitzer

Monsieur le Président Dwight
D. Eisenhower. Maison Blanche
Monsieur le Président

d'Albert Schweitzer
Lambaréné 27 jan-
vier 1957

J'apprends par mes amis dans le cercle gouverne-
mental de Paris, avec quelle anxiété ils considèrent
le sort de la question d'Algérie à traiter aux Nations
unies. Je partage leur anxiété. C'est ce qui me
donne le courage de vous écrire. Veuillez me par-
donner de venir vous parler des graves conséquen-
ces que cela pourrait avoir pour le gouvernement fran-
çais, si aux Nations unies il subissait une défaite
n'ayant pas le soutien de l'Amérique. Sa situa-
tion serait tellement compromise qu'il ne paraît
guère possible qu'il puisse rester au pouvoir. Cela
pourrait même entraîner un danger pour les insti-
tutions du pays de France qui aurait des réper-
cutions graves sur l'Europe en formation dont
M. Guy Mollet est un des plus remarquables prot

2.

a goutistes. La défaite de la France aux Nations
unies devant le ... à venir compromettrait gra-
nement la cause de l'Europe.

C'est l'angoisse qui me dicte ces lignes. Veuil-
lez me pardonner d'oser vous les faire parvenir.

Avec mon dévouement très respectueux

Albert Schweitzer

February 4, 1957

PERSONAL

The President
The White House
Washington, D. C.

Dear Mr. President:

 On my return from Africa, I want to thank you for your personal expression of good wishes on my departure and for your letter to Dr. Schweitzer which you were good enough to ask me to deliver to him, for you.

 I found Dr. Schweitzer in good health but terribly bogged down in his work. His ordinarily high good spirits are now considerably diminished as a result of added complications in the administration of his hospital. Most of these new complications are the result of changes in the colonial government of French Equatorial Africa. The government holds the power of life and death over the hospital and could invoke any one of a number of regulations that would make it impossible for the hospital to continue. Already, there are numberless forms for him to fill out; these are a great strain on his energies.

 I make a special point of all this as essential background for one of the two letters he asked me to transmit to you. This letter is concerned with the American position on the Algerian question. I owe it to you to say that a French representative made a special rush trip to Lambaréné to persuade him to write this letter to you. I think I can tell you, too, that it was not an easy letter for him to write, for it represented a violation of a basic operating principle of his life. Many years ago he decided that he would not involve himself in political affairs—though his personal interest in these matters was great—but would attempt to exert such influence as he might have toward building a world community in the world. It is self-evident,

I believe, that the circumstances of the present letter must have been unusual, to say the least, to cause him to forsake such a principle. It is also significant, I believe, that when the French representative asked if he would have any objection to having the letter made public, Dr. Schweitzer was absolutely firm in his opposition to public release of the letter. I find it significant, too, that he did not wish to send the letter to you directly, but specified that I transmit it. Whether this was because he felt I was in a position to explain the full background to you I have no way of knowing.

In any event, the letter is enclosed.

I also enclose another letter from Dr. Schweitzer. This one, in direct response to your own warm letter of birthday greetings to him, needs no special explanation. It is written out of the fullness of his heart and reflects his deep admiration for you as a person and world leader. To the expression of his good wishes, I of course add my own.

It goes without saying that I am at your command if you would wish further details about the situation at the Schweitzer Hospital.

<div style="text-align:right">

Sincerely,
Norman Cousins

</div>

P.S. In view of the possible embarrassment to Dr. Schweitzer if any of the foregoing should ever be published, I wonder whether the letter concerning the Algerian situation could be kept out of the regular files.

Despite Dr. Schweitzer's efforts to restrict his involvement in the Algerian crisis to his letter to President Eisenhower, and despite my request to the President, on behalf of Dr. Schweitzer, to keep his letter confidential, the French government betrayed its assurance to Dr. Schweitzer and released his letter in Paris, which was picked up by the world press and put Dr. Schweitzer in the position of supporting African colonialism. I sent the following cable to the doctor:

SCHWEITZER
Lambaréné
French Equatorial Africa

AM DEEPLY DISTRESSED THAT FRENCH SOURCES IN
PARIS HAVE VIOLATED YOUR DIRECT
INSTRUCTIONS AGAINST PUBLIC RELEASE YOUR
ALGERIAN LETTER. THIS DAMAGES YOUR
LAUDABLE HISTORICAL POSITION AGAINST
INVOLVING YOURSELF IN HIGHLY CONTROVERSIAL
POLITICAL MATTERS. RELEASE OF LETTER IS ALSO
EMBARRASSING FOR I ASSURED PRESIDENT
EISENHOWER IT WOULD NOT BE MADE PUBLIC.
UNDER CIRCUMSTANCES I SUGGEST ADDITIONAL
LETTER TO PRESIDENT STATING THAT RELEASE OF
LETTER IN PARIS WAS UNAUTHORIZED AND THAT
YOU HAVE NO DESIRE TO CREATE PUBLIC PRESSURE
IN ORDER TO INFLUENCE AMERICAN PUBLIC
OPINION.

<div style="text-align:right">Norman Cousins</div>

He immediately cabled in reply:

Lambaréné, February 8, 1957

DEEPLY SAD LIKE YOU. THANK YOU FOR YOUR
COUNSEL. NEW LETTER ON ITS WAY. CORDIALLY
AND SADLY,

<div style="text-align:right">Albert Schweitzer</div>

<div style="text-align:right">February 7, 1957</div>

To Norman Cousins
Dear friend:

I have just sent you a telegram in response to yours. In order that
you understand how the idea to write to the President came to me,

I tell what happened in Lambaréné on Sunday, the 27th of January. In the preceding days I had received telegrams and a letter from friends in the Academy and from my acquaintances in the political world to make welcome Mr. Lambert, who was coming to see me. He arrived with two gentlemen on Sunday, the 27th of January, at ten in the morning by special plane to talk to me of the anxiety of the French government on the subject of the situation in the Middle East, and submitted to me the text of an appeal to all interested nations with proposals with a view to persuading them to seek an understanding. I told them that I could not make known this plan as inspired by me. It treated concrete political questions. The men were very much disappointed by my refusal. They were about to discuss the question of the U.N. and Algeria. Well, I was profoundly impressed by the despair of these men. They confirmed to me the gravity of the position of the French government in case of a check. Then I happened to suggest writing a word to the President. But the hour of their plane's departure for the return to Paris arrived. They had come at 10:00 A.M. and must leave at 2:00 P.M. for the airport. I did not even have the time to write you a line.

I told Mr. Lambert (who had to leave for New York from Paris) that he must take the letter to you and that it would be you who would decide if you wanted to put it to the President or not. He promised me he would do it, as I said. From Paris, then, two days after, they telephoned me that they would like to be able to consider the letter as an open letter, of which certain people could have knowledge. I replied, "Letter absolutely personal. Impossible to consider it as open letter. Give it to Cousins to be transmitted to its destination." This telegram was addressed to Mr. Lambert. I was very vexed that they could have thought for an instant of making it known publicly. And here, in spite of everything, they have committed this unbelievable and stupid indiscretion which puts me face to face with the President and the American people in the situation of a man lacking the most elementary tact and wanting to play a public role. . . . I am disheartened. Really, one loses the courage to undertake anything whatever.

Please judge whether the letter enclosed can be sent to the President and can make him understand that I cannot surmise the usage that they have dared make of it without my knowledge. I wanted only to acquaint him with the anxiety that prevailed in the heart of the French government on the subject of the U.N. attitude on the Algerian question.

I thank you for your good letter of January 12. But at present I hesitate to make the declaration on the question of atomic tests. I have studied it thoroughly and I am convinced that one must warn the world of the danger of the continuation of these tests. But I wonder if after what has happened with the letter to the President I am still the man to speak to the world. I have now been discredited as one who wants to play a role in the world, and who wishes to speak to him anew. Yes, before this I could be the man to address myself to men of good will and believe myself charged with a mission that I could fulfill, leaving my solitude, feeling myself called. But at present I am someone who can be criticized as presumptuous, having already made myself noticeable by an unsuccessful entrance. I know nothing here of how the indiscretion at Paris is interpreted, and of how much it has been injurious to my reputation. When I am informed in the days to come, I will be able to judge better. Please let me know also your opinion. . . .

I leave you, late at night, very much depressed. And I have been so happy to know you and I occupy myself with conviction in the problem that you brought to my attention. I thank you for what you give me as regards advice.

With my good thoughts,

Votre devoue,
Albert Schweitzer

February 7, 1957

President Dwight D. Eisenhower
The White House
Washington, D.C.

Mr. President:

I am disheartened to learn of the indiscretion committed on the subject of the letter that I had the courage to have forwarded to you by Mr. Cousins in order that he decide whether it was advisable or inadvisable to transmit it to you. I did not in any way authorize that its contents be made known. On the contrary, I declared in confidence to the person who was to take it to Mr. Cousins that it was absolutely personal.

I suffer, at what one must think, that I lacked tact in communicating with you and that I wanted to influence American public opinion.

Please, I pray you, accept the assurance of my profoundly respectful sentiments and believe me.

Yours devotedly,
Albert Schweitzer

February 13, 1957

Dr. Albert Schweitzer
Lambaréné
Gabon
French Equatorial Africa

My dear Dr. Schweitzer:

You must not allow the fact that your trust has been abused to hurt you or sadden you in any way. I beg you to believe that nothing could ever interfere with your reputation or lessen in the slightest the profound love felt for you by people everywhere. Nothing has

been more impressive to me in my visits to many parts of the world than to see the evidence that your language of compassion is universally understood and that the lives of countless people have been enriched because of it.

The incident of M. Lambert is an unpleasant one, but the harm is not serious. I have explained the matter to the President and he understands fully. His limitless admiration for you is unimpaired. Incidentally, when M. Lambert telephoned me to say that he had a letter from you that I was to transmit to the President, I knew instantly why you had suggested that this procedure be followed. And so I asked M. Lambert: "Does Dr. Schweitzer wish me to be consulted about the advisability of his sending this letter to the President?" M. Lambert emphasized that my function was solely to transmit the letter. He said this had been made clear to him and he urged me to lose no time in carrying out my assignment.

Yet I knew deep in my heart that something extraordinary had happened in Lambaréné, and I could almost visualize the pressure and the confusion surrounding the hurried visit. And when the news story appeared in the *New York Times* even before the President saw the letter, there was no longer any doubt in my mind that there had been some misrepresentation to you. Hence I reassured the President that you were not in any way to be held responsible for the fact that the letter was given to the press even before he saw it, and that, indeed, this was a private communication and that you had specifically forbidden any publicity. The President understands fully, and you must feel completely reassured.

You must never use the word "discredited" about yourself. It crushes me to think that you would feel this way even for a moment. When you do something, the fact that you do it makes it right. I will never forget my first evening in Lambaréné, when you got up from the table and walked over to the piano to play a hymn. Earlier in the day, I tried to play the piano and gave it up immediately because so many of the strings were missing, the felt on the hammers was worn thin, and the volume pedal was stuck, to say nothing of the damage done to the instrument by the equatorial heat and moisture. And so,

when you walked over to the piano, I had a deep sense of shock.
Here was one of history's greatest interpreters of Bach, a man for
whom the finest piano ever made would be none too good, sitting
down to an instrument that was practically unplayable. Yet when
you touched the keys, everything seemed to come right again. And
it is this way with everything you do. Your doing it makes it pure.
You must therefore free your mind of any torment resulting from
the Lambert incident. Your standing is unimpaired. Your prodi-
gious power to do good for the entire human community is still with
you.

Do not feel under any pressure about the statement we discussed
at Lambaréné. If you are under any strain when you write it, its
purpose will be defeated. I believe that out of your thought concern-
ing the world crisis will come the large ideas that are necessary to
restore sanity to mankind. When you write these ideas your friends
everywhere will regard it as their mission to make them known. And
the ideas will be believed and acted upon.

I paid your respects to Martin Buber in Jerusalem. He felt deeply
flattered that you should think of him and he recalled the last time
he saw you with warm satisfaction. He spoke for almost an hour
about you and the meaning of your work. It was as fine a tribute by
one human being about another as I have ever heard.

In closing, my dear Doctor, let me tell you once again that there
is nothing in my power that I would not do if you would but ask it
of me. Please believe in my total readiness to serve.

Your friend,
Norman Cousins

*Prime Minister Jawabarlal Nehru, of India, had a strong admiration for
Dr. Schweitzer, as he had made known to me on one of my visits to India.
On the occasion of his visit to New York in 1956, we discussed ways of calling
to the attention of world public opinion the mounting danger of the nuclear
arms race. Mr. Nehru agreed that Dr. Schweitzer's voice might be a pow-
erful factor in this direction. After my return from Lambaréné, I wrote to the
Prime Minister about the visit to the hospital.*

February 13, 1957

His Excellency, Jawaharlal Nehru
Prime Minister's House
New Delhi India

My dear Mr. Prime Minister:

You may recall that the last time we spoke in New York you asked me to convey your good wishes to Dr. Schweitzer. I have just returned from Africa, and one of the first things I want to do is to tell you how deeply pleased the Doctor was to have your greetings. He recalled most vividly his meeting with you in Lausanne some years ago and said that he has followed your writings and your work with the greatest interest.

The Doctor seemed to me to be in remarkably good health. His skin is firm, his eyes are clear, his hands are steady. I can't think of a man half his age who could keep up with him in the physical labor he insists on doing every day under nearly impossible conditions. The heat and the moisture of the equatorial climate and the jungle have failed to slow him up.

He is, however, deeply distressed about the present drift in the world. He feels that we are rapidly approaching the point where the men who alone are in a position to act effectively will be caught up in the kind of despair that leads to desperation. The unlimited testing of nuclear weapons is by itself an inexcusable act of violence against the human community and the generations to come. He would like to do something about it but he is too modest to believe that anything he might do would have any useful effect. All his life he has refused to involve himself in matters concerning the politics of one nation or another, for he wished to identify himself with membership in the human family at its largest rather than with any of its groupings.

In any event, Dr. Schweitzer would like to give himself fully to the present crisis, feeling as he does that all men and the generations

to come are in grave danger. What do you think he might usefully do? It has been suggested by some of his friends that four or five of the world's political leaders might come together to meet with him, perhaps in Vienna. According to this idea, the members of this group would include yourself, President Eisenhower, Nikita Khrushchev, Chou En-lai, Prime Minister Macmillan, and one or two others. Dr. Schweitzer would attempt at this meeting to consider the world problem not in terms of the conflicting national interests but in terms of the overriding common interests of the human community.

I see many possible obstacles to such a meeting, not the least of which would involve getting President Eisenhower together with Chou En-lai. Nonetheless, I have agreed to seek your own opinion of the matter. Do you believe that such a meeting would be possible? Do you believe it might be productive of some good? If this does not seem to you to be too promising, is there any other way in which Dr. Schweitzer might have an important usefulness in the present situation?

I was delighted to see you and your daughter in such excellent health and spirits while you were in the United States.

With continuing good wishes, I am

Yours sincerely,
Norman Cousins

No. 227-PMS/57
New Delhi
February 19, 1957

My dear Norman Cousins,

Thank you for your letter of 13 February 1957, which I received today. We are in the midst of our general elections and I have to do a good deal of touring. I returned to Delhi only this morning and am going out again for a few days tomorrow morning.

I am happy to learn that Dr. Schweitzer is in good health. I can

well understand his distress at the present drift in the world. I suppose every sensitive person feels that way. I confess that I do not see any easy way out of this drift towards disaster. Apart from the actual dangers involved, what is distressing is the gradual acceptance by most people of this state of affairs as normal and almost inevitable.

None of the outstanding political leaders of today appears to have the vision or the strength to stop this drift. Every step that the leaders of the United States or of the Soviet Union might take, even though it may be a good one, is suspect by the other. That applies to the other big powers like the U.K., France, and China. The world atmosphere is thick with suspicion and fear. Everyone, I believe, recognizes that a major nuclear war is out of the question. And yet, in spite of this, the armament race goes on and atomic and hydrogen bombs are piled up. The testing of nuclear weapons continues, even though many eminent scientists believe that this may be poisoning the atmosphere.

I doubt if there is anyone in the world today whose opinion can carry more weight in these matters than Dr. Schweitzer. No one can accuse him of partiality, and whatever he says will at least command world attention. I welcome, therefore, his intention to try his utmost to deal with the present crisis. What steps he can take about this is difficult for me to suggest. A proposal for some outstanding political leaders to meet is, in theory, excellent. But I would be greatly surprised if the persons he mentions agreed to get together at present. Almost everything would depend on President Eisenhower. If he suggested such a meeting, it would come off. Obviously, no meeting would have much value if President Eisenhower was opposed to it or did not attend it. If, by some miracle, the meeting could be held, I think it would produce good results.

It would be difficult enough to get President Eisenhower to meet Khrushchev or Bulganin.[*] It would be, I think, next to impossible

[*]Nikolai A. Bulganin was premier of the Soviet Union from 1955 to 1958. Following the death of Stalin in 1953, Bulganin supported Nikita Khrushchev in a successful power struggle with Georgi Malenkov. In 1957, however, Bulganin joined Malenkov, V. M. Molotov, and L. M. Kaganovich in an attempt to oust Khrushchev. Although

for him to agree to meet Chou En-lai at present. When I had my talk with the President during my recent visit to Washington, the only subject on which he grew quite warm and rather excited was China. He was angry at China's behavior and, more specifically, at their refusal to release ten Americans. I think that the Chinese attitude in this matter is quite extraordinarily foolish. I have a high opinion of Chinese intelligence and foresight, quite apart from their policies. And so, it has surprised me that they still hold on to these ten Americans. The President told me quite definitely that he would have no truck at all with the Chinese so long as these ten were not released. Even after that, he would go very slow, but some small step might be taken.

It appears certain to me, therefore, that there is not the least possible chance of the President agreeing to meet Chou En-lai. That will mean a complete upsetting of American policy and a tremendous uproar in the United States. Personally I do hope that the Chinese government will release those ten and thus break this deadlock. Even if that happens, I doubt very much if the President or Dulles will take any forward step in a hurry.

Early last year, it seemed that the world was gradually getting out of this dreadful drift to war. There was a lessening of tension all round, and certain changes in the Soviet Union and the East European countries were full of promise. Hungary put an end to this and, as you know, produced violent reactions in the greater part of the world.[*] It was a great misfortune that what happened in Hungary

the effort failed, Bulganin remained in his official position as premier until 1958, when he was given an obscure position in Stavropol, which he held until he retired in 1960. He died in Moscow in 1975.

[*]The Hungarian revolution began on October 23, 1956, with a student demonstration in Budapest protesting Soviet domination of Hungarian political and economic affairs. When police fired on the crowd, student protestors were joined by angry Budapest citizens, as well as Hungarian army soldiers. Soviet troops were called out and fighting began, which spread throughout the country. A reform government was quickly created, headed by former prime minister Imre Nagy. When the Soviet Union sent several troop units into Hungary on October 30, Nagy protested, withdrew Hungary from the Warsaw Pact of 1955, and appealed to the United Nations. But on November 4 Soviet troops attacked Budapest and seized highways and railroads, crushing major Hungarian resistance. Janŏs Kadar, Hungarian Communist Party chief, was installed as prime minister, and Nagy was taken to Rumania and executed.

synchronized with the Anglo-French attack in Egypt.[*] It is possible, I think, that if this had not happened, Hungary might have come out of the crisis as Poland did. The Soviet Union was convinced at the time that the Anglo-French attack on Egypt had the approval of the United States and presaged a major war. This was not true, of course, but I have no doubt that the Soviet Union thought so at the time. Because of this, they decided to take no chances in Hungary and were prepared to face the odium which their cruel repression of the Hungarian nationalist movement brought them.

There has been a reaction in the Soviet Union and they have gone back to some extent on the more liberal policy that they had embarked upon. Personally I do not think that they can ever really go back upon it, because there are too many forces at play in the Soviet Union which will not ultimately tolerate this. I do not mean that the people of the Soviet Union want any basic change in their political or economic structure. Nearly all of them have grown up since the Revolution and accept that structure. But they want greater individual freedom and a lessening of the tensions in which they live. Also, more of the good things of life, commodities, etc. They do not want the secret police. There has been some improvement in these directions, in spite of Hungary. The measure of freedom and liberalization in the Soviet Union or the East European countries is directly related to war-scares and tensions.

The question, therefore, is how to lessen these tensions and remove the ever-present fear of war. I suppose this cannot be done at one jump, but step by step one may go in that direction.

Unfortunately, almost everything is thought of in military terms, and even the good deeds that are done have a military wrapping.

[*]In 1956, under Egyptian President Gamal Abdel Nasser, arrangements were made with Great Britain and the U.S. to finance the first stage of the Aswan High Dam project at a cost of $270,000,000. But on July 20, U.S. Secretary of State John Foster Dulles cancelled America's offer, and Britain followed suit the next day. Five days later, Nasser announced nationalization of the Suez Canal and threatened the state of Israel. On October 29, war broke out, and the Israeli Army invaded the Sinai Peninsula. Two days later French and British planes attacked Egyptian airfields. The Israelis occupied the Sinai and the Egyptian Air Force was virtually destroyed.

The Soviet government talks crudely and aggressively about their military might and indulges in cruel repression if this is challenged. At the same time, they do sometimes put forward proposals which appear to be reasonable and logical. But, because of this background, those proposals are rejected and are not even considered. The United States has given a great deal of much needed help to other countries. But, again, the military aspect is dominant. Also, the help often goes to the most reactionary ruling groups in backward countries. Thus, this help does not bring a sense of liberation or relief.

I do not know what to suggest. I have almost begun to feel that attempts at improving the world situation merely result in distressing entanglements which do little good to anybody. And yet, one cannot remain a passive spectator. Anyhow, Dr. Schweitzer is the one man who can take a lead. Perhaps, he could privately and informally make the approach he has suggested and then judge the results. I think he should first write to President Eisenhower. Any kind of a joint letter to a number of persons will probably irritate and make some of them feel that they are being embarrassed.

So far as I am concerned, I would gladly help in any little way that I can. But I have no exaggerated opinion of what I can do. Recent developments in regard to Kashmir[*] have not added to my belief in my capacity to do anything worthwhile in international affairs. I do not think that we have been in the wrong in what we have done in the Kashmir. And yet, as you must know, we have

[*]Following the partition of India and the withdrawal of British troops from South Asia in 1947, rulers of princely states, of which Kashmir was one, were given the option to accede to India or Pakistan. Efforts were made by Pakistan to take the Vale of Kashmir by force. The maharaja of Kashmir, Sir Hari Singh, appealed to India for help. Supported by Sheikh Mohammed Abdullah, Kashmir's leading political figure and prime minister from 1948 to 1953, the maharaja acceded to the Indian Union. Fighting began—the first war between India and Pakistan—which was ended by a United Nations cease-fire agreement in 1949. In 1956, the discovery by Indian patrols of a military road between Sinkiang and western Tibet, built by Chinese forces, led to border clashes. The Indian refusal to negotiate with China on boundary disputes in this area was in contrast to the willingness of Pakistan to reach a settlement with China on the course of a boundary lying within Pakistani-administered Kashmir.

been attacked with anger and malice, and every attempt has been made to humiliate us. I suppose this will pass. But this does demonstrate how every person who does not fall into line is suspect and is in peril.

This would not apply to Dr. Schweitzer. That is why I say that he is the one man who might bring some light into closed minds.

In this matter, I would like Dr. Schweitzer to trust his own judgment or, if I may use Gandhiji's phrase, his "inner voice." That will be a better guide than anything that I can say.

If you write to Dr. Schweitzer, please convey my deep regards to him.

Yours sincerely,
J. Nehru

Clara Urquhart, who had taken such a significant role in my first visit to Dr. Schweitzer, discussed with him the possibility of his partipication in the proposed meeting of world leaders. Dr. Schweitzer characteristically rejected it in favor of independent action for which he alone would be responsible. He had said that the people must build a "wall of resistance" against that which endangered life, and he wished to speak directly to them. "I have tried," he said, "to relate myself to the problems of all humankind rather than to become involved in disputes between this or that group. I wanted to be one man speaking to another man about the lasting problems inside men and between them."

He wrote me of his decision to make his own declaration, and his excitement about the possibility of reaching the greatest number of people by means of radio.

Lambaréné
February 23, 1957

To Norman Cousins
Dear friend,

Let us talk now about the question of the declaration which has to be made about the subject of the atomic bomb tests. I worked

rather hard on the question about the tests and how to write a state-
ment. If you really think that I could do something useful I will do
it, as tired as I am.

Let us talk about the way to make such a statement. Clara's pro-
posals don't agree with my intentions. For me it is not a question of
creating an opportunity for a meeting between Nehru, Chou En-lai
or Mao Tse-tung, Khrushchev, and Eisenhower. That is much too
complicated. I will write this kindly to Clara. For me it is a question
of saying a reasonable truth to the people of our generation to per-
suade them to bring pressure on their governments to face this tre-
mendous problem together. So, please, don't talk any more with
anybody about my plan, except the President, if you judge this in-
dicated. I have reason to believe that he takes an interest in my ac-
tion in this direction. But please judge for yourself if you want to
inform him confidentially. In any case, the undertaking must be
wholly personal. Only so can it have a considerable, or modest, suc-
cess. And if it is a failure only I myself will be compromised. So this
matter remains strictly between you and me. We both and only both
of us should meditate on the subject and its execution. After a long
consideration I abandon the plan to address myself to the people
through the press. That is too complicated. There is a possibility
that if I make use of the press, publication in one country's news-
papers might prejudice the newspapers of other countries and en-
danger the success. One does not know in which measure the others
would decide to publish a piece of which another had the priority!

So I return to the idea of having my message spread by radio, as
a message by radio can be heard over the whole world. But to which
radio can the mission of the publication be charged, without others
feeling indisposed? Answer: Radio Oslo, of the city of the Nobel
Peace Prize! That my voice departs from there where I delivered my
address of the Nobel Peace Prize will be found justifiable and rea-
sonable. In my message I will humbly ask the radio stations of other
countries to broadcast it too, and to consider addressing it to human-
ity.

I am on good terms with the president of the Commission of the
Nobel Peace Prize, and with Norwegian radio. I was happy to find

this solution. If you approve of it, please cable me: "Hospital Schweitzer. Lambaréné. Agree with you." (You can cable this in English.) If you feel you must make objections, please write me as soon as possible. I am fortunate and grateful to have you as adviser.

But, all this remains between you and me!

Heartily, yours devotedly,
Albert Schweitzer

In reply, I sent Dr. Schweitzer a copy of Prime Minister Nehru's letter of February 19, and expressed my enthusiasm for his proposal to broadcast his statement on Radio Oslo. In line with our discussions at Lambaréné, I included some background material for his use in preparing the statement.

At the same time, I wrote Nehru to tell him of Dr. Schweitzer's reaction to the suggestion to meet with world leaders, and Schweitzer's decision to make his declaration public by means of Radio Oslo. With characteristic insight, Nehru's response was an excursion through the background of East-West tensions.

No. 326–PMH/57
New Delhi
March 16, 1957

My dear Norman Cousins,

Thank you for your letter of 4 March 1957. I have read with great interest your article in *The Saturday Review*, which you sent me.

I am not, I think, a pessimist. Indeed, I do not think that any person can function effectively if he has no hope for the future. I have hope both for the world and for my own country, India, which I seek to serve. And yet, as I indicated to you in my previous letter, I have a feeling of depression growing within me, a feeling that the good things of the world are gradually being pushed out, that some slow disintegration is taking place in the collective mind of man in spite of the great advances that we see.

You refer in your article to this new possibility of our present generation having the power to put an end to everything that history has achieved. That is a terrible thought. What is worse, I think, is a creeping sickness of humanity which gradually leads it to this final destruction. Ultimately, this is of the mind, as I think the UNESCO Constitution says: Wars begin in the minds of men. In spite of the patent fact that a nuclear war may well end everything that humanity stands for, most people take preparations for it for granted, even though they wish to avoid it. Why do they do it? We go back to this all-pervading fear, which appears to them to make it incumbent on them not to be left behind in the race for the latest type of death-dealing machinery. The whole approach is patently illogical, and yet there appears to be no escape from it.

Essentially, the problem becomes one of psychology or of some kind of moral or ethical approach.

Politicians, however good they may be, do not frame their policies on this basis, even though they talk a great deal about morality. An individual might and does sometimes rise to high levels. But the mass thinks chiefly in terms of self-preservation and is much more prone to fear and anger and violence. Even the great advance of education has not got rid of these ever-present dangers, so far as the mass mind is concerned. Fear feeds upon fear, as violence feeds upon violence.

Oddly enough, in a democratic society, while the dangers of any sudden and terrible action are limited, the leader's ability to control the mass is also limited. There may be occasional exceptions for limited periods.

Any political leader has to function under these limitations. Occasionally, he may override them. But we seldom have a single leader with that power. So, a leader must not only feel what is right, but must also convince masses of people about it. Thus, he tends to compromise or else he would cease to be the leader. The only example in current history that I know of a leader who refused to compromise with what he thought was right is Gandhi, and Gandhi was assassinated in the end, as prophets often are. He was a rare

combination of a political leader who had something of the prophetic instinct in him.

I suppose the approach to the great problem of today has to be twofold. There should be the moral approach or the prophet's, and there has to be the political leader's approach. The latter should be in tune with the former, though it may not go that far. At any rate, every step taken, however short it may be, should be towards that moral goal preached by the prophet. It depends on the leader and the circumstances he has to face, as to how big the step he takes is. But, in any event, he should not go back or take a step in a wrong direction. It is not feasible to ask the leader to take a step which he cannot give effect to, because public opinion would not be ripe for it. In educating public opinion, both the prophet and the leader have to help in their respective ways.

All this is very well. But, time is short, and disaster hangs over us. Two great wars have brutalized humanity and made them think more and more in terms of violence. What progress, scientific and cultural, and in human values, that we have made is somehow twisted to the needs of violence. I think that the major disservice that Marxism and communism have done to the world is the encouragement of violence to achieve political or economic ends. But, of course, it is not Marxism alone that has done this. Fascism was, I think, even worse in this respect because it did not have the ideological element of communism. But, apart from communism and fascism, there is quite enough of this violent approach to problems even by others. I know that, the world being what it is, it is not possible to do away with some violence or coercion. At the same time, I have become more and more convinced that the way of violence and hatred is not the way of solving any problem. That is why I think that the "cold war" is something that is essentially bad, whatever the reasons of expedience that might be advanced for it. It takes us in a wrong direction.

Taking a practical view of things as they are, we see these two very powerful countries, the U.S.A. and the U.S.S.R., opposed to each other. Regardless of right or wrong, although we cannot, of

course, ignore them, it seems obvious to me that the cold war only aggravates their conflicts and spreads fear more and more. Some approach other than that of cold war has to be found, some approach other than that of military alliances.

As a politician, I cannot suggest, as Gandhi might have done, that a country should be brave enough to do away with armed forces for its defense. I recognize the inevitability at present of providing for defense and not leaving a vacuum which might tempt an evil-doer. Even so, I do not understand how defense is helped by the tactics of cold war or by the propagation of hatred and fear. It should be possible to take adequate steps for defense and yet seek for a removal of tensions and a friendly atmosphere in the world. After all, the great masses of people everywhere want that friendly atmosphere and to avoid all horror of war.

This leads one to the question of disarmament. Again, it is not feasible to talk about this in absolute terms. But there may be progressive steps, the main value of each step being a lessening of fear. Disarmament must inevitably take into consideration nuclear weapons. What can we do about them? I would suggest that two things can be done. One is stopping any further experiments, the other is stopping any further production of atomic or hydrogen bombs. This may be difficult now, but is going to be much more difficult in the future, when a number of countries can produce them. At present, there are apparently only three, the U.S.A., the U.S.S.R., and the U.K. Within a few years, it is likely that the process will become simpler, though the products will remain equally terrible, and a number of other countries might be able to make these bombs. Thus, delay in taking an effective step makes the position increasingly more difficult.

In regard to experimental explosions, I am convinced that these are a crime against humanity. I have received, as others have, appeals from various organizations in Japan protesting against the proposed British experimental explosion. As you point out in your article, nobody knows definitely what harm these explosions do. We do know that they do harm, and harm in a very vital way, which

may do infinite injury in the long run to large numbers of persons. If that is so, then it is surely a crime to continue them, and the least that we can do is to try to stop these experiments.

The rival powers or groups of powers are such today that neither of them can think of defeating the other without being largely destroyed itself. If that is so, then one has to accept a policy of tolerance of each other, of live and let live, and hope that the new atmosphere that is created may lead to a progressive lessening of tensions and fear. This, again, might and should lead to a lessening of the coercive apparatus of the state in authoritarian countries, that is, greater individual freedom. We shall not get the individual freedom in these states by threatening them. In fact, this policy of threats will inevitably result in a continuation of coercion and deprivation of freedom.

Instead of military pacts aimed against each other, one would imagine that a more sensible way would be for pacts between rival powers, something in the nature of the old Locarno Treaty between Germany and the other Western countries.[*] It is true that the Locarno Treaty did not bring peace, and Hitler came. That was not the fault of Locarno, because other circumstances prevailed. Anyhow, I see no other way except that there must be an agreement on the basis of live and let live, and that this should be backed by the United Nations. If any country breaks that agreement, then presumably the other countries will pull it back or deal with it. I know that no agreement is foolproof, and it is very difficult to trust some countries. Nevertheless, the position created by this mutual bond backed by the U.N. cannot possibly be worse than what we have today, and it will surely lessen tensions and fear, which will then enable the world to look at the problem in a more reasonable way.

If such an approach is made, it might be easier to solve the question of German unification, which is so vital not only to Europe, but also to the world. I do not think this reunification of Germany can be brought about by cold war methods, and presumably we rule out

[*]The Locarno Pact (December 1, 1925) marked a rapprochement between Germany and the Allies after World War I, whereby Germany, France, Belgium, Great Britain, and Italy mutually guaranteed peace in Western Europe.

war for the purpose, which would mean destruction of everybody. I hope you will forgive this jumble of odd ideas which I have placed before you. I have indulged in some thinking out loud. Coming back, however, to your letter, I entirely agree that Oslo will be the right and appropriate place for an appeal by Dr. Schweitzer, and it would certainly add to the value of that appeal for peace if it was made under the auspices of the Nobel Committee.

I agree with you that President Eisenhower is the one great political leader who has it in him to take an effective step. Natually any step that he takes cannot be taken in repudiation of the policies he has so firmly announced in the past. But there are many ways of doing it which can avoid that difficulty. I am sure that, if he did it, there would be a mass approval all over the world of such a brave step, and very few persons will sit down to argue as to how far it was in consonance with something else. Dr. Schweitzer might well approach him in this matter. Perhaps the right time would be after his appeal from Oslo.

I am afraid I have written to you rather a long letter. I had not intended doing so. But my mind ran away with me.

Yours sincerely,
J. Nehru

A series of letters from Dr. Schweitzer arrived in rapid succession, reflecting a growing conviction about the need to issue a "Declaration of Conscience" over Radio Oslo.

Lambaréné
March 25 1957

To Norman Cousins

Dear friend:

On the same plane as this letter is the text of the talk I will give in Oslo. It was hard work—the talk became too long. I almost had to sacrifice half, with the interesting details. But the main point was to have a talk that wasn't too long. I believe that it is simple and makes

the problem comprehensible for the public. I am waiting for another copy of the text, which is being made, and I will send it to you. But the English translation is made at Oslo, as all translations are, and it will be given to America from Oslo. Therefore, everything goes out from Oslo, which I believe is very advantageous for the reception that the talk must have. But I will do all I can to send you a copy of the text before the Oslo broadcast. Oslo is undertaking a great work. At the beginning of the talk I say: "I thank the Radio of Oslo, the city of the Nobel Peace Prize, for permitting that which I believe it is my duty to say to be circulated in the world."

This talk, to all intents and purposes, jumps back to my talk on the problem of peace in 1954! In working on the draft of the text, I quite often thought of you who gave me the idea of doing it. I hope that the text will give you satisfaction.

Imagine my surprise when an American gentleman recently came to see me and said, "I hear that you are working on a speech on the danger of atomic bomb testing." I asked him, "Where did you hear this rumor?" He answered, "I heard it spoken of in New York." Please be very careful therefore not to speak of what I have written you, for it could distress Oslo. Radio Oslo is treating the whole question very discreetly. They do not want the newspapers to speak of it before everything is ready for the broadcast.

The title of the talk is "The Danger that Radioactive Elements which Result from Testing of Atomic Bombs Signify for Humanity."

Well, the talk is now done. Ah, if now I could take two or three days of rest! But it will not happen. While I was working on the talk, I should at the same time have been doing my daily work. And now it is necessary that I still do it, without respite, and that I do in addition that which I could not do of the work while I needed the time to draft the talk.

From the heart,

Yours devotedly,
Albert Schweitzer

P.S. Pardon my handwriting. I am writing you after midnight.

Lambaréné, Gabon
French Equatorial Africa
April 12, 1957

To Norman Cousins

Dear friend:

I have just received a letter from Radio Oslo—all is arranged!

This is what they say: Radio Oslo will communicate with other radio networks and inform them that the president of the Parilamentary Committee of the Nobel Prize has asked, in my name, the assistance of the Norwegian Radio in broadcasting a speech on the dangers caused by the atomic bomb tests from as many radio stations as possible.

The Norwegian radio feels it to be its special mission to meet my request and to approach a number of network stations in Europe and in other parts of the world to do the same.

The Norwegian radio will send texts of the address to these institutions for broadcasting and will let them know that the Norwegian broadcasts will take place over Norwegian shortwave radio on the following dates and times over frequencies of 11, 13, 16, 19, and 25 meters—*Tuesday, April 23!* On April 23, 7:30 P.M.–8:00 P.M., Norwegian text (spoken by the president of the Parliamentary Committee of the Nobel Prize); from 8:00 to 8:30 P.M., French text; from 8:30 to 9:00 P.M., German text; from 9:00 to 9:30 P.M., English text; from 9:30 to 10:00 P.M., Russian text. These broadcasts will be repeated on April 24 between 3:00 and 5:00 A.M.

If other broadcast stations are interested in carrying this address, they'll be asked to reserve airwaves in the customary manner. No broadcast can take place before the one on April 23 from 7:30 to 10:00 P.M. over the Norwegian radio.

The text of the speech will be sent to the press for publication on April 24.

These are the contents of the message which the Norwegian radio sent to other broadcast networks. Radio Norway will also send this message to the two Americas, to Japan, to Australia, to Africa. It's

wonderful what Radio Norway has done to ensure wide exposure of the address.

First they made an arrangement for May 12. I telegraphed them that this would be too late. Then they changed everything to make an April 23 broadcast possible. I thanked them warmly for all the trouble they took. I hope you too find this satisfactory. It was a very difficult thing for me to reduce the text so that it will take no longer than 27 minutes.

<div style="text-align:right">With my best wishes, your devoted
Albert Schweitzer</div>

P.S. They were very pleased in Oslo with the clarity and simplicity of the text.

<div style="text-align:right">Lambaréné, Gabon
April 22, 1957</div>

To Norman Cousins

Dear friend:

Excuse the poor creature that I am for not having been able to send you the text of the speech earlier, as I would have liked to do. But time was pressing. I had to send it as quickly as possible to the president of the Nobel Prize Committee in Oslo so that he could decide if he could take the responsibility to ask the Norwegian radio network to undertake the great task of approaching the directors of radio networks of different nations so they would agree to broadcast it. These preparations had to be done in less than three weeks! It was an immense piece of work for the president of the Nobel Prize Committee and the director-general of the Oslo radio network. And I wanted the broadcast to take place by around April 20 at the latest, as I knew that an offensive against atomic tests was being prepared in Germany for about that time. We thus had no interest in coming on the air any later. But once my text was approved and accepted by the director of the Nobel Committee and the director-general of

the Norwegian radio, I no longer had the right to change it, no matter what the purpose. . . . And I had no copy to send you. I gave all the copies to Oslo and the French translator. I wasn't able to write you in time to explain the situation because I was so exhausted and so overcome by work that I could barely stand up any longer. And my eyes did not permit me to write as I would have liked or should. So, please excuse me.

What's essential is that what was due to your initiative has succeeded and that the attempt to awaken the attention of humanity to the subject of the danger that atomic bomb tests already convey for human existence is being undertaken under the best of conditions, thanks to the Nobel Prize Committee and the Norwegian radio. This appeal had to come from a completely neutral place. This was the great problem. In reality, the U.N. should have been the one to undertake the matter. But it is an organization that functions in complicated ways. Perhaps it is better that the U.N. will not undertake it and that this is a spontaneous movement which is manifested outside the U.N. I beg you to present my respects to the President. My best regards to Mme. Clara if you see her. From my heart your devoted

Albert Schweitzer

The text of the Declaration arrived in time for me to make some editorial corrections, as Dr. Schweitzer had requested, which were returned to him for his approval. The complete text of that statement follows.

A Declaration of Conscience

Since March 1, 1954, hydrogen bombs have been tested by the United States at the Pacific island of Bikini in the Marshall group and by Soviet Russia in Siberia. We know that testing of atomic weapons is something quite different from testing of non-atomic ones. Earlier, when a new type of giant gun had been tested, the matter ended with the detonation. After the explosion of a hydrogen bomb

that is not the case. Something remains in the air, namely, an incalculable number of radioactive particles emitting radioactive rays. This was also the case with the uranium bombs dropped on Nagasaki and Hiroshima and those which were subsequently tested. However, because these bombs were of smaller size and less effectiveness compared with the hydrogen bombs, not much attention was given to this fact.

Since radioactive rays of sufficient amount and strength have harmful effects on the human body, it must be considered whether the radiation resulting from the hydrogen explosions that have already taken place represents a danger which would increase with new explosions.

In the course of the three and a half years that have passed since then [the test explosions of the early hydrogen bombs] representatives of the physical and medical sciences have been studying the problem. Observations on the distribution, origin, and nature of radiation have been made. The processes through which the human body is harmfully affected have been analyzed. The material collected, although far from complete, allows us to draw the conclusion that radiation resulting from the explosions which have already taken place represents a danger to the human race—a danger not to be underrated—and that further explosions of atomic bombs will increase this danger to an alarming extent.

This conclusion has repeatedly been expressed, especially during the last few months. However, it has not, strange to say, influenced public opinion to the extent that one might have expected. Individuals and peoples have not been aroused to give to this danger the attention which it unfortunately deserves. It must be demonstrated and made clear to them.

I raise my voice, together with those of others who have lately felt it their duty to act, through speaking and writing, in warning of the danger. My age and the generous understanding so many people have shown of my work permit me to hope that my appeal may contribute to the preparing of the way for the insights so urgently needed.

My thanks go to the radio station in Oslo, the city of the Nobel Peace Prize, for making it possible for that which I feel I have to say to reach far-off places.

What is radioactivity?

Radioactivity consists of rays differing from those of light in being invisible and in being able to pass not only through glass but also through thin metal discs and through layers of cell tissue in the human and animal bodies. Rays of this kind were first discovered in 1895 by the physicist Wilhelm Roentgen of Munich, and were named after him.

In 1896 the French physicist Henry Becquerel demonstrated that rays of this kind occur in nature. They are emitted from uranium, an element known since 1786.

In 1898 Pierre Curie and his wife discovered in the mineral pitchblende, an uranium ore, the strongly radioactive element radium.

The joy caused by the fact that such rays were at the disposal of humanity was at first unmixed. It appeared that they influence the relatively rapidly growing and relatively rapidly decaying cells of malignant tumors and sarcomas. If exposed to these rays repeatedly for a longer period, some of the terrible neoplasms can be destroyed.

After a time it was found, however, that the destruction of cancer cells does not always mean the cure of cancer and, also, that the normal cells of the body may be seriously damaged if long exposed to radioactivity.

When Mme. Curie, after having handled uranium ore for four years, finally held the first gram of radium in her hand there appeared abrasions in the skin which no treatment could cure. With the years she grew steadily sicker from a disease caused by radioactive rays which damaged her bone marrow and through this her blood. In 1934 death put an end to her suffering.

Even so, for many years we were not aware of the grave risks involved in X-rays to those constantly exposed to them. Through operating X-ray apparatus thousands of doctors and nurses have incurred incurable diseases.

Radioactive rays are material things. Through them the radioactive element constantly and forcefully emits tiny particles of itself. There are three kinds. They are named after the three first letters of the Greek alphabet, *alpha*, *beta*, *gamma*. The gamma rays are the hardest ones and have the strongest effect.

The reason why elements emit radioactive rays is that they are in a continuous state of decaying. The radioactivity is the energy liberated little by little. There are other elements besides uranium and radium which are radioactive. To the radiation from the elements in the earth is added some radiation from space. Fortunately, the air mass 400 kilometers high that surrounds our earth protects us against this radiation. Only a very small fraction of it reaches us.

We are, then, constantly being exposed to radioactive radiation coming from the earth and from space. It is so weak, however, that it does not hurt us. Stronger sources of radiation, as for instance X-ray machines and exposed radium, have, as we know, harmful effects if one is exposed to them for some time.

The radioactive rays are, as I said, invisible. How can we tell that they are there and how strong they are?

Thanks to the German physicist Hans Geiger, who died in 1945 as a victim to X-rays, we have an instrument which makes that possible. This instrument is called the Geiger counter; it consists of a metal tube containing rarefied air. In it are two metal electrodes between which there is a high potential. Radioactive rays from the outside affect the tube and release a discharge between the two electrodes. The stronger the radiation the quicker the discharges follow one another. A small device connected to the tube makes the discharge audible. The Geiger counter performs a veritable drum-roll when the discharges are strong.

There are two kinds of atom bomb—uranium bombs and hydrogen bombs. The effect of an uranium bomb is due to a process which liberates energy through the fission of uranium. In the hydrogen bomb the liberation of energy is the result of the transformation of hydrogen into helium.

It is interesting to note that this latter process is similar to that which takes place in the center of the sun, supplying it with the self-renewing energy which it emits in the form of light and heat.

In principle, the effect of both bombs is the same. But according to various estimates the effect of one of the latest hydrogen bombs is 2,000 times stronger than the one which was dropped on Hiroshima.

To these two bombs has recently been added the cobalt bomb, a kind of super atom bomb. It is a hydrogen bomb surrounded by a layer of cobalt. The effect of this bomb is estimated to be many times stronger than that of hydrogen bombs that have been made so far.

The explosion of an atom bomb creates an unconceivably large number of exceedingly small particles of radioactive elements which decay like uranium or radium. Some of these particles decay very quickly, others more slowly, and some of them extraordinarily slowly. The strongest of these elements cease to exist only ten seconds after the detonation of the bomb. But in this short time they may have killed a great number of people in a circumference of several miles.

What remains are the less powerful elements. In our time it is with these we have to contend. It is of the danger arising from the radioactive rays emitted by these elements that we must be aware.

Of these elements some exist for hours, some for weeks, or months, or years, or millions of years, undergoing continuous decay. They float in the higher strata of air as clouds of radioactive dust. The heavy particles fall down first. The lighter ones will stay in the air for a longer time or come down with rain or snow. How long it will take before everything carried up in the air by the explosions which have taken place till now has disappeared no one can say with any certainty. According to some estimates, this will be the case not earlier than thirty or forty years from now.

When I was a boy I witnessed how dust hurled into the air from the explosion in 1883 of the island Krakatoa in the Sunda group was noticeable for two years afterwards to such an extent that the sunsets were given extraordinary splendor by it.

What we can state with certainty, however, is that the radioactive clouds will constantly be carried by the winds around the globe and that some of the dust, by its own weight, or by being brought down by rain, snow, mist, and dew, little by little, will fall down to the hard surface of the earth, into the rivers, and into the oceans.

Of what nature are these radioactive elements, particles of which were carried up in the air by the explosion of atom bombs and which are now falling down again?

They are strange variants of the usual nonradioactive elements. They have the same chemical properties, but a different atomic weight. Their names are always accompanied by their atomic weights. The same element can occur in several radioactive variants. Besides iodine-131, which lives for sixteen days only, we have iodine-129, which lives for 200,000,000 years.

Dangerous elements of this kind are phosphorus-32, calcium-45, iodine-131, iron-55, bismuth-210, plutonium-239, cerium-144, strontium-89, and cesium-137. If the hydrogen bomb is covered by cobalt, cobalt-60 must be added to the list.

Particularly dangerous are the elements combining long life with a relatively strong efficient radiation. Among them strontium-90 takes first place. It is present in very large amounts in the radioactive dust. Cobalt-60 must also be mentioned as particularly dangerous.

The radioactivity in the air, increased through these elements, will not harm us from the outside, not being strong enough to penetrate the skin. It is another matter with respiration, through which radioactive elements can enter our bodies. But the danger which has to be stressed above all the others is the one which arises from our drinking radioactive water and our eating radioactive food as a consequence of the increased radioactivity in the air.

Following the explosions of Bikini and Siberia, rain falling over Japan has, from time to time, been so radioactive that the water from it cannot be drunk. Not only that: Reports of radioactive rainfall are coming from all parts of the world where analyses have recently been made. In several places the water has proved to be so radioactive that it was unfit for drinking.

Well-water becomes radioactive to any considerable extent only after longer periods of heavy rainfall.

Wherever radioactive rainwater is found the soil is also radioactive—and in a higher degree. The soil is made radioactive not only by the downpour, but also from radioactive dust falling on it. And with the soil the vegetation will also have become radioactive. The radioactive elements deposited in the soil pass into the plants, where they are stored. This is of importance, for as a result of this process it may be the case that we are threatened by a considerable amount of radioactive elements.

The radioactive elements in grass, when eaten by animals whose meat is used for food, will be absorbed and stored in our bodies.

In the case of cows grazing on contaminated soil, the absorption is effected when we drink their milk. In that way small children run an especially dangerous risk of absorbing radioactive elements.

When we eat contaminated cheese and fruits the radioactive elements stored in them are transferred to us.

What this storing of radioactive material implies is clearly demonstrated by the observations made when, on one occasion, the radioactivity of the Columbia River in North America was analyzed. The radioactivity was caused by the atomic plants at Hanford, which produce plutonium for atomic bombs and which empty their wastewater into the river. The radioactivity of the river water was insignificant. But the radioactivity of the river plankton was 2,000 times higher, that of the ducks eating plankton 40,000 times higher, that of the fish 15,000 times higher. In young swallows fed on insects caught by their parents in the river the radioactivity was 500,000 times higher, and in the egg yolks of water birds more than 1,000,000 times higher.

From official and unofficial sources we have been assured, time and time again, that the increase in radioactivity of the air does not exceed the amount which the human body can tolerate without any harmful effects. This is just evading the issue. Even if we are not directly affected by the radioactive material in the air, we are indirectly affected through that which has fallen down, is falling down,

and will fall down. We are absorbing this through radioactive drinking water and through animal and vegetable foodstuffs, to the same extent as radioactive elements are stored in the vegetation of the region in which we live. Unfortunately for us, nature hoards what is falling down from the air.

None of the radioactivity of the air, created by the explosion of atom bombs, is so unimportant that it may not, in the long run, become a danger to us through increasing the amount of radioactivity stored in our bodies.

What we absorb of radioactivity is not spread evenly in all cellular tissue. It is deposited in certain parts of our body, particularly in the bone tissue and also in the spleen and in the liver. From those sources the organs which are especially sensitive to it are exposed to radiation. What the radiation lacks in strength is compensated for by time. It works day and night without interruption.

How does radiation affect the cells of an organ?

Through being ionized, that is to say, electrically charged. This change means that the chemical processes which make it possible for the cells to do their job in our body no longer function as they should. They are no longer able to perform the tasks which are of vital importance to us. We must also bear in mind that a great number of the cells of an organ may degenerate or die as a result of radiation.

What are the diseases caused by internal radiation? The same diseases that are known to be caused by external radiation.

They are mainly serious blood diseases. The cells of the red bone marrow, where the red and the white blood corpuscles are formed, are very sensitive to radioactive rays. It is these corpuscles, found in great numbers in the blood, which make it possible for it to play such an important part. If the cells in the bone marrow are damaged by radiation they will produce too few or abnormal, degenerating blood corpuscles. Both cases lead to blood diseases and, frequently, to death. These were the diseases that killed the victims of Xrays and radium rays.

It was one of these diseases that attacked the Japanese fishermen who were surprised in their vessel by radioactive ashes falling down

240 miles from Bikini after the explosion of a hydrogen bomb. With one exception, they were all saved, being strong and relatively mildly affected, through continuous blood transfusions.

In the cases cited the radiation came from the outside. It is unfortunately very probable that internal radiation affecting the bone marrow and lasting for years will have the same effect, particularly since the radiation goes from the bone tissue to the bone marrow. As I have said, the radioactive elements are by preference stored in the bone tissue.

Not our own health only is threatened by internal radiation, but also that of our descendants. The fact is that the cells of the reproductive organs are particularly vulnerable to radiation, which in this case attacks the nucleus to such an extent that it can be seen in the microscope

To the profound damage of these cells corresponds a profound damage to our descendants.

It consists of stillbirths and of the births of babies with mental or physical defects.

In this context also, we can point to the effects of radiation coming from the outside.

It is a fact—even if the statistical material being published in the press needs checking—that in Nagasaki, during the years following the dropping of the atom bomb, an exceptionally high occurrence of stillbirths and of deformed children was observed.

In order to establish the effect of radioactive radiation on posterity, comparative studies have been made between the descendants of doctors who have been using X-ray apparatus over a period of years and descendants of doctors who have not. The material of this study comprises about 3,000 doctors in each group. A noticeable difference was found. Among the descendants of radiologists a percentage of stillbirths of 1.403 was found, while the percentage among the nonradiologists was 1.222.

In the first group 6.01 percent of the children had congenital defects, compared to only 4.82 percent in the second.

The number of healthy children in the first group was 80.42 per-

cent; the number in the other was significantly higher, viz., 83.23 percent.

It must be remembered that even the weakest of internal radiation can have harmful effects on our descendants.

The total effect of the damage done to descendants of ancestors who have been exposed to radioactive rays will not, in accordance with the laws of genetics, be apparent in the generations coming immediately after us. The full effects will appear only 100 or 200 years later.

As the matter stands we cannot at present cite cases of serious damage done by internal radiation. To the extent that such radiation exists it is not sufficiently strong and has not lasted long enough to have caused the damage in question. We can only conclude from the harmful effects known to be caused by external radiation those we must expect in the future from internal radiation.

If the effect of the latter is not as strong as that of the former, it may become so, through working little by little and without interruption. The final result will be the same in both cases.

Their effects add up.

We must also remember that internal radiation does not have to, in contrast to that coming from the outside, penetrate layers of skin, tissues, and muscles to hit the organs. It works at close range and without any weakening of its force.

When we realize under what conditions the internal radiation is working, we cease to underrate it. Even if it is true that, when speaking of the dangers of internal radiation, we can point to no actual case, only express our fear, that fear is so solidly founded on facts that it attains the weight of reality in determining our attitude. We are forced to regard every increase in the existing danger through further creation of radioactive elements by atom bomb explosions as a catastrophe for the human race, a catastrophe that must be prevented.

There can be no question of doing anything else, if only for the reason that we cannot take the responsibility for the consequences it might have for our descendants.

They are threatened by the greatest and most terrible danger.

That radioactive elements created by us are found in nature is an astounding event in the history of the earth and of the human race. To fail to consider its importance and its consequences would be a folly for which humanity would have to pay a terrible price. We are committing a folly in thoughtlessness. It must not happen that we do not pull ourselves together before it is too late. We must muster the insight, the seriousness, and the courage to leave folly and to face reality.

This is at bottom what the statesmen of the nations producing atomic bombs are thinking, too. Through the reports they are receiving they are sufficiently informed to form their own judgments, and we must also assume that they are alive to their responsibility.

At any rate, America and Soviet Russia and Britain are telling one another again and again that they want nothing more than to reach an agreement to end the testing of atomic weapons. At the same time, however, they declare that they cannot stop the tests as long as there is no such agreement.

Why do they not come to an agreement? The real reason is that in their own countries there is no public opinion asking for it. Nor is there any such public opinion in other countries, with the exception of Japan. This opinion has been forced upon the Japanese people because, little by little, they will be hit in a most terrible way by the evil consequences of all the tests.

An agreement of this kind presupposes reliability and trust. There must be guarantees preventing the agreement from being signed by anyone intending to win important tactical advantages foreseen only by him.

Public opinion in all nations concerned must inspire and accept the agreement.

When public opinion has been created in the countries concerned and among all nations, an opinion informed of the dangers involved in going on with the tests and led by the reason which this information imposes, then the statesmen may reach an agreement to stop the experiments.

A public opinion of this kind stands in no need of plebiscites or of

forming of committees to express itself. It works through just being there.

The end of further experiments with atom bombs would be like the early sunrays of hope which suffering humanity is longing for.

On April 27, I wrote Dr. Schweitzer about his broadcast.

April 27, 1957

My dear Dr. Schweitzer:

Late last night, I was on my way home when I saw people looking up in New York's crowded Times Square in the heart of the city. They were looking up at the large electric sign that ran around the *Times* building on which something was being flashed. I looked up and saw in large letters powered by thousands of electric lights the news of your statement released in Oslo. An hour later the first edition of the *New York Times* was published. The account of your declaration was prominently featured on the front page. Then inside, a large portion of the text was carried verbatim. I read it carefully, word for word, four or five times over. I cannot tell you how impressed I was by what you said. It was the fullest account of the scientific basis for the case against the explosions that has yet appeared in America. Never before have the American people been given such concisely stated facts on this critically important problem. And you write your Declaration from a vantage point completely outside the political arena. You wrote with the ethic and culture of man uppermost in your mind.

The timing of your Declaration was most propitious, from the standpoint of events in America and the world itself. The disarmament talks in Europe have raised hopes that this might be a good time for a fresh attack on the problem. The controversy over hydrogen bomb tests by Great Britain has re-focused world attention on the entire question. Meanwhile, the special Japanese envoy, Masa-

toshi Matsushita, has been traveling around the world, making known the concern of his government about the nuclear tests. He came out to our house last Sunday to report on the results of his trip so far. He had an extremely good audience with the Pope, who said that he felt the gravest apprehensions were about both the effects of radiation through nuclear testing and the danger of a nuclear war. In London, Ambassador Matsushita spoke to all the government leaders, including Prime Minister Macmillan, Sir Winston Churchill, and Clement Atlee. He came away with the feeling that the British government is waiting for the United States to make the basic decisions concerning any cessation of nuclear testing. There was a tendency in Great Britain to avoid any action that might result in the displeasure of the American government. No doubt this is the result of the Suez incident and the near-break with the U.S., creating the need to subordinate almost everything today to winning back the favor of Washington.

Ambassador Matsushita discussed two points. The first concerned appropriate steps or initiatives Japan might take at the United Nations. The second concerned his approach to Secretary Dulles, whom he was scheduled to see in Washington the following day. On the first point, I urged him to use your Declaration as the basis for a full presentation to the United Nations. I told him that your statement should be called officially to the attention of the delegates in the General Assembly. It also seemed to me that Japan should attempt to get several other nations, Norway among them, to join in urging that your statement be proposed as the substance of a general resolution. He favored this idea. In this connection, some additional Declarations, signed by a member of the world's moral leaders, might be useful. I shall write to you again as matters develop.

Concerning his second point—his meeting with Secretary Dulles—I told him I was certain that his own ideas on this subject were far better developed than my own. I did, however, urge him to make clear to Secretary Dulles that Japan believes the danger from nuclear testing to be real and not hypothetical, and to document this statement with actual facts concerning the contamination of soil and water

in Japan. I also expressed the opinion that no country should feel obligated, because of its connections to the United States, to avoid the larger obligations to the health and safety of its own people. Ambassador Matsushita said he anticipated that Secretary Dulles would agree in principle but would say that the United States had no choice but to continue nuclear testing in view of the fact that the Russians were developing nuclear weapons. In that case, I suggested it might be pertinent to point out that the easiest way for the United States to force Soviet Russia's hand would be for the U.S. to declare before the entire world that we were giving up our nuclear tests because of the danger to vegetation, water, and human and animal life. Having abandoned the tests for that reason, we would shift the burden of good faith to all other nations. Any nation which proceeded with its own tests would alienate itself from the human community and face a difficult situation with its own people.

Mr. Matsushita saw Mr. Dulles in Washington the following day. The meeting went off as expected. Mr. Dulles was polite but said that the United States had no choice. Mr. Matsushita left Washington in a mood of concern and discouragement. From Washington he went to Chicago to see Adlai Stevenson, who discussed the meeting with me by telephone the following day. Mr. Stevenson was somewhat apprehensive about the lack of imagination in the State Department. He will discuss this entire question with you when he visits Lambaréné in a few weeks.

Part of the discouraging picture in the United States, as I wrote you some time earlier, may be due to the fact that President Eisenhower has not been well recently. His staff is apparently seriously worried about his health and almost no one can get through to him except a few intimates.

It is for all these reasons that your Declaration was so essential in the United States. I believe it carries a scientific and moral authority that must make a profound impression. Indeed, now, for the first time in several years, I feel genuinely hopeful that a fundamental change with respect to the nuclear problem can be brought about. It may take another few months for the cumulative effect of your Dec-

laration to be fully felt but I believe that the nations will be forced by the pressure of the world public opinion to abandon nuclear testing. Beyond that, of course, is the larger problem of world tensions and war itself; but as you say, the light that can result from this one gain can make visible other objectives and the means of reaching them.

It was for me a matter of great good fortune that Clara was in the United States at the time your Declaration was released, for we could both rejoice in the tremendous contribution you have made to the human community. I am especially grateful to her for having persuaded me to go to Lambaréné in the first place, and now I am looking forward to seeing you in Gunsbach late in August or early September. My heartfelt thanks for your letters keeping me informed about developments at Oslo.

With continuing good wishes, I am,

Faithfully yours,
Norman

Lambaréné, Gabon
May 5, 1957

Norman Cousins

Dear friend:

A thousand thanks for your dear letter of April 25th. I am so relieved that you agree with my text. Everything was so rushed once it had been completed, because I expected Oslo to transmit it on April 20th. Radio Oslo thought that they would be able to do it only in May, as otherwise they would have had too little time to make the necessary contacts with the other radio stations. . . . But I knew that April 20th was the right psychological moment and asked Oslo to make the impossible possible. What the Nobel Committee and Radio Oslo managed to achieve in three weeks is magnificent. One hundred and fifty transmitters throughout the world broadcast the

address: in the East, in Asia, Australia, South America . . . these are all of value to me. It must reach the point where there is an open public opinion among mankind; that is why the address had to have as wide a range as possible. Also it must have been generally understandable: that is why it appears to have been written by a shoemaker. It was with intent that I restricted myself to the cessation of atomic tests. One must have the right beginning. And right at the end I spoke quite quietly of the political and diplomatic side, and of the need to encourage that aspect by means of an open public opinion. But I don't count much on that. . . . Now oftentimes I think of you. Without your coming here I don't think I should have decided to make the statement. You were right to encourage me to do it. I will not forget that.

Thank you a thousand times for the news that you give me. The fact that the President withdraws further and further is a serious historical factor. . . . We will talk of all this when you come to visit me in Europe in the autumn. I hope I will be able to get away from here.

So aufwiedersehen. If you have anything interesting about the nuclear situation please send it on to me. You can write in English; I can read it well.

Should you see the President please give him my best wishes and kindest regards.

<div style="text-align: right">

Cordially yours,
Albert Schweitzer

</div>

P.S. I had to use a wide soft nib so as not to strain my arm; hence the bad handwriting.

Concerns were mounting in the United States in regard to the radioactive contamination of food and water resulting from the atmospheric testing of hydrogen bombs. Despite efforts by the Atomic Energy Commission to reassure the public, research showed a definite increase in the leukemia rate as a result of the testing.

I wrote Dr. Schweitzer to this effect, and enclosed copies of issues of The

Saturday Review *containing his statement and that of Dr. Libby, as well as some additional materials on the research being done. Not long afterward, I received a letter from Dr. Schweitzer expressing concern about President Eisenhower's health, and enclosing a letter from him to the President with instructions for taking some medicine he felt sure would be of benefit. The medicine and instructions were promptly delivered to the White House.*

<div align="right">

Lambaréné, Gabon
May 17, 1957

</div>

Mr. Norman Cousins

Dear friend:

I was disheartened to see in the newspapers photographs of the President where one can see him pressing his handkerchief to his nose because of a bad cold. I was disturbed first of all that photographers are permitted to show a chief of state in this condition, but also disturbed that he was obliged to travel in this state. It's for this reason that I have sent you four tubes of powder of rhino lactic acid, which is the best treatment for a mounting cold. I am writing him on the attached sheet as to how to use it. Over the years I've found for myself and my patients that if this medicine is taken like tobacco at the first signs of a cold and that if a pinch is taken in each nostril every half hour over a period of several hours the cold will not develop and the ensuing grippe will also be avoided. Thus, if you think it opportune to send on these four tubes which you will receive to the President, please send him a translation of the instructions for treatment that I've noted for him. If you don't feel it's indicated to give the medicine to the President, keep it for yourself and profit thereby if you feel the beginnings of a cold. For every grippe begins with a cold and is avoided if the cold is cured.

<div align="right">

From my heart, your devoted
Albert Schweitzer

</div>

P.S. The packet with the four tubes will probably come a little later than this letter.

Albert Schweitzer
Lambaréné
French Equatorial Africa
May 17, 1957

President Eisenhower
Washington

Dear Mr. President:

I was chagrined to see a photograph of you in the newspapers where you were seated in an automobile with a bad cold, gripping your handkerchief in your hand. Permit this ancient doctor to send you through Norman Cousins a simple remedy which can keep you from colds, if you take it in time. It's a powder of lactic acid, thus inoffensive, to take the same way one takes tobacco. As soon as you sneeze or feel that your nose is beginning to drip or clog up you must take pinches of this powder in the two nostrils, *each half hour at least a dozen times and even more often than that.* This powder disinfects the mucous membranes of the nose and prevents the cold from developing. To get the powder properly in the hand for application, you have only to turn the perforated cover until the small perforation of the metal (O) is superposed on the identical perforation of the tube (O). The powder comes out when you tap the tube with your finger. Afterwards, you reclose the cover. It is a simple and efficient way to combat colds which I have tested on myself and on my patients.

Please excuse me, Mr. President, for being so bold as to give you advice for your health.

With assurances of my respectful sentiments,
your devoted Albert Schweitzer

May 20, 1957

My dear Dr. Schweitzer:

First of all, let me thank you for the letter and the medicine you asked me to send to the President. It was a characteristically thoughtful act by you and will, I am sure, endear you even more to the President's heart.

Now about your Declaration: So much has happened with respect to its impact in the United States that I hardly know where to begin. As you know, there was some slip-up or confusion at the time of the release of your Declaration with the result that it was not broadcast by the American radio stations. Only the *New York Times* was able to get enough information about it in time to publish a reasonably complete account of it. Even at that, the *New York Times* received only half the text of the Declaration. That was why *The Saturday Review*, in its next issue, published the statement in full. Never before in the history of the magazine have we had such a response to anything that appeared in our pages. Countless thousands of reprints have been ordered. Newspapers around the country are republishing the statement in full as it appeared in *The Saturday Review*. Senator Neuberger[*] read your statement on the floor of the Senate and it now appears in full in the United States Congressional Record. Individuals throughout the country have been inspired to act in behalf of it. Ministers have delivered sermons on it, literally by the hundreds. Church groups have passed resolutions in favor of it. Teachers in colleges and high schools have asked for permission to mimeograph the statement for distribution among their students.

Meanwhile, a joint committee of the Senate and House of Representatives has started to hold hearings on the entire question of radioactive fallout. The hearings started yesterday. I am enclosing some news clippings relating to the hearings.

More and more, public opinion is swinging against the tests. More and more, it is being realized that the people have a right to know

[*]Richard Neuberger was U.S. Senator from Oregon from 1955 to 1960.

what the truth of the situation is. More and more, it is being understood that there is much that the government does not know; i.e., what the tolerance limits of human beings are to strontium radioactivity; what the contamination factor is with respect to food; what happens when a confluence of winds causes an abnormally high fallout; the increased sensitivity of children, etc., etc.

It may be asked, What is the President's role and position in all this? I say to you advisedly that the President has not been thoroughly informed. One of the great tragedies in the development of atomic energy form the very start is that it has been carried out in an air of great secrecy and mystery—so much so that its full implications have hardly been understood by the people at the head of government. On an important matter such as this, where conscientious research is required on a vast scale, and where the fullest possible public debate is required to bring out the moral and sociological implications, there has been up until now very little public information with the result that not only the public but the lawmakers themselves have been confused.

For at least a year, the President has had before him material on the danger of contamination and suggesting the need for a highly imaginative policy which would recognize that not only the American people but all peoples were now in jeopardy. The President said he agreed. Then unhappily, during the presidential campaign, this became a political issue and the Administration felt it was a politically wise policy to endorse continued hydrogen bomb testing.

Now the attempt is being made to justify the present effort to tell the people there is very little danger, on the grounds that if the people know what the real situation was there might be a panic. It is very curious reasoning and I am confident that the people will demand, and before long, to receive the truth concerning the radioactive situation. The current Senate hearings, for example, will keep this issue in the forefront of the public consciousness for several weeks at least.

Last Saturday, Clara left for London. She had a most productive visit in the United States and is now looking forward to her visit to

Lambaréné with Adlai Stevenson. She will be in a position to tell you directly of the impact of your statement in the United States.

I am enclosing six additional copies of *The Saturday Review* containing your Declaration. I am also enclosing several copies of the following issue of *The Saturday Review* analyzing Dr. Libby's reply.

It is now definite that I shall be in Europe late this summer, and I am looking forward to seeing you in Gunsbach.

With prayerful good wishes for your continued health and well-being, I am

Faithfully yours,
Norman

May 29, 1957

His Excellency, Jawaharlal Nehru
Prime Minister's House
New Delhi, India

Dear Mr. Prime Minister:

This will supplement my earlier report concerning Dr. Schweitzer's Declaration on the danger of radioactivity from nuclear explosions.

Various newspapers around the country have reprinted the Declaration in full. Thousands of individual reprints have been ordered. More important is that the Declaration has started off something of a chain reaction. Each day some additional research by universities is announced that underlines the danger. Many scientists have been encouraged by Dr. Schweitzer's example to come forward and raise vital questions. Members of Congress are giving the situation the serious attention it deserves. The Senate was informed fully about Dr. Schweitzer's Declaration by several of its members.

Congressional hearings on the subject, as you know, are now being held. While the official position will receive a large share of the

attention, the Schweitzer viewpoint will be given an adequate hearing. Evidence will be presented to show that there has been more than a 1 percent increase in the incidence of leukemia already as the result of the tests, and that this rate may be expected to increase fivefold within a few years. The fact that children have a much lower tolerance will be brought out. It is also planned to call attention to the fact that an unhappy confluence of winds over the state of Minnesota two weeks ago brought about a fallout more than one hundred times the national average.

There is now strong reason to believe that a change in American policy with respect to the nuclear explosions may come about some time before the end of the year. The accumulating evidence is too strong to resist; public opinion is moving very solidly and is being strengthened by the support of leaders in science, religion, and education. Indeed, for the first time since the end of the war in 1945 I have some measure of confidence that the disarmament negotiations, now going on in London, are being conducted by each side with truly serious intent and not for the purpose of jockeying for the kind of position that will make it seem that the other side is responsible for any failure to arrive at agreement.

The overriding question, of course, involves not merely cessation of nuclear testing but the possible danger of a war in which the stockpiled nuclear weapons will be used. While Dr. Schweitzer did not address himself in his statement to that general issue, it is his hope that the crack in the door that might be created by cessation of nuclear testing might be widened for larger and more basic purposes.

Dr. Schweitzer is very eager to learn what you believe his next step in this matter should be.

With continuing good wishes and the highest esteem, I am,

Yours faithfully,
Norman Cousins

No. 1074–PMH/57
New Delhi
June 6, 1957

My dear Cousins,

Thank you for your letter of May 29th and the copy of *The Saturday Review* containing Albert Schweitzer's statement.

I agree with you that there is now a far greater realization all over the world of the effect of these test explosions than there was previously. I am sure that Schweitzer's statement has helped in this process.

In India, there is strong and widespread feeling of this subject. Indeed, one preaches to the converted here. Both our Houses of Parliament separately passed resolutions in regard to these test explosions and the harm they were doing.

I do not know what to suggest as to the next step. Clearly, the pressure must come from awakened and, where possible, organized public opinion. This has been aroused, but there is always the danger of its relapse in quiescence. We should take advantage of all legitimate methods of keeping the public informed. Unfortunately, the so-called peace conferences and congresses, usually organized by Communists and their friends, do more harm than good in this respect. They have patently political objectives in view and they irritate many people outside their fold. Fortunately, others now are also playing an important part in this vital question.

I agree with you also that there is some small measure of hope now in the partial success of the disarmament negotiations. But I have been disappointed so often that I do not rely too much on them at this stage.

I wonder if you saw a book which one of our scientists, Dr. D. S. Kothari, prepared last year on nuclear explosions. This was probably the first connected account, accurate and yet not too technical, and it was welcomed in many countries as such. That book is some-

what out of date now, because more facts are known. Kothari is now preparing a new and revised edition of that book. I am asking him to send you copies of the old and the new editions. Perhaps, you could send a copy to Dr. Schweitzer.

All I can suggest to Dr. Schweitzer is that he might, perhaps some little time later, follow up his broadcast.

Yours sincerely,
J. Nehru

Nehru's concerns about the dangers of atmospheric testing, and his lack of confidence in disarmament negotiations were mirrored in these letters from Dr. Schweitzer.

Dr. Albert Schweitzer
Gunsbach
Haut-Rhin
France
October 14, 1957

Mr. Norman Cousins
Dear friend:

I've been following the debates at the United Nations on disarmament with great attention. I find it sad that Henry Cabot Lodge, deputy of the United States of America, declares in his speech that the nuclear explosions do not present a grave danger. He makes a very bad impression on the entire world in relying on a theory which real scholars and physicians recognize as absolutely false, especially in view of the disastrous effects for human beings still to be born. I wonder if American scholars and physicians can accede to it without protesting against an American representative who professes such a false opinion in the name of America. . . . It's up to them to decide

if they will tolerate it or not. One could think that it would be better that the protest came from them than from abroad. What a sad time we're living in! Falsehood rises up in the name of facts against truth, while the latter cannot manifest itself as it should because the lie is joined with well-organized publicity.

What will be the result of the United Nations debates? Considering how they're engaged now, there is little hope that they will arrive at a solution. . . . Congratulate Stassen and Flanders[*] on my behalf if you have the chance. I think a great deal about them these days. . . .

But treat the contents of my letter as completely personal. I don't want to give the impression that I am meddling in U.S.A. affairs.

<div style="text-align:right">

From my heart, your devoted
Albert Schweitzer

</div>

Writing a month later, Dr. Schweitzer referred to a suggestion I had discussed with Clara Urquhart. It was our hope that the momentum begun by the Radio Oslo Declaration could be sustained by a meeting between Dr. Schweitzer and highly respected members of the American press, including Edward R. Murrow from CBS and a representative of NBC. He continued to stress the necessity of his independent action in affairs of state, always with the conviction that genuine political movements must be initiated by the people themselves. References to his own role reflected his reluctance to become involved politically. As he said in this letter, "The fire must be lighted in the U.S.A.; and I will then be able to help other men of other lands to bring the wood to throw onto the fire . . ."

[*]Harold Stassen, former governor of the state of Minnesota, was a member of the U.S. delegation to the San Francisco Conference that created the charter of the United Nations. He had served as a special assistant to President Eisenhower on disarmament problems. Ralph Flanders served as a U.S. Senator from Vermont from 1946 to 1959 and took an active role in congressional investigations in regard to the Atomic Energy Commission.

Lambaréné, Gabon
November 11, 1957

Mr. Norman Cousins

Dear friend,

Clara has submitted your proposal to me. It was good news to me to know there are persons in the U.S.A. who disagree with the proposition made by the people at the U.N., and with the ideas of the government of the U.S.A. Because this negation of all so as to negotiate for new bases was, during these last days, agonizing. I suffered much from it. And I am relieved that an unofficial public opinion is manifesting itself besides the official one. That was absolutely necessary. But I cannot accede to your proposition to receive the two gentlemen. It is necessary that this unofficial public opinion has an absolutely American origin and a completely American character. Otherwise its enemies could diminish its importance, saying that it was inspired from abroad. That would be very grave. American opinion must pronounce itself with complete sovereignty on the situation that has been created at present by my Declaration—insofar as American opinion is known, it does not yet allow for this new situation, but in a general sense it contains the spirit of this new unofficial attitude. It asks for the suspension of nuclear tests as a first act. But one could say that it was I who asked for this first step, and that it is not the people in America alone who proclaim it. I attach great importance to the fact that the Russian proposal calling for a meeting of American and Russian scientists goes back to something inspired by Cyrus Eaton a year ago. One must not obscure this American origin by mixing with it the name of this Mr. Schweitzer or by any meetings that he might have with three American personalities. [Translator's note: "Schweitzer means Murrow and NBC but in the letter writes of 'three men.' "] The strength of the manifestation of this unofficial opinion lies in the fact that it is completely American. Avoid everything that could attenuate this characteristic; encourage that which will enable it to become popular. Reflect well

on this and you will see that I am right. That Americans come out against the opinion of American politics is the beginning of the beginning. And a general movement in Europe could grow out of that example. Once things are that far I could then help in the creation of the general movement, if I judge that my intervention could serve a purpose. The fire must be lighted in the U.S.A., and I will then be able to help other men of other lands to bring the wood to throw onto the fire and to give it the importance it should have to enable it to create a different atmosphere. All this between ourselves. Sustain the movement in America and it will propagate itself in Europe, and in the world. And count on me for everything that I will be able to do to propagate the movement.

From the heart, your devoted

Albert Schweitzer

I replied to Dr. Schweitzer, informing him that a group of distinguished Americans had come together to work for a responsible policy on nuclear energy. The group, which came to be known as SANE (National Committee for a Sane Nuclear Policy), had just issued a public statement in the New York Times, *a copy of which was being personally delivered to Dr. Schweitzer by my friend and physician, Dr. William Hitzig. At the same time, I wrote Prime Minister Nehru, reporting on conversations I'd had with Dr. Schweitzer in Gunsbach a few weeks earlier.*

No. 997–PMO/57
New Delhi
November 27, 1957

Dear Norman Cousins,

It is good of you to keep me in touch with your talks with Dr. Schweitzer. I quite agree with you that we cannot retire into our shells because the response is not adequate and the prospect not good. Dr. Schweitzer should certainly continue to press his views before the public and I am sure that they will affect people's thinking.

I am inclined to think that large numbers of people all over the world have begun to realize the dangers inherent in the cold war approach allied to modern developments in the production of weapons of mass destruction. But all these people function rather as individuals without much direction and their fears can be played upon. If a little twist was given to their thinking which removed this element of fear, then progress in the right direction would be rapid.

Yours sincerely,
Jawaharlal Nehru

Lambaréné, Gabon
December 12, 1957

Mr. Norman Cousins

Dear friend,

I'm writing you from the ship "Brazza" on which I'm returning to Lambaréné. We are south of Dakar. If I'm writing you so late (since the departure of Mme. Clara Urquhart, who was the one who had us meet), it's that I had an accident, a fracture of a bone in the right hand in mid-September, and it's taking a long time to heal. Writing still demands an effort and I have to be very careful with this hand. I've been following events with full attention as much as I can. I believe you must be pleased with the echo found by your appeal to reason. I particularly appreciated the opinion expressed by the former American ambassador to the U.S.S.R. This testimony has particular importance. Now we must await the results of the Paris meeting. It is very interesting that Chancellor Adenauer has spontaneously declared that he would not consider the question of installations for American weapons on German territory as an actuality. Norway and Denmark also have the same attitude. This means that the Paris conference will not succeed in mobilizing Europe. What is curious is that England has declared herself ready to receive American nuclear weapons on her territory without waiting until the Paris

conference takes place. I don't know whether the news that Sweden and France want to build nuclear arms has real foundation. Given the French financial situation, one wonders how she can find means for this enterprise. . . . Thus we must wait to see how the situation works out in Paris. But I would judge that the decisions will be less serious than one would have feared a little while ago.

Concerning this you can inform me about what is happening in the United States; this would be of great service to me. I admire you for all you've undertaken and succeeded in. You've created a movement that did not exist before. When will we see each other again? I won't forget you. With my best wishes.

Your devoted
Albert Schweitzer

December 30, 1957

My dear Dr. Schweitzer:

I am grateful to you for your letter. It distresses me, however, that you should have put yourself to such discomfort in order to write to me, for I know how painful and awkward it must be to work with one finger in splints. I trust that by now your finger has completely healed and that you are able to play the piano again. How sad I was when I learned from Erica that your accident interfered with your organ playing at Gunsbach.

Concerning the situation in the United States at the present time, I venture to offer the following estimate:

1. The official position of the government on the matter of nuclear testing is hardening, but public understanding of the basic issue is growing.

2. The President has been persuaded by the State Department that it would be inadvisable to agree to a cessation of testing, even though the Russians might agree to monitored controls.

3. The State Department does not, of course, state publicly what

204 ALBERT SCHWEITZER'S MISSION

are probably real reasons against cessation. Those reasons are two-fold: first it fears that any cessation would produce a letdown and a feeling of complacency among the American people and blind them to the continuing danger from the Soviet Union. The second reason is that American policy towards the Soviet Union seeks to convince the Soviets beyond a shadow of a doubt that, in the event of a war between the two countries, we will use every weapon at our disposal. In short, the U.S. is still proceeding on the basis that its main chance for peace is through the nuclear deterrent. A few people in government, however, have now come to recognize that the policy of the nuclear deterrent is now obsolete. The Soviet Union now possesses superior means of delivering atomic weapons on target. The danger of a first strike by one side because of uncertainty over what the other side may do cannot be dismissed. As I say, some people in government now recognize the changed situation and re-alize that there is no longer any truly workable military security and that we shall have to look to a moral consensus in the world for the creation of necessary restraints.

4. The feeling is growing in some quarters in the United States that war is inevitable and that we should not wait for the bombs to fall on us. This view can of course only have the effect of intensify-ing the same feelings in the Soviet Union.

Taking all these facts into account, I should say that the danger of contamination from radioactive fallout is great, but that an even greater danger is represented by the fact that the world situation is getting out of control. A few months ago, there seemed real reason to believe that the best place to take hold in an attempt to arrest the mounting tensions was in an agreement to stop the tests. Today, however, the growing feeling of war inevitability is so great that it may become necessary to attempt a broader and more inclusive ap-proach to the problem of the peace. President Eisenhower cannot retreat on the matter of testing without losing face. If, however, some broad demand or public mandate could be created for a basic settlement that would include cessation of testing but not be con-fined to it, the President would probably welcome it. The State

Department would have to be convinced, however, that the Soviets would not interpret a conciliatory spirit as weakness.

Any comprehensive approach to the problems of the peace, of course, must have some place in it for direct discussions between the United States and the Soviet Union. I believe it would be a mistake, however, for the two countries to seek to resolve their differences only in face-to-face negotiations without adequate preliminary discussions. Rather, the initial discussions should be strictly directed to the basic principles that should obtain in the effort to resolve outstanding issues. It may be easier to achieve agreement on the machinery to be used in reconciliation and the rules of the game that are to be applied than on the actual issues.

I submit these ideas to you for your consideration. I confess I have no clear ideas as to how they can be best implemented, but I persevere in the conviction that powerful voices such as yours can be a vital factor in creating the public mandate that is the pre-condition for any basic change in the present situation.

You touch me deeply in your invitation to me to revisit Lambaréné. It would mean much to me to do so. At the moment, it may be that I should devote myself to the Committee for a Sane Nuclear Policy, now growing very fast, and to the magazine. But later in the spring, if the conditions are propitious, I should like to make the trip.

With every prayer for your good health and welfare, I am,

Sincerely yours,
Norman Cousins

Nehru had written public letters to President Eisenhower and Premier Bulganin in efforts to advance the cause of world peace in general and the cessation of nuclear testing in particular. Writing to congratulate him on his letters, I put some questions to him. First, a proposal had been made by the head of the U.S. Atomic Energy Commission that a world conference of leading scientists, philosophers, and theologians be held on the subject of world peace. I asked him about the possibility of holding such a meeting in New

206 ALBERT SCHWEITZER'S MISSION

Delhi. Second, President Eisenhower had written to Premier Bulganin of the need to strengthen the United Nations in order to resolve some of the unanswered questions relating to world peace. I asked Nehru if he felt any purpose would be served by an exchange of views between the U.S. and Indian governments as to what measures could be initiated in that direction. Third, prospects seemed dim for substantive talks between the U.S. and the Soviet Union.

1958

New Delhi
February 9, 1958

My dear Cousins,

Thank you for your letter of January 27th, which I have read with great interest.

I have a feeling that the situation in regard to disarmament, and, more especially, nuclear weapons and the like, is slowly taking a turn for the better. There is undoubtedly a widespread demand all over the world for what is called a high-level meeting. That demand itself represents the urge of people everywhere and the hope that something will be done soon to stop this mad race. Even governments are being affected by this tide of public opinion, though they move slowly and with great caution. I realize that such a top-level meeting may lead nowhere unless some adequate preparation is made for it. I do not think a foreign ministers' meeting is that type of preparation. Foreign ministers are by their very nature very rigid and they might well make matters worse. I agree with you also that a meeting of the United States and the Soviet Union right now may not be desirable and will not yield results. But I suppose some kind of a meeting will take place, probably on a wider basis and after informal contacts have been established.

It seems to me that any new proposals of the type you have men-

tioned will probably not be helpful at this stage. A conference of scientists, philosophers, theologians, etc., would no doubt pass some vague resolutions and, to that extent, add to the public opinion already existing. But any such attempt may well delay a closer and more intimate approach to the problem.

As for strengthening the United Nations, I do not quite understand what this means and how it will help. Even a consideration of problems of world peace by the United Nations, helpful as it well might be, should take place after some informal approaches have been made.

The general tendency, not only among the Communist countries, but also among those that might be called anti-Communist, is to function on the bloc level. I want to avoid that. I feel that the situation ought to be allowed to develop a little and informal approaches and contacts should be established. No progress can be made if either party puts forward proposals which it knows are unacceptable to the other. That is the present tendency, but I think that it is possible to explore a field where agreement is not ruled out. We are trying to do this insofar as we can. With all good wishes,

Yours sincerely,
Jawaharlal Nehru

In order to maintain the momentum generated by his Declaration, Dr. Schweitzer prepared a series of three appeals which were sent to Radio Oslo.

April 14, 1958

Mr. Norman Cousins,

Dear friend,

At last, you are receiving the appeals which you have been expecting for a long time. There are three appeals, each for a different night. They were finished as early as mid-March. But then came the negotiating with Oslo because I inquired if they intended again to

broadcast my appeals. After all, there is a certain significance in the fact that they are broadcast from Oslo, the seat of the Parliamentary Commission for the Nobel Peace Prize. Oslo is very kind and will do it again although the three appeals are much more political than last year's appeal. Then there were negotiations about the date. Oslo will now broadcast the three appeals on April 28, 29, and 30. Before that time they must not be disseminated anywhere by newspapers or radio—I had to make this promise to Oslo. You must therefore keep the text in a safe place so that nobody can pass it on to the press or radio.

I am sending you the first appeal in the English translation which I received from Oslo. As to the other two appeals, you will have to arrange for them to be translated there. So, on April 28, you may give the texts to the newspapers and to the radio if you have a station at your disposal, and later you may do anything you like.

The text is intended for Europe where we have to keep the NATO generals from forcing launching pads and nuclear weapons on the governments, which would amount to a military isolation of the Soviet Union and which could lead to war. We cannot and will not tolerate this NATO domination, which does not at all consider the abolition of nuclear weapons but only the continuation of armament. What is also on our minds is that the military presence of America in Europe which was brought about by the two world wars is unnatural and must gradually come to an end. This question has become an issue already because America by resisting the abolition of nuclear weapons exposes Europe to the danger of becoming the battlefield of a nuclear war between the Soviet Union and America. But sooner or later this idea of a slow emancipation of Europe from American weapons would have come up anyway. It has been in the air since the creation of NATO, which exercises military power over Europe, and especially since NATO has wanted to force nuclear weapons on us. America's wrong policy on nuclear weapons has triggered off this development. It is necessary that America's rulers take note of this and take in into account. We no longer wish to be associated with the idea that America keeps the free world free by

the threat of a nuclear war. This theory fails to appreciate the meaning of a nuclear war with contemporary arms. But I talk with affection about the U.S.A. and the help she has given Europe. If you think a phrase about the U.S. policy on nuclear weapons is too strong for the American readers and listeners, just leave it out. The same applies to all three appeals. But the American government may know that public opinion does not agree with its policy on nuclear weapons for NATO and that it puts pressure on the European governments from which they cannot escape.

My third appeal deals in detail with the top-level negotiations. I hold the opinion that nuclear weapons are against international law and that they have to be abolished for that reason irrespective of whether or not the three atomic powers have come to a satisfactory disarmament agreement, because in peace and in war they harm the uninvolved people and even humanity. I think this thesis will be considered important during the top-level negotiations. If the abolition of nuclear weapons is not achieved during these top-level negotiations, we will be in a serious situation. . . .

Please regard this letter as strictly personal. If you write to me about your opinion on the three appeals, I shall be pleased. I worked hard on them during the nights.

<div style="text-align: right;">

Devotedly,
Albert Schweitzer

</div>

<div style="text-align: right;">

May 9, 1958

</div>

Dear Dr. Schweitzer:

Erica Anderson is sitting with me at this moment so that in effect we are writing this letter to you together.

A few days ago I wrote to you via Clara in the thought that she was still in Lambaréné. Shortly after that letter was written, however, I received word that Clara expected to leave Lambaréné before

the letter would reach her; hence, the information in that letter which I had hoped that Clara would read to you I should now like to repeat.

1. *Coverage of the Three New Appeals*

The thing that I was hoping a new statement would achieve was manifestly successful. What was necessary was to supply the growing millions of people all over the world who are becoming increasingly concerned over this question with new inspiration and nourishment. It is vitally important, and I am sure you will agree, that you furnish continued leadership on a world scale. The fact that you are concerned, the fact that you are giving your deepest thoughts to this problem, the fact that you are investing most of your energies in this cause—all this is a powerful and indispensable contribution. I stand in greater awe than ever of you for this accomplishment. I think I have some idea of the personal sacrifice that was required to produce the three documents. You have every reason to feel that your vast efforts have been justified.

2. *The General Situation in the U.S.*

The picture here is mixed. As before, the government is divided on this question. The President's natural inclination is to move towards agreements; the State Department and the Atomic Energy Commission have done everything possible to block any agreements. A few days ago I lunched with Arthur Larson, special aide to the President, in Washington.

At lunch, Larson spoke about the President's dilemma: the fact that he wanted to reach some accord on nuclear testing and arms control but that there was overwhelming fear by the American military and also by the British and French that once we reduced or gave up our nuclear weapons we would be left exposed to the clear superiority of the Russians in armed manpower. I got the impression that the President's determination to resolve the impasse was not as strong now as it was two or three years ago. Indeed, I came away from the lunch with the feeling that one of the main problems was

fatigue. The men at the top seem intellectually and spiritually tired. The kind of inventiveness and restless courage that alone can create a new climate for fresh attempts at the peace seems to be wanting.

As it concerns Stassen, Larson went into the details of the split with Dulles. He said Dulles feared that Stassen was too eager to reach an agreement with the Russians at London last September. When I observed that I had thought Stassen was actually attempting to achieve the arms control that the President had thought was essential and that therefore it was strange that he should have been penalized for being successful, Larson said that Dulles felt we had to go very slowly with the Russians. For the same reason, he said, we had no choice except to go ahead with nuclear testing. The President has been told that we are on the verge of perfecting the clean bomb and also that we have some defensive missile devices that have to be tested.

I still cling to the hope that somehow the President's natural desire to be the architect of peace in the world will be tied to specific action. In fact, there is one approaching fact that might have this effect.

I refer to the probability that the Chinese government will soon develop nuclear weapons. Against the historical background of Russia's relationship with China, it is doubtful whether the Soviets would welcome this development. Indeed, there is every indication that the Soviet Union has been trying desperately to get a plan for a world ban of nuclear weapons established before China gets into the act. The very fact that Russia has not shared atomic information with the Chinese, or given them any weapons from its nuclear arsenal, now very substantial, gives strength to this hypothesis.

Now, this is the kind of plot-and-counterplot situation that may conceivably cause the State Department to make a switch in its policy. On the manipulative and reactive level where anyone short of your biggest enemy becomes your friend, it is possible that Dulles may find the reasons to seek immediate agreement with the Russians. This is something that could happen very soon. The one man

in the United States Senate who has been best informed and most effective on the entire question of nuclear arms control is Senator Hubert Humphrey. He is a veteran in the Senate but is fairly young (not quite fifty) and has widespread support throughout the Midwest. It is not beyond the realm of political possibility that he could become a candidate for the presidency. In any event, we have been working closely with him and the benefits have been substantial. Several weeks ago I drew up a list of questions concerned with the effects of radioactive fallout. These were questions the answers to which were vital before deciding to proceed with nuclear testing. They had to do with the effects of cumulative fallout, especially under conditions of testing by other nations, projected over the next fifteen years. Senator Humphrey, as chairman of an important Senate committee, put these questions to the A.E.C. The astonishing thing is that the A.E.C. did not have the answers and asked for considerable time in which to attempt to work them out. It seems outrageous to me that the A.E.C. would have sanctioned testing without specific knowledge as to even the probable long-term effects. But this is the kind of insanity that is now so common that we seem to live with it easily.

3. Next Step

Would it not be useful if an appeal were to be filed with the World Court, in Geneva? This appeal should be signed by no more than half a dozen of the world's moral leaders, including you and Pope Pius XII. The appeal would be concerned with the present acts now being committed against the human community—acts that have nothing to do with the legitimate requirements of national sovereignty or national security. As more and more evidence is developed on the long-term dangers to the genetic integrity of man, the moral issue grows in proportion. The fact that the nature of human life is being violated makes this an issue on which the world's spiritual leaders must come together.

What we need, first of all, is a letter from you to the Pope. This

letter would reflect your mutual concern, describe the danger in graphic terms, and suggest an appeal that should be made to the World Court.

4. *Miscellaneous*

[a] Discrepancies in the public statements of the United States Atomic Energy Commission continue to appear. For example, the U.S. Public Health Bureau made public three days ago some findings concerning radioactive fallout. These figures revealed that the fallout was twice as heavy as had been reported previously, as Erica has already informed you by way of a clipping, I understand.

[b] You are already familiar, I am sure, with the earlier claim by the A.E.C. that it would be unwise to have any agreements banning nuclear tests because of the ease with which secret violations could take place. As evidence, the A.E.C. declared that its own underground Nevada test was not detected more than 235 miles away. Then, by accident, it was learned that the underground test had been detected almost 2500 miles away and that this fact had been reported to the A.E.C. at the time.

[c] The A.E.C. has tried to minimize the significance of radioactive strontium in the bones of children by dealing in terms of the average. Now it comes out that some of these children have 50 times more strontium-90 than the average.

[d] It is too early to talk about this with any certainty, but some scientists are now doing research, the net effect of which may be to prove that both the United States and the Soviet Union have deliberately tested bombs into which high radioactive additives have been packed. In short, some of the high-megaton bombs have contained much more uranium than was required to trigger the explosion. I will write you about this in greater detail as more information develops. . . .

Meanwhile, my dear Docteur, I think you will be interested and perhaps amused to learn that the readers of *The Saturday Review* have selected you as the greatest living human being. Also, in the somewhat larger competition among the great of all time, you run second

only to Abraham Lincoln. This may give you some idea of the power of your voice in America—and, for that matter, all the rest of the world.

Incidentally, on the question of who among living world leaders is best qualified to deal with the human crisis today, again you come out No. 1. What you have been doing, therefore, in this appeal, is fulfilling the obligations of leadership in accordance with the expectations of your fellow human beings.

<div style="text-align: right">

Sincerely,
Norman Cousins

</div>

<div style="text-align: right">

Lambaréné, Gabon
May 17, 1958

</div>

Norman Cousins

Dear friend,

Finally I am writing to you. I am still very tired by the work on the three appeals for which I had to read many newspaper articles in small print and to make excerpts from them. My eyes have suffered from this. Sometimes now they refuse to work. Also my hand is exhausted and refuses sometimes to serve me. However, more important is that the appeals catch the attention of people and awake them. And how good it is that I was allowed to use Radio Oslo, and by it a hundred radio stations in the world, for the atomic issue. The whole enterprise did not cost a cent. It is incredible.

Now my opinion on your plans. I do not agree that we should appeal to the International Court in The Hague. First, it deals only with governments and not with private persons. Second, if ever it should make a sentence or an expert statement, it would be expressed in judicial language full of clauses, with the effect that nobody would know what to think of it. It would not be of any use in the struggle against atomic arms. The lawyers would have been the ones

to use and raise the argument that atomic weapons contradict the law of humanity; but they were silent and have failed. Therefore we will leave them out of the game. They would be but unreliable allies. Keep away from lawyers, keep away from courts. . . .

Also the Pope we will leave alone. He is a great sir, and he owes consideration to the Church. He may be a good man, but he is no fighter. Or did you ever read anywhere that he condemned the atomic and H bombs in the name of Christian religion? Protestantism does it, but there is no Catholic declaration so far. . . .

My opinion is to group the whole thing about the International Court in The Hague. If this court were efficient it would raise its voice by itself. But it is not allowed to do so. It is allowed only to judge complaints brought before it by governments. My hope is that among the lawyers in the world there will be some to open their mouths.

Our purpose in expressing the argument that atomic weapons contradict international law is to arm the hands of the opponents of atomic weapons, or their mouths, in order that they may shout it all over the world. It is evident that atomic weapons are contrary to international law. People will believe it because of its evidence and because it is based on human and moral reflections. We don't need the lawyers' blessings. History shows how it is their role to pour water into the neat wine of the law of humanity and to construct compromises.

Our task is to raise our voices permanently in order to awake those who are still asleep and to build up a public opinion which is capable of bearing pressure upon the governments, as is happening already in Germany.

And just because in my appeals this argument—that atomic weapons contradict international law—is mentioned over and over again, I want it to be published in a paperback booklet with the title *Peace or Atomic War?* in many countries. I ask you to find a good courageous publisher for it in the U.S.A. I had written previously to you about this in the beginning. It is difficult for me to do this from

Europe. You can believe me that the appeals will have their best effect only after being spread to the people, in an inexpensive edition. Magazines and groups must be allowed to reprint them at low costs. If you have a publisher tell him to send me at once a contract for me to sign. I want 8 percent of the price as royalties (of the price in shop sale). It has to be quite a simple, cheap edition. The sooner it is published the better. Don't lose much time. Another thing. You can tell your friends that I do not think much of an appeal to the International Court in The Hague, and that I will not join it; and also that I do not think it the right thing to contact the Pope; the Pope should speak in his own way against atomic weapons. So much you may tell your friends. But the reasons for this opinion of mine they need not know, and should not quote them in public. I am fighting against the atomic danger; but it is not up to me to judge the lawyers and the Pope.

With best thoughts
A.S.

P.S. Radio and the press are the small firewood to kindle a fire; booklets which are passed from one hand to the next are the big logs to keep the fire burning and to bring it to its full effect.

In reply, I was happy to inform Dr. Schweitzer that his appeals had been heard in America by millions of people over the radio and that his regular publisher, Henry Holt, would proceed with publication on his terms. Also, that the texts had been reprinted and distributed in great numbers, including insertion in the Congressional Record. *A few weeks earlier I had been in Washington to meet with people in the government with respect to Schweitzer's position on nuclear weapons, and I reported on the results of these meetings.*

Lambaréné, Gabon
June 15, 1958

Mr. Norman Cousins

Dear friend,

How pleased I am to learn that Henry Holt is publishing the bro-
chure: *Peace or Atomic War?* I will write to them directly. It is so
important that the brochure will receive the widest and most *constant*
distribution by a good publisher. I thank you for having handled the
matter well. After all, you know the conditions in the U.S.A. better
than I. The fact that Strauss and Teller[*] are no longer employed
by the government is a good sign for the assumption that Dulles now
expects to have to give in with regard to the questions of test explo-
sions. But, as far as the abolition of nuclear weapons is concerned,
he will try to remain unyielding. . . . The situation in Germany is
good. The campaign against the acceptance by NATO of nuclear
weapons is gaining popularity among large sections of the popula-
tion and there are good leaders in Germany. As far as de Gaulle is
concerned, it is feared that he will submit to the wishes of NATO
and that he will include in his program the plan that France should
have nuclear weapons of her own. But I believe that he has other
worries that are bigger than this. He must think about how to stay
in power. His position is not secure. Now to the question of *Harper's*
wanting to print several speeches under the title: "Albert Schweitz-
er's Speeches on Peace." I am quite for it. It does not matter if the
three last speeches are published twice . . . provided the publishers

[*]Admiral Lewis Strauss left his post as chairman of the Atomic Energy Commission
on June 30, 1958. Dr. Willard Libby, a member of the Commission, and Dr. Edward
Teller, who held an advisory position with the Commission, strongly supported Admiral
Strauss's opposition to any ban on nuclear testing and to any agreement on nuclear
arms control. The AEC had taken the position that such agreements would be unen-
forceable because of the difficulties they foresaw in detecting nuclear explosions. Later,
a congressional investigation showed that underground explosions were detectable at
great distances. Although the AEC was aware of this from its own Nevada under-
ground testing, it had continued to issue reports to the media to the contrary. Dr.
Libby and Dr. Teller resigned from the Commission early in 1959.

agree. And see to it that the motto, "nuclear weapons are against international law," he propagated well because it is the simplest and most effective motto.

Cordially yours,
Albert Schweitzer

Lambaréné, Gabon
August 15, 1958

Norman Cousins

Dear friend,

I take the opportunity while I am writing to Erica [Anderson], also to write a letter to you, especially about the nuclear situation, which quieted down because the newspapers are occupied with the adventures of Dulles and Macmillan in the Middle East.[*] But that does not mean that all is well. On the contrary. This unexpected and senseless sending of troops to the Middle East has shown the people in Europe that the danger of an atomic war, which can start at any time, really exists, and it has shaken the authority very considerably of the two statesmen, who count this danger as small, especially so in Germany. And the people have had to admit that Khrushchev kept calm and that he did not answer the unnecessary sending of troops with sending troops on his part. This led many people to think about the question, whether the free world is really so much endangered by the Soviets as it is being preached all over the West. And that neither the USA nor England thought it necessary to let the other countries belonging to NATO know about their decided adventure has harmed the reputation of NATO very much,

[*]Although significant progress toward Arab unity was made during 1958, pressure from Egyptian president Gamal Abdel Nasser on Middle Eastern countries to take a neutralist position in the cold war situation began to take effect, weakening the Baghdad Pact. In January 1958, U.S. Secretary of State John Foster Dulles attended the fourth session of the Baghdad Pact Council, assuring the members of U.S. support. Great Britain, one of five members of the Baghdad Pact Council, was represented by Prime Minister Harold Macmillan.

again especially in Germany. That the U.S.A. and England took such a long time to arrive at an agreement with Russia for the taking place of a conference about the Middle East situation has brought about an estrangement in Europe, and that it has given Red China an opportunity and time to force Russia also to talk in its name, is being judged as a very bad thing indeed, because the mixing Chinese politics into Middle East politics and also into European situatiore is a fact of which one cannot foresee the results. You do remember that I have written to you for quite a while that Khrushchev has a difficult time with China and that America and England should take this to heart and not make more difficulties. Now, what could have been avoided has happened, become fact. Through America's refusal to recognize the real government of China, the situation does not get easier. There is now an uneasiness in Europe that the policy of Dulles is not satisfactory. That American newspapers criticize him very much also makes an impression in Europe. All this brings with it that those who plead for the use of atomic weapons do not have the authority now as they used to. What is important is that the argument that atomic weapons are against the law of the people (Volkerrecht) finds more and more recognition, and that the meaning of this is being well understood. Recently I received from a lawyer of a German university an article, which he has published in an important newspaper. In this article he proves legally that all weapons which produce radioactivity, *even those which are being praised as clean*, have to be looked on as opposed to the "Volkerrecht" and must be abandoned. I will try to send you a copy of this article. Until now the lawyers have shied away from questions that were unsympathetic to the governments; they have just not lived up to occupying themselves with this. But now, when everywhere this question has been discussed, they cannot do otherwise but to occupy themselves with it. Whenever I could I have in letters talked about this argument that atomic weapons are against the laws of the people. The text of the pamphlet *Peace or Atomic War?* has come out also in Korea. I received a copy yesterday. So calmly and confidently carry

on with the battle. . . . Write much about it and open your mouth.
That is better than to hold many conferences . . . and cheaper. . . .

Your devoted,
A.S.

*In August 1958, I sent a cable to Dr. Schweitzer telling him that the
U.S. government had announced a temporary suspension of nuclear testing
for exploratory purposes.*

Albert Schweitzer
Lambaréné
Gabon
French Equatorial Africa

UNITED STATES JUST ANNOUNCED PROVISIONAL
SUSPENSION OF NUCLEAR TESTING.
CONGRATULATIONS. ALL GOOD WISHES TO YOU
FOR THE COMPLETION OF YOUR OBJECTIVE FOR
WORLD PEACE.

Cousins

*Erica Anderson had produced a film biography of Dr. Schweitzer and, in
collaboration with Eugene Exman, vice-president of Harper & Bros., a pic-
ture-and-text book about Dr. Schweitzer and the hospital. She later founded
the Albert Schweitzer Friendship House in Great Barrington, Massachu-
setts. Dr. Schweitzer was grateful for her support and loyalty, frequently
entrusting her with matters of importance, including his correspondence. The
letter of August 24 was sent to Erica for translation, with the following
message to her:*

Letter to Erica Anderson
From Dr. Albert Schweitzer

. . . . Norman was so dear to send me a telegram about the decision
to renounce the tests by America. I believed that it was something

which would be put into force at once and definitely. Now I learn from the clippings of the newspapers that it will be only for one year and will not start until the 31st of October. How poverty stricken and full of clauses is this thing! A thinking process in installments! But, quite rightly, a French newspaper writes, "The U.S.A. has seen itself forced to renounce the tests by public opinion. This public opinion will not allow it to go back on its decision." I believe that England was responsible for the way the renouncement was formulated and claused.

Now there is work for you again in this respect. In answer to Norman's telegram, I sat myself down to write him a letter of thanks, and quite by itself it turned into a short report about the battle in which we were standing together. I felt the need to write all this down in the moments of the first triumph, for both of us (and for you, too). Make him a translation of it. You have also worked much and hoped much in this. Make yourself a copy. In a few months, all the details of this battle may not be as clearly in my head as they are now. . . .

August 24, 1958

Mr. Norman Cousins

Dear friend,

How beautiful that I received the good news, especially through you! I was sitting just then at the table in my room when Mlle. Mathilde came and said: Just now a telegram arrived with a very wonderful message. Then she put it in front of me. I read it with deep emotion. And then I looked at the table next to me, at which you, at your first visit here, were sitting, when you tried to convince me that I should speak in regard to atomic weapons. Before, others had talked to me, asked me to do so, without my being able to make a decision. Then you came and asked me the same and it impressed me. So it was you who made me do it, to take up the word for the

cause. I remember well the letter in which I told you and also the letter I received from you, your kind answer. Our pact in Lambaréné has surely contributed to the fact that the powers possessing atomic weapons had to give in, at least as regards this question. And Radio Oslo has also a great merit. That the director of Radio Oslo, Mr. Fostervoll, and the president of the Parilamentary Commission of the Nobel Peace Committee mustered up enough courage (and courage it needed) to give me permission to speak, in complete freedom, through their radio station has given our opinion in the public eye a great esteem. And moreover, Radio Oslo had moved ninety other stations in the world, at the same time, to make my appeals known, which caused great notice everywhere.

And then, after the first success of our pact followed months in which we changed between fear and hope, because the American "calming" propaganda, with Teller and Strauss and the Atomic Energy Commission, had such a terrific success in America and in Europe, that public opinion was chloroformed and the press were apathetic. It meant a lot that Pauling was successful in getting a manifesto from 9,326 scientists, which, in a certain sense, instead of the U.N. Commission scientists (who until August 1958 were condemned to silence), put forth an opinion that was sent to the U.N.—all this, despite the president of the U.N. burying it in a drawer and letting it lie there. . . . Yet it made an impression. And then Strauss and Teller made such blunders that Dulles could not hold with them anymore. . . . And still the press remained apathetic and public opinion did not know how to decide, and did not want to make decisions. That the Soviets renounced the tests was put down as propaganda and made hardly any impression. It mattered greatly that your magazine again and again backed the truth.

On the boat which carried me back to Africa, in the middle of December 1957, I decided to take up the word again and this time to occupy myself also with the political aspects of the problem, as well as the political situation and how this situation had developed. To begin with, Radio Oslo did not want to cooperate in my expression of somewhat temperamental (temeramentvoller Wise) views. But

when the two gentlemen had read the three appeals, they changed their minds and gave permission so that the appeals would be sent over the stations unaltered. Again Radio Oslo was able to get ninety other stations to publicize these appeals simultaneously, all over the world.

This happened on the 28th, 29th, and 30th of April, a year after the first appeal (23rd of April 1957). Since it was quite clear to me that in the atomic nations as well as in the NATO countries everything to repress these appeals would be done, in radio as well as in the press, I undertook the big task of trying to place these appeals under the title *Peace or Atomic War?* in as many countries as possible in book form. In this respect my publishers in all countries helped me greatly. So, during the course of four months the appeals became known in America and in Europe, partly through the aid given by your magazine and also through the help of others which published parts of the appeals in short or long form. Much good work was done by the courageous and knowledgeable Pauling, who kept questioning Teller and did not rest until it was proved that, in regard to the underground explosion in Las Vegas on September 19, 1957, a seismograph as far as Alaska *had* registered the disturbance—contrary to what was said at the time. Teller was the bad spirit to which President Eisenhower and Dulles had bowed. He was the one who influenced them to shatter the London conference, which had been going along all right, under the direction of Stassen, during July 1957. He had made them think that by continuing the tests one would arrive at the production of a "clean" hydrogen bomb, which would have no radioactive fallout and which would not hurt civilians. That it was necessary for Dulles to separate himself from Teller refuted the "calming" propaganda, which had tried to create the idea of an idyllic atomic war as well as the fiction of "purity of air" with the new tests.

Later the slogan appeared in America and in Europe simultaneously that one *must* be able to live with the atomic bomb and that one *can* live with the atomic bomb.

Generals and philosophers let this message be spread in the world

and public opinion let itself be impressed with it. But the saner statesmen began to understand that they must follow their consciences and resist the movement to continue the tests.

That the conference called by scientists of both East and West agreed that test explosions, even small ones, could not happen without their being noticed opened the way for President Eisenhower to announce that the United States would discontinue these tests. England could not do differently.

How sad, though, that it took so long for these two states to come to this conclusion! To listen to the voice of reason and humanity! A real joy, to have been victorious, cannot rise within us, who have fought the battle of reason and humanity. . . . The disaster which has overcome the world because of the powerful explosions held up till now fills us with sadness, in which there is no room for contentment because of the success finally appearing on the horizon.

Again, we have to keep on fighting the battle for the abolition of the tests . . .

<div style="text-align: right">

With my best thoughts, your devoted
A.S.

</div>

P.S. When I received your telegram I thought of Einstein—what it would have meant to him if he could have lived to see the day which he longed for so much! As the best answer to your telegram it seemed to me I should give a short report on paper of the developments in the battle in which we are standing together. When will I do the same for the coming second part of the battle?

<div style="text-align: right">

September 4, 1958

</div>

My dear Dr. Schweitzer:

This morning Erica brought your letter. I was deeply moved by it. This is a historic account you have written; I shall treasure it.

The fact that there were conditions attached to the American decision to halt its nuclear tests was primarily to satisfy the objections of England and France. The President had intended some weeks

earlier to make an unequivocal declaration on this issue, but Prime Minister Macmillan made a hasty visit to the United States and prevailed on him at least to wait until after the British completed their tests on October 31. The President felt obliged to concur since his own military officials had prevailed on him to delay his proposed announcement until the end of the American series of nuclear tests. The British further suggested that the President delay his statement until October 31. The President felt, however, that the United States could defer its position no longer. Hence the announcement. The reason for putting a time limit on the suspension was a technical one and was designed to satisfy Congress. Under the circumstances, therefore, the particular announcement made by the President was perhaps the best that could be made.

As I say, you must not allow these conditions to detract from the great meaning of your contributions to civilization. True, the United States should have stopped its tests two years ago. True, its failure to do so resulted in a serious increase of radioactive poisons in the atmosphere. True, the U.S. gave the Soviet Union an enormous propaganda advantage by delaying as long as it did. Yet, incalculable harm would have resulted if the President had listened to those of his advisers who implored him to continue the tests. And the nature of your victory becomes all the more dramatic when we take into account the fact that the two chief figures of the United States Atomic Energy Commission were forced out of their offices. Admiral Strauss was not reappointed as chairman and Edward Teller, who is the real architect of the H-bomb policy, is no longer connected with the A.E.C. These things are significant.

In any event, the world's peoples can be grateful to you for the way you threw yourself into this fight, summoning all your moral imagination and energy in your appeal to the conscience of mankind. And I am prouder than I can say to have been permitted to stand at your side.

> With continuing good wishes, I am,
> Faithfully yours,
> Norman Cousins

September 24, 1958

Norman Cousins

Dear friend,

Your friendly writing in answer to my description of our fight against the test explosions has deeply moved me. But you must not regard my cooperation as something so extraordinary. Each of us has done what he could, be it in Europe or in the U.S.A. For this reason we were able at last to create a public opinion which forced the politicians to capitulate. The opinion of the scientists in Geneva allowed them to capitulate with dignity, but it is a sad thing that the scientists of the West did not have the courage to say that the tests must be stopped on account of the scientific reports. They were forced by their governments to take that attitude, to leave the decision to the politicians. It does not give honor to the West that its scientists were resigned to leaving the verdict to the politicians and not to expressing their views based on scientific findings.

A thousand thanks for the information about the President in these matters. It does hurt one that the U.S.A. will continue the tests until the 31st of October. The terrible storms in Mexico are a result of these tests, I assume. It is strange that all nations accept these storms, which are resulting from the atomic tests, without complaining. But the politicians have been able through the propaganda they started to stop any questions about these atmospheric disturbances of our time, as much as they have been able to silence the lawyers who would deal with the question of atomic weapons in regard to international law. The politicians have also succeeded in preventing people from knowing how great is the amount of damage that has already been done. . . . Everywhere a surface view and lies against which the public opinion does not dare to stand up. Public opinion cannot do anything because the press which should deal with these things does not dare to pick up the word. One cannot understand how humanity keeps on living under these circumstances. They know they are kept in ignorance in regard to the radioactive dangers but

they accept this because the press—which should discuss these questions—has failed to bring them up.

And it is our culture which tolerates these circumstances, and does not acquire any knowledge because those who reign feel uncomfortable about it—they don't like to be open about it, they don't allow the public to know the truth about the dangers of the atomic age. These are strange circumstances under which we live . . . and the people in general do not ask themselves to account for all this. I write as many letters as I possibly can to shake the public from their sleep and to clarify for them that the atomic danger concerns not only Europe but all nations. In South America I have had success with these letters and with the publication of *Peace or Atomic War?* The main thing now is to distribute as widely as possible the idea that the atomic weapons are against international law, because the cessation of atomic weapons can only be achieved with this argument.

> With loving thoughts your devoted
> Albert Schweitzer

Erica traveled with Dr. William Hitzig to Warsaw in connection with a project initiated by The Saturday Review *to provide assistance to Polish victims of Hitler's medical experimentation, continuing on from Poland to Lambaréné. Her letter describing her stay with Le Docteur provides a vivid picture of the physical and emotional demands on Dr. Schweitzer. In spite of the pressure of long hours and responsibility, he took the time to add a short handwritten note at the end of her letter to me.*

Sunday, October 12, 1958

Dear Norman:

I did not write to you from Warsaw because I knew you were well supplied with news from Bill, by letter and by phone. Now, having arrived in Lambaréné and enjoying the stillness (in spite of the noise) of this place I want to give you a report of my impressions. But

before I do this I hurry to tell you that I found the Doctor in good health again. . . . Sometimes one thinks that by sheer willpower alone he can stand the amount of work he is attending to. . . . Though his first reaction was a definite no to my suggestion to let Bill come, he modified it and sent a telegram of invitation to him (to come as a visitor only). Later he said, I don't want to hurt him by not letting him examine me. . . . So I think, I hope we will succeed. I had a long talk with Dr. Friedmann and he said that Bill's report would be invaluable, in case another emergency arises . . . apart from the avalanche of correspondence in connection with the atomic question as many other things occur which take up his time. The day before yesterday a truck turned over three times on the new road which lies behind the leper village, and ten people were gravely injured. A.S. standing for hours in the operating room holding each one's hand and talking to them while they screamed during the time the doctors were trying to stitch them together again. My cameras, which I sent by freight to save money, have not come yet and I was desperate that I was not able to record these scenes, except indelibly in my heart. . . . Since the patients were all in shock, no sedative could be given them, that's why they screamed so and there was A.S. talking to them telling them that the doctor was here to help, that it will be over soon and holding their hands, bending over their faces. One of them died that night, the others were saved. A.S. stayed with the dying one until the end . . . went to bed in the early hours of dawn. . . . It is then that one asks oneself how long can he stand this? And yet one knows: this is the only way he can and has lived. . . . I have touched only on the plan of the interview, so far, but, as usual, he was against it. He says he has said all he has to say publicly and that now he is carrying on in letters, privately, to practically everyone he can write to. . . . But I have had this first NO reaction from him so often that it does not make me feel the battle is lost . . . I have to keep explaining to him how many more people would have a chance to understand what he means could his words be heard and his face be seen on T.V. . . . He does not believe it yet . . . and I think it might be good if you in one of your

next letters might back me up on this. He is convinced that his appeals in book form are the backbone of information. They, as he terms it, are the continuous torch which will keep on burning . . . but he does not realize how comparatively few people reach for a book on a bookshelf, or even buy it. . . .

Well, I am working at it and will keep you informed. I do want also to wait for Bill's report before shooting all cannons, because if Bill says that A.S. looks better than he actually is, one must conserve his strength and not add any additional burden . . . however much it would mean. . . . As long as he lives, here in Lambaréné, there is one focal point of moral strength and goodness . . . one stronghold in a shaky world.

This is a very disorganized account of the Lambaréné news, but I trust your being so familiar with everything here will enable you to make head and tail out of my scrambled English. . . .

With all best intentions I did not yet get around to finishing the letter—but in the meantime it has been arranged that Bill is coming. . . . I consider it so vitally important . . . will write you soon . . .

Erica

Albert Schweitzer to NC
[note at end of letter by Erica Anderson]

Sunday, October 12, 1958

Norman Cousins

Dear friend,

This is just a brief hello. I hope to write to you at length in the future. As you must know, Pablo Casals will be giving a talk at the U.N. celebration. This is important because it will draw attention to our cause. I continue to write letters to make others aware of the argument that atomic weapons are against the international law with which most civilized countries have complied. It seems to me that this is very important. I am not certain yet if Mr. Dulles' military

adventure in the China Sea[*] is ending in a happy manner although I know Mao Tse-tung is trying to negotiate with Chiang Kai-shek and his terms are reasonable.

Your devoted Albert

Following his talk at the United Nations, Pablo Casals received this letter from Dr. Schweitzer.

November 22, 1958

To: Pablo Casals

Dearest friend,

Thank you for your moving letter. Your speech is notable. Never would I have imagined that you would become advocate and orator of this cause. They wanted to keep a barrier up by which you would not talk, only about peace in general—as if there did not exist the problem of atomic peace! It is a miracle that they let you pronounce the word "atomic" at all. And the good people don't even know what it is about! There exists the great danger that the pro-atomic governments may give the impression that they search for the same thing as we do, when fundamentally they pursue nothing but to sabotage all that precisely can be done for peace in our day. But, after all, the miracle has been produced, and they let you talk with clarity. And they allowed you to pronounce my name.

It has touched me deeply that you have quoted me. But you ran the risk of not being authorized to declare the argument that atomic weapons are against international law. It is this very argument which has been suppressed so far.

The jurists, in common secret accord, have not occupied them-

[*]Quemoy and Matsu, small islands in the Formosa Strait off mainland China, were heavily bombarded from the mainland in 1958, which caused the redeployment of the U.S. 7th Fleet and provoked an international diplomatic crisis. The islands had been occupied by the Nationalist Chinese when they were driven from the mainland to Taiwan by Chinese government forces in 1949.

selves with this question in order not to be obliged to give evidence as to the illegality regarding the international law, which they say is the duty of governments, according to the constitutions of their countries. I, on my part, have been able to raise the coward's mask, because I had the privilege, as winner of the Nobel Peace Prize, to speak with absolute liberty about all questions pertaining to world peace, via Radio Oslo (because the Nobel Prize is given in Oslo), particularly about the fact that, because atomic weapons are a violation of international law, this means a threat to the continuation of such armament. Therefore the irrefutable legal adherence starts to become recognizable and will become a matter of serious discussion. Never, in our earlier meetings in Europe, would we have imagined that one day we would together descend in the world arena to fight against those who constitute the greatest danger for mankind of the whole world. Thank you, dearest friend!

With my most loving thoughts for your wife and for you, your devoted

(A.S.)

P.S. Isn't it curious that Switzerland, well-known soil of hospitality to liberties and generosities, should play such a perplexing role in the great discussion!

In connection with arms negotiations being held in Geneva, Switzerland, The Saturday Review of November 22, 1958, published the following open letter on its editorial page:

To the Men at Geneva

What we offer you is the most precious thing human beings have to give. We offer you our hopes.

We want you to feel you are representing not just a nation, powerful though it may be, but two billion human beings who represent the ultimate authority on earth.

No group of men in history have had a bigger or nobler chance to serve their own age and all other ages to come.

We know there may be many times during your meetings when further discussions will seem fruitless.

We know there will be in the background many voices actually pushing you in the direction of failure—for it is hard for some men to comprehend the needs and dangers of our times.

But this is not the source of your mandate. Your mandate comes from one and only one source—the sovereign will of the human community. It is to this community that you are primarily responsible.

Naturally, the peace of the world depends on many things besides control of nuclear weapons. It depends on the control of the basic causes of war—injustice, hunger, oppression, aggression, ambition. To meet these dangers, we must look to the cause of a stronger United Nations into which has been built the required powers of world law.

But, meanwhile, an important beginning has to be made on one vital part of the problem of world peace—the permanent internationally inspected ending of nuclear weapons tests.

This vital beginning is now your responsibility. To that beginning we now invest our hopes, make known our mandate, and wish you well.

(signed)

Albert Schweitzer (Lambaréné)	*Max Born (Germany)*
Martin Niemoeller (Germany)	*Clarence Pickett (U.S.A.)*
C. Rajagopalachari (India)	*Lord Boyd-Orr (Great Britain)*
Toyohiko Kagawa (Japan)	*Bertrand Russell (Great Britain)*
François Mauriac (France)	*Mrs. Franklin D. Roosevelt (U.S.A.)*
Trygve Lie (Norway)	*Gunnar Myrdal (Sweden)*
Carlos P. Romulo (Philippines)	*L. John Collins (Great Britain)*
Herman J. Muller (U.S.A.)	*Tadao Watanabe (Japan)*

November 24, 1958

Norman Cousins

Dear friend:

I must tell you how right you were to send an open letter to Geneva. It was necessary that the world hear that a cessation of test explosions was still discussed, that a discussion about the cessation of

nuclear weapons production was still going on. The political happenings of recent times have pushed the atomic question completely into the background, which is a fact of great value to those who are pro-atom. It is indeed very sad, as I have written to you already, that the atomic question steps back behind political questions; contributing to this surely has been the political adventure of Dulles in the Middle East and also that in the China Sea. The atom question became a dish of soup which one removes from the table to warm up in the kitchen. And again propaganda dared to advocate holding on to atomic weapons, trying to calm public opinion.

Typical of this is the talk of air protection in the case of an atomic attack. In England, such a paper was published (from the government) which, with photographs, tries to show that there could be *millions of survivors!* Also in Germany the same melody is being heard. It is incredible. . . .

A new political happening has to be cited: Macmillan, Adenauer, and de Gaulle want, together, to put up a war-ready Europe, and encircle the Soviets in this manner. At the moment they do this by making propaganda for a better organized NATO and by suggesting that NATO prepare itself for an atomic war. The original aim of NATO in Europe was to form a force with *ordinary weapons* which could confront the force of the Soviets. But this plan was abandoned because England needed to minimize its army on account of the cost, aiming towards having a professional army rather than a people's army. This the government declares quite openly, however incredible this is. It promises an early halt to compulsory military service, which is only possible if the arming is entirely reduced to atomic weapons. The army of France does not count, because it is, to such an extent, needed in Algeria. The German army, because still small, is also supposed to be modernized with atomic weapons, as far as possible. Belgium reduces military service to one year. So NATO has arrived at a point where only an atomic war is being considered. But atomic weapons are not defenses . . . they are aggressive. Russia's situation is that it has given up its tests in March, probably because of a great accident which has happened during its last tests.

During the fall it had to realize that the U.S.A., in the production of tactical small atomic weapons in its tests, has made great progress. Therefore Russia made up its mind to go as far, also to make tests again. Through this, it has now lost the prestige it had gained through its cessation of tests. On the other hand, Dulles, because of his two military adventures (of which the second is in no way finished), has also lost influence in the world. The one thing balances the other a little. A good factor is that the scientists in Geneva, those from the U.S.A. as well as those from Russia, agree as far as the danger is concerned—that is, a mounting radioactivity in the atmosphere. This is the basis for public opinion in the world. This opinion we have to create, everywhere, and we have to back it with the argument that atomic weapons are against international law. This is the road on which we may succeed. [He possibly means "we will succeed"— Erica's note.]

Now the new happenings in Europe. The Soviets continue to follow their policy to avoid being encircled. This has to be taken very seriously now. A great rocket base exists in Italy; very important bases also in Germany. Now Khrushchev intends to retaliate by needling the European powers in every way possible. A genial shi-kan *[I don't know whether this word exists in English . . . it means to make angry, to bother, to needle—Erica's note]*, he withdraws the Soviet troops from Germany and then he leaves the supervision of all the powers which have their troops in Germany to East Germany. Now the U.S.A. and England are forced to discuss everything which concerns Berlin, and the territories which have so far been supervised by the Russians, with the East Germans, which until now have not been recognized. This is a great humiliation for them, especially for Adenauer. I believe that the silly word by Dulles, that Berlin is the Quemoy of Europe, is responsible for Khrushchev's action. He wants to show that Berlin is something quite different than Quemoy. How this whole situation will clarify itself cannot be predicted now. Naturally this is a very unfriendly action on the part of Khrushchev, not a bit suited to helping the situation in which we live. The pact which Adenauer and de Gaulle are making is not helping either. De

Gaulle's plan to give France atomic weapons and the fact that Adenauer wishes atomic weapons from NATO for his army cause Khrushchev to show Europe that this opposition to the Russians could have grave disadvantages.

In Germany in recent years opinion has spread that one has to tie in with East Germany. This opinion will now become stronger. The public opinion for Adenauer is not quite as strong as two years ago. This is the situation today. The main thing is that the Geneva conference express their opinion clearly. Then one will see further and act specially and fight. It is interesting that Adenauer during the last few days, in a speech, uttered, as an accusation towards Khrushchev, that what he now does in regard to Berlin is *against international law*. This was not very wise. Because with much more reason one can declare that the arming of the German troops is against international law. But it is good that Adenauer commits himself, publicly, to international law.

All this I write to you completely confidentially. But I thought that it would be interesting for you to look at the situation as it appears from the European viewpoint. And again: The address you sent to the conference in Geneva was a very valuable undertaking. It was a declaration which made the world conscious of the fact that the atomic question exists, a question with which public opinion has to occupy itself. Despite all the political happenings which have pressed themselves into the foreground, the nuclear question demands prior attention.

From my heart
A. S.

In connection with The Saturday Review *project in Poland, I planned to visit Warsaw and Berlin to make arrangements for medical care and rehabilitation for the women, and to seek reparations and compensation from the German government. I asked Dr. Schweitzer's help in making it possible for me to achieve this latter purpose.*

Lambaréné .
December 4, 1958

Norman Cousins

Dear friend,

I am glad that you go to Europe. But I don't believe that it will help to see the heads of governments. The president of Germany is in the same position as the Queen of England: he does not control politics. The politics are being handled entirely by Chancellor Adenauer. For this reason the president avoids talking to anyone, except his intimates, about politics. He would resent it if I asked him to receive you. With Adenauer it is like this: He does not want to talk to anyone. He can bear only people who speak according to his opinion. He feels that many in Germany, concerning the two great problems which are being discussed, do not agree with him and demand that he does not accept atomic weapons from NATO. This worsens the relationship with Russia. They also want him to take up the existing Berlin problems. This public opinion creates great worries in him, more than he is willing to admit. And in me he sees the big enemy, who, because I enjoy great respect in Germany, contributes to this public opinion. Before that, we had a very good relationship with each other. But now I would not dare to visit him because it would cause him pain, and I dare even less to ask him that he see someone whom I recommend.

Altogether I would try, in your place, to contact other persons in Germany. From the outside, one cannot too well influence things in Germany. The Germans want to solve these things by themselves. I am looked upon as a German, in spite of my being a French citizen, on the basis of the Versailles Treaty. But a foreigner can do nothing in Germany. He could only make people who are against Adenauer's nuclear policies and against his East-West policies more antagonistic and in this way give the impression that he is being influenced from the outside. Because the Germans were under foreign sovereignty they are resentful of everything foreign.

You will remember how I refused to step into the anti-atom move-
ment with my name, in the U.S.A. The same principle holds every-
where. In England, they became very resentful for this reason. The
Rev. Niemoller has participated in anti-nuclear demonstrations. We
who fight against nuclear weapons must remain in contact all over
the world. But the fight in one's own country has to be fought by
each one in its own country.

Don't forget that you are always welcome in Lambaréné!!! Here
we can talk with each other. Here you can rest.

From my heart
your devoted
Albert Schweitzer

December 29, 1958

My dear Dr. Schweitzer:

Clara and I recently visited Berlin and Warsaw. While in Berlin,
we had a brief opportunity to sense some of the cross-currents of the
city. As you once said so vividly: Khrushchev has all the cards. He
can play upon the deep-seated desire of the German people, both
East and West, to reunite their country and to get rid of all foreign
troops. If the West withdraws, Berlin goes to East Germany sooner
or later. If it doesn't withdraw, Khrushchev at least has made the
gesture and can use the presence of armed foreigners in Germany as
a powerful argument against the West. Either way, he holds the
initiative and the advantage.

In Warsaw, we attended strictly to our principal business, which
was to bring out of Poland some three dozen women in need of
medical, surgical, and psychological help. We were grateful that the
purpose was accomplished without undue complications. The women
are now in this country; they are in good homes and should have a

wholesome experience. At least, every effort is being expended in that direction.[*]

It is not easy to assess the political situation in Poland today. Conditions are considerably better than they were before the October 1956 uprisings, so far as freedom of action and conscience are concerned. Economically, the country has had at least a slight improvement. Food is more plentiful, though still fairly expensive. But everyone seems fully aware of the fact that such freedoms as now exist must be kept within carefully circumscribed bounds. Moreover, the tensions seem to be increasing again. So far as the relations between Poland and Russia are concerned, the present policy of the Polish government is to do everything possible to convince Moscow that it is not necessary to send in Russians to operate the government and the country. The Poles are nationalists first, last, and always.

Back here in the United States, the political currents are mixed. There is no unified government policy. The White House continues to be more idealistic and far-seeing than the State Department; but even within the State Department there are significant differences. Our job—the job of private citizens—it seems to me, is to work unceasingly to strengthen those elements of the government that are struggling in behalf of world law and the other ideas that you have expressed with such insight and inspiration.

With this letter go my heartfelt good wishes for your birthday and for the New Year. The human situation has never been more precarious, but I am profoundly grateful that there is at least one moral leader in the world today—Albert Schweitzer—who can speak for man.

Sincerely,
Norman Cousins

[*]The negotiations in West Germany for providing war-damage compensation to the victims of Nazi medical experimentation were successful—thanks in large part to the support we received in the Congress and the U.S. State Department, with Senator Edmund Muskie playing a leading role.

1959

Dear friend:

Something important and interesting has happened in the nuclear question: A German law professor from the University of Munster in Westfalen has published, in the October 1958 edition of the famous Munich illustrated "Hochland," a thesis about the question of nuclear weapons, in which he comes to the conclusion that nuclear weapons are against international law. This does not only apply for the big but also for the small and for the so-called clean weapons of this kind. This is the first time that a European lawyer has expressed his opinion officially. I will let you have a pamphlet of this study through Erica by ordinary mail and I believe that it is extremely important that this becomes known in the U.S.A. *Public opinion in the U.S.A. must realize that judicial objective is condemning nuclear weapons according to international law.* This verdict cannot be contradicted. All cultural states (even the half cultural states) have committed themselves to accepting international law as the highest law and to *act accordingly.* No state can ignore it. It is good if public opinion becomes familiar with this idea. Therefore please help. I am so overburdened and tired therefore I cannot write to you as I wish. All good wishes for 1959.

Your devoted
Albert Schweitzer

Despite the distractions of his hospital, Dr. Schweitzer kept himself informed on world affairs; in particular, European matters. He became increasingly concerned about the mounting tension in Berlin, and the tendency of politicians to use this issue to side-step the more ominous and pressing nuclear issue. The problem of a mutually acceptable German peace settlement was the chief issue of contention between East-West powers in the mid-1950s. Repeated attempts to resolve the problem through high-level conferences failed. Western leaders wanted a unified, sovereign German state, but Soviet authorities were reluctant to subject East Germany to the test of free elections and were concerned about renewed German militarism.

Lambaréné
March 3, 1959

Dear friend:

Forgive me for not writing sooner. Not only do I have much work to do but I suffer deeply from exhaustion. Also, I must once again take care of my hand that suffers from writer's cramp. Otherwise it might become quite unusable.

That which we are experiencing in the world is sad. How much harm the military undertakings in the Middle East and in Quemoy have done to the cause of stopping nuclear testing. And how much harm they have done to the work in relation to the whole nuclear issue, because they have forced it into the background and have created an atmosphere unsuitable for negotiations. And now we have the question of Berlin added to it all. And that has ruined the atmosphere. The Berlin question gives the politicians who are the virtuosi of madness an opportunity to withdraw from the nuclear issue. They also never stop to ask themselves whether it is morally right to risk an atomic war over the Berlin question. I wonder how many people are really prepared to die because of Berlin. But I still believe that the negotiations to end atomic tests will end well. Most of the difficulties were overcome before the talks were broken off. I

believe that no atomic power would now dare to start testing again. Of course that would mean that the peoples of the earth would be aroused and would no longer be prepared to subject themselves to such danger. And we have no reason not to continue our fight against atomic weapons, even under present unfavorable conditions. *We must carry on with our new argument that they are against human rights.* I believe that in this regard much too little has been undertaken. I have been following the various congresses. None of them have taken the position that these arms are against human rights. That the press remains indifferent also in this issue is quite natural, but we, the fighters, must keep shouting about it. The professor of the University of Münster also made the point that such arms violate natural law. Because the press is silent, it is we who must bring this point to bear at the meetings and congresses and *we must stress the legal moral argument.* The human rights declaration was based not only on legal but also on moral grounds, and it is for moral reasons that we must make our stand against extinction. *The fact that law is based on morality is the decisive thing in this case and must be brought to the fore.* Only if we keep stressing these facts can we fight the good fight, can we arouse public opinion—a public opinion that is common to all peoples. That must now be our only goal—to create this enlightened and cohesive public opinion. It is in this arena that the battle must be joined. Otherwise, our cause will not be successful. Could you not publish the Münster professor's talk in your journal? It would be good if such a sensible jurist could be the means of an open debate such as took place as a result of his talk in the German press.

The great anxiety I feel about the issue which we are fighting together causes me to write you in this way. I had hoped to see you in Lambaréné and I go on hoping.

Heartily,
Albert Schweitzer

My response to the March 3 letter referred to the nuclear situation in the United States, and included a copy of The Saturday Review *editorial for*

April 4, 1959, entitled "The Debate Is Over." The editorial reported that Dr. Willard F. Libby, who had just resigned as Atomic Energy Commissioner, had acknowledged "real concern" over contamination resulting from the testing of nuclear explosives. Dr. Libby had been one of the most influential spokesmen in blocking any serious effort to arrive at a worldwide ban on nuclear testing.

In the weeks that followed my letter to Dr. Schweitzer, I went to the Soviet Union at the suggestion of President Eisenhower. I arrived in Moscow on June 16, 1959. The first talk took place on June 25 before the Presidium of the Soviet Peace Committee. The text of that address, along with a report on the response to it, was printed in The Saturday Review *of July 25, 1959. On August 6, 1959, I reported to President Eisenhower, and left with him a memorandum detailing what I felt to be the most important information resulting from the visit. Thinking that my observations on the trip might be of some interest, I sent Dr. Schweitzer a copy of my memorandum to the President. The substance of the memorandum reviewed the principal factors affecting U.S.-U.S.S.R. relationships.*

1. Q. Given Marxist belief that war is inherent in the nature of capitalism, does Soviet leadership believe peace to be possible?

 A. Due to changes in fundamental Marxist doctrine, made largely under Premier Khrushchev, Soviet leaders see no doctrinal obstacles in the way of a workable peace.

2. Q. How far can the Iron Curtain be raised?

 A. The Iron Curtain has been replaced by a Red Magnet, which has more significant and challenging implications for the U.S. than the Iron Curtain.

3. Q. How do historical and economic changes within the Soviet Union affect the United States?

 A. With the upgrading of the standard of living of the Soviet Union, it gains in strength as a nation. This strengthening could produce an increased challenge to the U.S. in the struggle for world balance of power. Or, if the security of

both the U.S. and the U.S.S.R. were to be guaranteed by mutually acceptable commitments, the increasing prosperity of the Soviet Union could become an important factor for world peace and stability. Without such agreements, it is likely that there will be a continuing polarization of force.

4. Q. Are there any present trends and factors in the Soviet Union that might have a long-term effect on Soviet policy?

A. The primary domestic trend is economic. The Soviet Union seeks strength through increased productivity, which has resulted in the adoption of some capitalist techniques, especially incentives, albeit under state auspices. More important, perhaps, are the sub-surface geo-political factors affecting the long-term relationship of the Soviet Union and the PRC. The views of Mao Tse-tung are not necessarily shared by the present Kremlin leadership, and growing membership in the Chinese Communist Party along with the growing general Chinese population represent major historical factors that weigh importantly in the thinking of the present Soviet leadership. Just as the contest with the United States is now seen on a national rather than an ideological level, so the relationship with the People's Republic is being inevitably viewed on the same plane.

5. Q. What specific agreements in the American interest and the world interest are now within negotiable reach?

A. The Soviet Union may be ready to agree to basic enforceable measures of mutual security, assuming it is possible to arrive at reasonable guarantees concerning the long-range pacification of Germany. In addition, it would be essential for both the U.S. and U.S.S.R. to reexamine the structure and functions of the United Nations, in order to deal with its demonstrated weaknesses in peace-making and peace-keeping. It is difficult to see how genuine peace can be created and maintained without adequate world organization.

1960

The following spring, I cabled Dr. Schweitzer to ask his permission to proceed with the publication of a book I had written about my first visit to him at Lambaréné.

April 25, 1960

Dear friend:

How could you ask me by telegram whether I am willing that you publish a book you have written about me? This is so nice of you that you did it! And Clara and Erica had written me that you did it so solidly and that you write so vividly about me.

I did not realize that you were waiting for an expression from me about publication. But my correspondence has become chaotic because I have to attend to so many varied tasks. I get to my letters only at night. Last evening I wrote until one thirty in the morning. I also spend a lot of time with newspaper clippings to make notes of them, to stay informed scientifically and politically on nuclear matters. I consider this *important even if letters have to remain* unanswered because of it.

Now I have to scold you. It was agreed between us that you would come to see me soon. And I was awaiting you, but you *did not come!* And why didn't you come? Because people told you it would be a

bad time during the weeks around my birthday. And I had at that time almost no visitors and would have so much liked to see you. What a shame! Remember: you are always welcome! And if you want to ask someone whether it is a good or a bad time for your arrival—don't ask anyone but me! I still think so much of the days when you were here. So, come when you can free yourself. And don't postpone your trip without asking me.

I have just read that Stevenson begins to involve himself politically again and that he believes the U.S. has to start serious discussions with the Soviet leaders. It really is necessary that the U.S.A. give up the policy which Dulles started. It cannot keep up the great military expenditures year after year without ruining itself financially. President Eisenhower understands this but, since his office is not going to be held by him for a long time, he does not feel himself concerned to arrange for different approaches. England also cannot keep up with its armament arrangements! The problem of defending against attacks by remote-controlled fast atomic weapons is strategically unresolvable. . . .

And all nations need and want peace.

So, do something to arrive soon in Lambaréné!

<div style="text-align: right">

From the heart
Albert Schweitzer

</div>

<div style="text-align: right">

October 4, 1960

</div>

Dear Dr. Schweitzer,

My purpose now is to inform you about a conversation I had last week with President Eisenhower. He had come to New York in connection with the special session of the U.N. General Assembly and was staying at the Waldorf Astoria apartment of the American ambassador. I received a message at my office inviting me to meet with the President at the apartment for an afternoon snack.

Let me say right away that I had never seen him in such high

spirits, at least not since he became president. As you know, he is not running for re-election and, in less than three months, will return to private life. Whether his buoyant mood was the result of anticipatory relief in relinquishing the burdens of the presidency I cannot say. When I commented on the fact that he seemed to be in fine shape, he gave me his characteristic grin and said he had no complaints. He had improved steadily since his serious illness more than a year ago.

In your role as physician, you will be interested in the account he gave me of the onset of that illness. He said he had been desk-bound in Washington for a number of weeks and pined to stretch his legs and fill his lungs with good air. Finally, his workload lightened somewhat and the White House physician suggested he go to Denver, Colorado, for a golfing weekend.

Again, President Eisenhower grinned and said this was precisely the kind of medical advice he had hoped his doctor would give.

Denver, Colorado, as many golfers know, has some of the most beautiful golf courses in the country. The countryside is spectacularly beautiful. The President started to play in a general mood of release, but it took him four holes to get loose. At this point I'll let DDE tell the rest of the story in his own words:

"On the fifth tee, I took a few practice swings and was beginning to get back in the groove. Just as I was about to address the ball, someone drove up in an electric cart and said an emergency telephone call from the White House was waiting. I rushed back to the clubhouse, wondering what in blazes the emergency was all about. But when I picked up the phone, no one answered. I called the White House. No one at the switchboard knew anything about the earlier call. Nor did any members of my staff. I waited perhaps 15 minutes while they tried to run the call down. Finally, I hung up and went back to the fifth tee, where the rest of my foursome was waiting.

"I kept wondering about the phone call, trying to figure out what it was all about. I proceeded to scatter my shots all over the landscape. It was two holes before I felt relaxed again and able to enjoy

my freedom. While we were on the eighth fairway, the courier in the cart sped up to us again and said that the call had come through and the party in Washington was waiting to speak.

"By this time, I was mumbling to myself. When I picked up the phone, it was an assistant secretary of state saying the Pakistani ambassador had an urgent message to deliver personally.

"I asked whether Pakistan had gone to war against India or anything of that import. The fellow on the phone said, 'Oh no, nothing that crucial!'

" 'Well, then,' I said, 'I'm sure Foster [John Foster Dulles] can handle it.'

"I was then told that the Secretary had left his office early and had stopped off somewhere on the way home and they didn't know exactly where to reach him.

"I exploded. My old army training really erupted at this point and I barked at the assistant secretary and told him he had better brief himself on what an emergency is. By the time I caught up with my foursome I was angry at myself for having chewed out the young man who was only trying to do his duty. My playing was half-hearted. In fact, I never played worse. After about 15 minutes of hacking at the ball, I broke off and went home—still angry. Angry at the bumblehead, angry at Foster, but mostly angry at myself for having lost my temper. I tried to call the young man to apologize but they couldn't reach him.

"I didn't sleep well that night. The next day I felt those terrible pains in my chest and stomach. That was when they took me to the hospital. Anyway, I feel fine now. And I'm looking forward to leaving the White House so that I can devote myself full time to the cause of world peace."

He waited for this anomalous remark to sink in, then said that the multiple pressures on the presidency made it difficult for any man in that office to move forward in a straight line towards his goals. As he spoke, I had a picture of the presidency as a complicated balancing act. On all sides are the pressures, many of them competing. The public has a rather simplified impression of the president con-

sulting with the secretary of state in deciding upon foreign policy matters. What most people don't understand is that there are a half-dozen foreign policy centers inside the government. First of all, of course, is the State Department with its thousands of employees all over the world. But inside the White House is a smaller-scale built-in State Department with desks for different areas of the world. Then there is the C.I.A., which is not just a vast intelligence bureau but an operating agency as well. These C.I.A. operations have foreign policy significance. Now comes the military, which has its own assessment officers in different parts of the world. The pressure from the military is carried out in the name of national security. Then, of course, we have the National Security Council, to say nothing of the National Security Agency.

But this is not all. The Congress of the United States has its committees, one of the most formidable of which deals with foreign policy. The hearings and findings of the congressional committees can be a potent factor in the President's own approaches. I haven't even mentioned the press or public opinion, which at times can outweigh everything else.

The surprise to me is not that the making of foreign policy in the United States often seems inconsistent and convoluted but that it makes any sense at all.

I found it both interesting and significant that the President's comments about the proliferation of foreign policy agencies seemed to place special emphasis on the pressure from the military, by which he also included the sector of the economy involved in weapons manufacture. He said he had no illusions about the threat from the Soviet Union, and he believed that the United States should not allow itself to weaken its defenses through unilateral actions. At the same time, he recognized the dangers inherent in the arms race—dangers that pertained not just to risk of war but to our economy and way of life. He could also recognize that it was not in the interest of the Soviet Union to be caught up in a nuclear war. Both sides had no choice except to work as hard as they could to reduce the very real dangers inherent in the nuclear arms race. Beyond that, he

said, both sides had to be concerned about the need to create a workable relationship.

Basically, therefore, the President sees a phased and orderly program in the direction of a structured peace accompanied by corresponding reductions in weaponry.

It was very difficult, the President said, for some military leaders to accept any limitation on their authority to make and accumulate whatever weapons they thought necessary. There was also a tendency by the military to involve themselves unduly in policy matters.

He said he was urged only recently by some military advisers to pursue an arms race with the Soviet Union as an end in itself. They supported the arms race as a means of bringing heavy pressure on the Soviet Union economically, thus contributing to its political downfall. He was appalled at this simplistic, incompetent, and dangerous reasoning and said he did what he could to block it. Even as an economic strategy against communism, he said, the policy is bound to backfire because of the devastating effects of an unlimited arms race on the American economy itself. When heavy industry and the American military combine their influence, he said, the result is not very pretty.

The President agreed on the need to make the pursuit of world law the underlying aim of American foreign policy. He believed that our willingness to negotiate seriously for arms reduction and control can help create a stage for a genuine program of world security under world law. I discussed with him the work of Grenville Clark and Louis Sohn[*] in this direction. He reminded me that he had made a speech before the American Society of Newspaper Editors in which he stressed his belief that military force was not enough to create security and that it was essential to start thinking in terms of effective world organization. You would have been pleased, in view of your own emphasis on world law, to have heard him reiterate his

[*]Grenville Clark and Louis B. Sohn were co-authors of the book *World Peace through World Law*, published in 1958 by Harvard University Press, Cambridge, Massachusetts.

contention that nations have to find their way out of the jungle of anarchy to a workable framework for their relations with one another.

The President was in a reflective mood and said that only in the past year did he feel he was serving as a president in his own right. He had resisted the initial pressures to accept the nomination for the presidency because of his strong feelings against having military men in high political office. He didn't think that military training was the best preparation for dealing with the pluralistic problems of a free society. When he yielded to the efforts to get him to run for office, he made up his mind that he would bring in strong persons from outside the military to run the government. His job would be to maintain an even course.

I believe he came to realize he had gone too far in this direction for he found himself more in the position of a regent than a president. It seems clear he also found himself in disagreement at times with his secretary of state, who made the most of the authority given to him.

The result, I believe, is that Dwight Eisenhower was not exactly happy in the role he cast for himself in the presidency during his first term. However, after the departure of Sherman Adams, as chief domestic officer, and the death of John Foster Dulles as chief architect of foreign policy, Eisenhower came into his own. I think he surprised himself by his ability to do a good job as active president. It is too bad that he has to leave just as he begins to feel comfortable in the office and has the means to do what means more than anything else in the world—carrying out the steps that might lead to genuine peace.[*]

[*]Following the election of John F. Kennedy in 1960 to the presidency, the world alternated between crisis and opportunity. In October 1962, the United States and the Soviet Union came perilously close to war over Soviet missile sites in Cuba. The crisis was broken when Khrushchev dismantled the missiles. President Kennedy followed with a series of measures designed to ease the tensions between the two countries. The most far-reaching and effective of such measures was the Limited Nuclear Test-Ban Treaty, ratified by the Senate on September 23, 1963. The period of better relations probably dates from June 10, 1963, when the president, speaking at American University, extended an outreached hand to the Soviet people. Premier Khrush-

Eisenhower's main flaw, if it is a flaw, is that he was so eager to avoid being a man on a white horse that he held back unduly from doing the big and imaginative things that had to be done and that he, because of his great popularity, would have been able to do perhaps better than anyone else. I like the man. I like him very much. And I think you would, too.

Devotedly,
Norman

In 1959, at the request of President Eisenhower, I began making arrangements for a meeting between prominent and knowledgeable citizens of the U.S. and U.S.S.R. The first meeting was held at Dartmouth College in early November 1960, just prior to the election of John F. Kennedy to the presidency. The "Dartmouth Conferences" have been held thirteen times in subsequent years, with meetings held alternately in the United States and the Soviet Union. I was certain that a report of this meeting would be encouraging news for Dr. Schweitzer.

November 28, 1960

Dear Doctor:

Warmest greetings! I hope all is well with you. Reports reaching me indicate that your spirits and general health are excellent.

Now for some news. Recently I was involved in a conference at Dartmouth College which brought together, under informal circumstances, a number of Soviet and American leaders in the arts, sciences, economics, politics, and religion. A warm and friendly atmosphere characterized the frank discussions of complex issues. The meeting did not seek to represent the official policies of either sides; nor did it represent a group attitude taken by either delega-

chev's response was positive and it appeared, at long last, that both countries were embarked on a course that might lead to the making of a durable peace. These prospects were retarded, if not impaired, by the assassination of President Kennedy on November 22, 1963.

tion. It represented the thinking of twenty-seven individuals deeply concerned with the future of the planet.

We tried to hold a planetary frame of reference as we discussed an agenda covering: (1) disarmament; (2) structured peace; (3) the psychological gap in understanding; (4) economic aid to developing nations; (5) the role of the citizens in foreign policy.

Many areas of agreement were found, and some of disagreement. In general, we agreed that nuclear war must be prevented no matter how difficult the task; we differed sharply about ideological theory but agreed that this should not prevent accord in other matters, such as steps toward disarmament and aid to emerging nations.

We agreed that a non-violent relationship between the two countries was mandatory; that there is no serious conflict between the two nations concerning raw materials, boundaries, or land area; and that a realistic program for peace must allow for the emergence into freedom of the once-dependent nations. We further agreed that, along with controlled disarmament, steps must be taken to set up structures for world law, world courts, and a world security force to carry out the mandates of the courts and to halt incipient armed conflicts between nations. We agreed that even with complete disarmament, disputes would continue, and that there must be world machinery to deal with them by orderly and legal methods. This machinery would operate not so much to bring nations together as to keep them apart—apart from clashing in armed combat.

The banning of nuclear tests, with adequate inspection, was regarded as a step toward disarmament. We approved the present informal ban and urged that it be made permanent. We agreed, too, that inspection of delivery systems for nuclear-tipped weapons is simpler and as effective as inspection of stockpiles. We were also of the belief that "first use" of atomic weapons should be banned by agreement between the U.S. and the U.S.S.R.

In discussions about the United Nations, we stressed the need for strengthening the organization. Lawyers at the conference decided to engage in further meetings aimed at specific problems in the area of international law.

Areas of disagreement were recognized and defined without anger. Primarily they revolved around the interpretation of democracy, capitalism, freedom of the press. It was recognized that vast ideological differences exist; that the determinism of the Soviet thinkers presents a stumbling block to Westerners who tend to contemplate an "open" future. We could not agree on the timing of disarmament even within our own American group; nor could we reach a consensus about the phasing out of weapons. The Soviets have invited us to come to Russia this spring to continue and enlarge the discussions. We plan to take advantage of this opportunity. We thought you might be interested in this report.

With warm regards,
Norman Cousins

1961

The major concern of the National Committee for a Sane Nuclear Policy in its early years was in regard to nuclear testing in particular and the arms race in general. Routinely, copies of statements issued by the Committee were sent to world leaders. The following letter from Chairman Nikita Khrushchev was in response to such a statement.

February 8, 1961

Mr. Norman Cousins
Mr. Clarence Pickett
Chairmen, National Committee for a
 Sane Nuclear Policy
17 East 45 Street
New York 17, New York

Esteemed Mr. Cousins and Mr. Pickett,

I acquainted myself very fully with the statement of your Committee, which was sent to me as well as to the Prime Minister of Great Britain, Mr. Macmillan, newly elected President of the U.S.A., Mr. Kennedy, and President of France M. de Gaulle.

We are well aware of your concern about the still growing danger

caused by futher intensification of the arms race and the increasing chances of war related to the growing number of nations possessing the nuclear weapons. I have had to point out more than once that the Soviet government is profoundly convinced that the dangerous and devastating arms race should be ended as soon as possible, and therefore the Soviet Union makes and will make every effort to achieve the solution of the problem of disarmament and other urgent international issues. We sincerely seek that the new year of 1961 become the year of achieving successes in the cause of securing peaceful and quiet life on our planet.

The address of your Committee mentions several measures which could be realized in the year 1961. Almost all of them are connected with the problems of disarmament. As to us—we consider that the problem of disarmament is the most important, cardinal problem which the world faces at the present time.

As is known the problem of general and complete disarmament was being considered at the XV session of the United Nations General Assembly in September—December of 1960. The Soviet government submitted to this session new proposals in which it met halfway the Western powers in a whole number of questions. These proposals also include detailed provisions on control that secure effective realization of a treaty on general and complete disarmament.

On behalf of the government of the Soviet Union I made a statement at the XV session of the General Assembly that, if the Western countries accept our proposals on disarmament, we shall without reserve accept the proposal of the other side on control over disarmament. And this I am repeating once again in my letter to you. The Soviet government stands for the widest control with understanding existing on disarmament.

In the course of work of this session India and several other countries made an attempt to come to an understanding over agreed directives for further negotiations on the problem of disarmament. The Soviet Union deemed it possible to support a draft resolution of twelve states on the directives on general and complete disarma-

ment, in spite of the fact that, in our opinion, this draft resolution contains a number of insufficiently precise and inadequately clear formulations and some important provisions are missing. However, a representative of the former government of the U.S.A., as is known, opposed the draft resolution, and by doing so, set himself off against all peace-loving forces who are speaking in support of the quickest solution of the problem of general and complete disarmament.

We would like to hope that at the second part of the XV session of the General Assembly the Western powers would change their negative position and by doing so would create an opportunity for the resumption of constructive negotiations on general and complete disarmament. The Soviet government and myself as the Chairman of the Council of Ministers of the U.S.S.R. are ready to do everything we can in order to facilitate the achievement of an agreement on this great problem.

Some measures, mentioned in the address of your Committee, are related to the problem of cessation of the nuclear weapons tests. We have always paid a great attention to this problem, though, and this is a matter of course, the cessation of the testing of nuclear and hydrogen weapons—this measure alone—would not solve the problem of removal of the menace of an atomic war and stop the arms race. The straightforward and unmistakable way to this goal is general and complete disarmament. The Soviet Union patiently and persistently has been striving to achieve an agreement at the Geneva conference of the three powers, which has already been in session for more than two years. And in spite of the fact that we have made a number of serious concessions to the U.S.A. and Britain, in spite of our factual acceptance of many proposals of our partners to the Geneva negotiations, so far an agreement on the problem of the cessation of the nuclear weapons tests has not been achieved. In particular, the problems of a moratorium on small underground nuclear tests and of a research program to improve methods of detecting such tests, which were mentioned in the address of your Committee, have not been solved.

Upon the resumption of the Geneva conference the Soviet Union

will, as before, strive in every way for an agreement to cease forever the testing of nuclear weapons of any size.

I hope that the activity of your Committee directed toward the strengthening of the world peace will bring real fruits and will help to solve urgent international problems and, first of all, the problem of disarmament.

I can assure you that in 1961 the Soviet government will continue to fight tirelessly for securing the lasting peace on earth.

With respect,
N. Khrushchev

March 8, 1961

Chairman Nikita Khrushchev
The Kremlin
Moscow, U.S.S.R.

Dear Chairman Khrushchev:

A member of your United Nations delegation visited my office this afternoon to deliver your letter dated February 8. Mr. Pickett joins me in thanking you for your full and considered reply to our earlier letter.

Because of the absolute necessity for complete understanding, we beg leave to seek clarification of several key points in your letter:

1. Are we correct in interpreting your letter to mean that the Soviet Union is prepared to accept adequate inspection and enforcement as an essential part of any disarmament agreement?

2. Are we correct in interpreting your letter to mean that the Soviet Union will accept adequate inspection and enforcement as an essential part of any agreement to end the testing of nuclear weapons, whether underground, in the atmosphere, or in space?

3. Are we correct in interpreting your letter to mean that the Soviet Union will permit access to its country to any extent that may be

required, in connection with any disarmament agreement or agreement to ban the testing of nuclear weapons?

In view of the widespread use we intend to make of your letter, we believe it would be helpful if we could obtain your personal confirmation of these points. . . .

> With all good wishes, I am,
> Sincerely yours,
> Norman Cousins

[undated]

Dear Mr. Cousins:

Recently you wrote a letter to me asking some questions about the nuclear arms race in the context of critical world tensions.

There can be no doubt about the gravity of this problem. I don't think that any human being on this earth, whether he is the head of a government or just a plain citizen, can sleep soundly at night knowing how delicately balanced the scales are between destruction and survival.

The one stark fact we all have to face is that adequate means to insure the peace do not now exist but the means for destroying mankind do exist and are instantly available. Therefore the problem before all of us is how to develop the means to prevent war before the present momentum will become so great that no one can stop it.

In emphasizing the reality and the seriousness of this problem, you are entirely correct. But the main question you ask, in effect, is this: what do the world's leaders propose to do about it?

Naturally, we all have our own views as to how to meet such a fiercely important problem. In my talk before the United Nations last year, I tried to stress the need for getting rid of all the weapons before the weapons got rid of us. Since leaders of your government had previously spoken of the need for total disarmament, I did not feel there would be any occasion for debate on the question.

But the issue of disarmament got bogged down just the same. I don't think there is any point now in saying why this has happened; what matters now is that we find some way of going at this question again with real seriousness of intent.

I like to think that my proposals last year, if accepted, would have served as a sound beginning. But they were not accepted and I want to make clear that I take no hidebound approach to the problem. The Soviet Union was therefore heartened by President Kennedy's call for a fresh start. I accept the call. I just want to assure President Kennedy and the American people that I will consider with the utmost care and respect any proposals he may make about ending the present arms race. I will go into such discussions with an open mind and open heart, and I am certain that the President is prepared to do the same.

It has been said that any agreement to end the arms race is bound to be a failure if the specific issues that divide the nations are not resolved.

Here, too, there is no quarrel. We must deal with the basic causes of tension and not just with the weapons that will be used if these tensions get out of control. Yet I think we can also recognize that the very fact of the arms race produces tensions which can markedly increase the danger of war. My hope, therefore, is that we will not ignore the terrible problem posed by the spread of these weapons to nation after nation.

Here, however, we come to a vital fact. Both the United States and the Soviet Union need peace if they are to serve their peoples properly; in fact, both need peace if these two great nations are to continue to exist. But neither nation can create the peace by itself. If peace is created, these two great nations are going to have to work together.

In fact, we owe it not just to ourselves but to the entire world. If we two countries fail to work together for peace, all mankind will suffer. Therefore the rest of the world has a right to demand that we put aside our quarrels for the greater good.

This doesn't mean that the American people have to accept communism or that the Russian people have to accept capitalism. It means that each of us follows his way of life but that both of us join in these things that are essential for creating a condition of safety on earth for the human race.

Let me give you an example. Few people in the United States have spoken more critically of the Communist philosophy or the Soviet economic system in particular than you have. We recognize you as an ardent American patriot and exponent of the American way of life. You believe in the superior wisdom of the American economic system and you have confidence in its ability to meet the challenges of peace in competition with whatever we have to offer.

I disagree with you. I happen to believe that the Soviet economic system is more up-to-date than you own and that we can demonstrate without war the superiority of our system.

But the important thing is that we both recognize that neither your system nor ours can possibly win through war. You can work for peace without becoming a Communist. And we can work for peace without becoming capitalists.

Incidentally, I often see references to the fact that I once said about the United States: "We will bury you." This quotation is used by people to prove that we in the Soviet Union intend to murder the United States and all its citizens.

The way this quotation is used is an example of the difficulty of taking an expression from one language and giving it literal meaning in another. When I was in the United States, I watched an American television program. It was a dramatic sketch. Two good friends were talking. One of them said something slightly impolite and the other told him to drop dead. I could hardly believe my ears and I told my interpreter he must have made a serious mistake. Then he told me not to take it literally. It's just a casual expression. Many people in the United States go around telling even their best friends to drop dead. No one thinks anything of it.

In the Soviet Union we have an expression that is sometimes used

when two men happen to disagree. One of them, feeling certain he will ultimately be proved to be right, will say to the other that he will attend the other's funeral.

When I said that communism will bury capitalism, I meant that ultimately capitalism will cease to exist in its pure form and that we socialists will be around when it happens. But I don't believe we can do it by force. As I said, I don't believe war is the proper means for proving the superiority of either of our systems. All war can prove is how stupid we are and that we prefer suicide to everything life has to offer.

Against this background let me take up some of the specific questions you have asked in your letter.

1. You ask if the Soviet Union will accept inspection in connection with the abolition of nuclear testing or disarmament in general.

The answer is yes. We will accept inspection. We will accept inspecting teams on Soviet territory. I state without reservations that we have no objection to adequate on-site inspection.

In terms of practical application, I must assume that the purpose is to make sure that neither we nor anyone else will set off secret nuclear explosions, underground or anywhere else. I must assume, too, that the purpose of inspection is to make sure that any agreement seeking to reduce or eliminate nuclear weapons or all weapons, for that matter, will not be secretly violated.

Inspection for these purposes we agree to, on the assumption that others will submit to inspection, too.

The only thing I object to is inspection that has nothing to do with the prevention of secret violations. Wouldn't it be ridiculous if we all thought the danger of war was behind us, just because dozens of inspectors were wandering around who had nothing to do with carrying out a ban on nuclear weapons?

I assume, therefore, that when you ask about inspection, you are not asking about a system of legalized espionage. If you mean by inspection the specific machinery that can guard against secret violations of agreements in the field of nuclear testing or disarmament, my answer is that we are willing to accept inspection adequate to do

the job, on condition that your country is willing to do the same.

2. You ask if the Soviet Union will submit to enforceable measures to back up any agreements on nuclear weapons or other weapons in general.

The answer is yes. Enforcement means legal procedure. It also means punishment for the guilty parties. We accepted this principle at the Nuremberg trials. We accept it today. If a nation should engage in the secret manufacture of armaments once an armaments agreement is consummated, then the men responsible for such violations have committed a crime against the world's peoples and should be dealt with in the severest manner. I would be glad to propose an amendment to the Soviet Constitution that would make me subject to the punishment of a world court in those matters concerning the proper enforcement of genuine agreement to end the arms race. The same would apply to all Soviet officials involved in any such violation. Naturally, the same would have to apply to those responsible for similar violations in other countries.

3. You ask if we will accept disarmament only on the terms I have stated before the United Nations.

The answer is that we will rule out no serious proposal in advance having to do with putting an end to the arms race. Despite what some of my critics have said, I do not believe I possess all the answers to all the important questions in the world. Any government that has ideas as to how the arms race can be stopped should lose no time in making those views known. We for our part, as I said earlier in my letter, will give such proposals the most serious and deliberate consideration of which we are capable. The one hope I wish to express, however, is that we get moving at once. Each day that passes complicates and intensifies the problem. If we do not act soon, the spread of nuclear power to a number of other nations may substantially alter the world positions of both the United States and the Soviet Union. Even more serious is the fact that it would increase the number of fuses that could accidentally go off and start a world war. Any man who is in a position to help keep this from happening but who holds back does harm to the whole of the human race.

4. You ask if the Soviet Union would be willing to modify its ideology having to do with world revolution, in order to advance the cause of world peace. In particular, you ask if we would be willing to "call off" our Communist parties throughout the world.

The answer is that events have already modified the ideology. The Soviet Union does not believe in world revolution as the means of advancing the cause of world socialism. The world has changed substantially since Karl Marx wrote *Das Kapital*. Marx had no way of anticipating the problems of a world in which great nations could destroy one another within a few minutes. He had no way of anticipating the fact of a missile that could cross an ocean in ten minutes—a missile that could contain more destructive power in one bomb than had been used in all the wars in history combined up to the time Marx wrote his great book.

I might also add that Karl Marx failed to anticipate many of the important changes that have occurred in capitalism. Capitalism in the United States today is much different from what it was in the time of Marx. The American government is already a partner in any profitable American business. Enlightened business leaders like the young Fords and Rockefellers are helping to change the predatory image that existed some years ago. Moreover, your government has engaged in social services of a kind and on a scale that was unheard of at the time of Karl Marx.

About our "calling off" the Communist party in your country or elsewhere. If you will forgive me for saying so, you make it sound as though I had a pack of dogs at my disposal that I could call off just by whistling them to heel. I just want to assure you that I have no special whistle that can send Communists scurrying in this direction or that. In fact, if I were able to "call off" a political party, then you would indeed have reason to be alarmed, for this would then also give me the power to call them back again. What happens to the Communist party of the United States is not the business of the Soviet government. It is your business; that is, the business of the American people. How you handle your internal political organization is your business, not mine.

5. You ask if I agree with Karl Marx that war is inevitable in the nature of capitalism.

As I said a moment ago, Karl Marx is not infallible. I believe the idea of the inevitability of war under capitalism was completely valid at the time Marx made his observations. I do not believe that idea holds true today. I have held to the view that war is not inherent in the nature of a capitalist society. If it is, then God help us all. For then we are all doomed. I don't happen to like any ideas that say the human race is doomed. I like the human race. I like my own people. I like the Americans. It is nonsense for grown people to allow themselves to be governed by bogeys from the past or by superstitions concerning notions of "inevitability." We do what we have to do in the world to stay alive and be healthy and make sense as grown human beings.

I came to the United States in 1959 for one main reason: to hold out my hand to the American people and take off my shirt, if need be, just to prove there was nothing up my sleeve. I liked what I saw in the United States. I liked your vigor, your sense of independence, your energy, your capacity for progress. And I was eager that the head of your government see our country, for we, too, have made progress. I still hope that the man who has the honor to be President of the United States will give us the privilege of meeting him on our own soil so we can show him not only the warmth of our hospitality but the extent to which our people have increased their share of the good things of life in recent years.

Incidentally, there is something else I don't believe is inevitable. I don't think depression is inevitable in the United States should you disarm and should there be real peace in the world. In fact, I became convinced on my trip to the United States that there are limitless opportunities for peacetime expansion for your industries and for your economy in general. You have the means, in fact, to create an even greater prosperity than you now enjoy.

Just because I believe our own economy can move even faster than yours and that I believe we can catch up with you doesn't mean I believe you are stagnating. Far from it. You are giving us high goals

to shoot at. We wish you all the luck in the world in making them even higher.

6. You ask if the Soviet Union would be willing to support measures designed to strengthen the United Nations, and also, whether we would accept the compulsory jurisdiction of the United Nations in those matters concerned with world peace and world security.

The answer is that it all depends on what kind of measures you have in mind. In principle, we agree that the world organization should be strong enough to keep the peace. But it is also important for the individual nations to have confidence in the devotion of the United Nations to justice. A United Nations that can be manipulated by a few powers is not a United Nations in which justice is going to get very far.

I think your own government probably agrees with me on this. Both of us recognize the need for a greatly improved United Nations and I think that we might both start thinking and talking about what the specific measures are that could best achieve this objective.

I hope you feel I have answered your questions. At least, I have tried to indicate that I am aware of the seriousness of these questions and that I agree we should do something about them right away.

Men like President Kennedy and yourself are young and vigorous. You believe in the greatness of your country and its system and you want to dedicate yourself to its future in a world at peace. That is all to the good. I respect that spirit. Speaking for myself, I may be getting along in years but I still am full of enthusiasm and excitement when I think of what a wonderful future the human race has ahead of it if only we face up to our job to build a good peace now.

> Sincerely,
> (signed) Nikita Khrushchev

Dr. Schweitzer had received a letter from an old friend in Europe suggesting that he and I might appear on public television in the United States to discuss matters related to the nuclear arms race. The proposed meeting never took place.

April 7, 1961

Dear friend,

I am unable to come to the U.S.A. I cannot leave the hospital and, at eighty-six years old, I must not risk the fatigue that a long trip and stay in the U.S.A. would involve for me. But I shall probably send a text that will be read.

It was suggested that you and I ought to have a public discourse about peace and disarmament. If we proceed with this idea, I think that you ought to speak first and then I would respond. The latter, as Mme. Evian has probably told you already, would concern the nature of meetings which have already taken place on the question of peace and disarmament, and on the future of these conferences. I am asking thirty-five minutes to do this appearance. And as the Nobel Peace Prize winners are invited to this reunion, they must also express their opinions on such and such a question on the subject of peace and disarmament. It would also be possible to cite such and such a famous page about peace, or such and such a poem about peace, about the longing for peace. This reunion must express our aspiration for peace. That is the reason for this meeting of May 5. It must help to change the mentality of the men of our era. Let us do all we can for its success.

De coeur,
Albert Schweitzer

I sent him the first copy of Dr. Schweitzer of Lambaréné.

April 22, 1961

Dear friend:

I have to tell you once more how grateful I am for the book about me, which proves so interesting and which is going to be translated into many different languages.

Again, a thousand thanks, and also for the great gift. I have already thanked Mrs. Clara for her gift and for the wonderful photographs which she has given.

Forgive me that the text which you would have liked has not been sent yet. The text is only halfway written. When the message came that the program, planned for the 5th of May, was postponed till the fall, I did not finish it but got to other pressing work now, so that I can then later finish it in peace. And look, as things are now, when Kennedy carries on with such a strange and dangerous political course—I am really scared about it—no stranger should take up the word in America. Because it has to be a hard word which has to be spoken to the Americans to enlighten them not to accept such a dangerous political course. This is a pressing American concern where foreigners must not interfere, because if they did, one would say, the inspiration came from the outside. And this in turn one would use to discredit this opposition. Americans have to oppose in powerful and valuable words such a policy. I hope this opposition starts to roll before it is too late. Is it really true that Kennedy said, that, if the agreement to disarm is not reached in a few days, America would start with new and mightier tests? I cannot believe it; has Kennedy really talked like that? But he must know that if he navigates towards war the Americans would not go with him. You are face-to-face with enormous tasks, dear friend, I dare not think it to the end. Give me some message soon. I thank you from my heart for the beautiful opinion you expressed about me in your book.

> With best thoughts, your
> Albert Schweitzer

October 2, 1961

My dear Dr. Schweitzer:

As you know, Mr. Gromyko is here in the United States conferring with Secretary Rusk on Berlin. I had a visit the other night with

Mr. Rusk and came away with some somber reflections. Mr. Rusk made it clear that his approach to Mr. Gromyko is conciliatory and that the U.S. is eager to come to a genuine settlement. Rusk was not talking for effect. I have known him a long time; I have no doubt he was describing his real feelings. He said that what makes the present situation so fiendish is that a war over Berlin would release more nuclear force "than the human race could tolerate." Yet he wasn't sure that the Berlin problem could be satisfactorily resolved, though he would do all in his power to avoid a failure.

The heart of the problem, of course, is that the statesmen are aware of the nature of nuclear force but find it difficult to face up to the implications. We now live in the first period of human history when it is no longer possible to save freedom by fighting for it, or to save the nation by fighting for it. This is a distasteful idea and people prefer not to think about it or talk about it. Instead, they allow themselves to be governed by the same old conditioned reflexes produced by long centuries of struggle between nation and nation. They speak of the need to avoid appeasement or surrender, using terms that are meaningless alongside the fact of suicide. More and more, it appears that their ultimate value is saving national face, rather than the actual good of their society.

Many things now need to be said, openly and clearly. One thing that has to be said is that the welfare of the human race comes ahead of the welfare of any single nation. Another thing is that no nation has the right to use weapons whose effects bring harm to people in other countries who are in no way involved in the dispute. Radioactivity converts the entire earth into a single battlefield. Therefore, the only policy that makes sense is for a nation to say that it would prefer to die rather than to fight a war that would kill millions of innocent people outside their own countries who have no part in the argument.

By a curious turn of events, it may well be that the only defense against nuclear weapons in our time is bare hands and an embattled conscience.

These things should be said against the background of the kind of

moral imperative that a demonstration by world moral leaders would produce.

I give you my heartfelt thanks for your good letter and send you every good wish for your continued good health.

Devotedly,
Norman Cousins

Lambaréné, Gabon
October 10, 1961

Mr. Norman Cousins

Dear friend:

I have just received your letter of October 2. I make haste to write these lines to tell you that you are much too pessimistic! The question of Berlin is basically very simple. Basically it is a question of formalities. Until now, the Allies were obliged to notify the Russians of the passing of their troops over the territory of East Germany in which Berlin is situated. Until now all that was going well. After the declaration that East Berlin is free, the Allies would no longer have to deal with the questions of formalities with the Soviets, but with the East German authorities. America does not want to deal with this little country. To me this seems incompatible with her [America's] honor. In my opinion she [America] should have dealt with the East German authorities. It would have been the simplest way.

But the Soviets would never think of preventing America from keeping troops in Berlin! That doesn't interest them. At present we are seeking a solution for the creation of the free city of Berlin. This would irritate Bonn and Adenauer. The Soviets have nothing against the project of the free city of Berlin. What complicates everything is that we want to treat all the Soviet-American questions together. The question of Berlin and the question of the Secretary General of the U.N.! And so we get no further.

But there is no danger at all that the Soviets want to go to war over Berlin. And we in Europe are surprised that in the U.S.A. there is talk of going to war because of Berlin and of the question of fighting and, eventually, dying, for Berlin. I do not understand why the diplomats speak of this eventuality. One must be out of one's mind to speak in that fashion.

So, rest easy. One can speak a lot of foolishness in politics, but we have to remember that we can all be wiped out by a bomb in a few minutes. *In public I never discuss the problem of Berlin, because it is stupid. It does not merit the importance it is being given. I give my opinion only on the problem of disarmament and peace!* This is the real problem. And it is there that the people ought to raise their voices!

I am writing you late at night. I do not see why world opinion should be taken up with the problem of Berlin!

<div style="text-align: right">

Your devoted
Albert Schweitzer

</div>

<div style="text-align: right">

October 23, 1961

</div>

My dear Dr. Schweitzer:

I share completely your view that the fundamental danger proceeds out of the fact of the nuclear arms race and its spread to other nations. You are quite right when you say that it would be preposterous to allow the Berlin question to flare up into war. Obviously, Berlin would not be saved and everything else would be lost. But it is unhappily true that a war of nerves over Berlin is in progress, and the fuses lie close to the sparks.

In any event, the heart of the problem remains what it was. The world's two largest power blocs each possess absolute destructive force. The same irrational thinking which caused each bloc to amass this kind of power may lead to the use of the power. It is this stark fact that calls for dramatic counteraction. Day by day, the drift towards the edge continues. If it is to be stopped, people everywhere

may have to experience something on the order of a spiritual awakening. It was in this connection that I wrote to you earlier.

With profound good wishes,
Norman Cousins

[undated]

Dear friend,

Here is my opinion about the European situation. However, it is only for you personally. The Berlin crisis is slowly cooling off. It developed because Kennedy, instead of simply negotiating with the Soviets directly, started a mobilization and a tremendous strengthening of the army and sent even more American troops to Berlin, among which were some trained in street-fighting! Even England and France sent more troops to Berlin, and suddenly there was the Berlin airlift and a great panic in East Berlin. Kennedy should have been able to anticipate this.

Now one hears in Europe that Kennedy has to explain his actions to a prowar faction that has developed in the U.S., and that he does so with considerable energy. One also hears that he, unlike his predecessors, will not continue to support Adenauer's policy to let the Berlin question continue to exist with all its inherent danger, instead of solving it. It is assumed that he will agree to Russia's making peace with East Germany and that the Berlin program will not continue to exist in its current form. This peace means that East Berlin will become a free state and that Adenauer and West Berlin must put up with the fact that they won't have any further claims against East Berlin, which is something they dislike very much. But nothing can be done about it, since there is such a "distance" between the two German states, so that East Germany will never agree to be united with West Germany in today's conditions. England as well is for East Germany's independence. However, France, i.e., de Gaulle, stands closer to Adenauer and his policy about Germany. France has increased the number of troops in Germany.

In some German circles it is not considered impossible that Adenauer would attack the freed East Germany to unite it by force with West Germany. It is possible that de Gaulle will help him with this. Whether or not NATO will go along with this plan I don't know. There is a small circle in West Germany who would agree to a war to conquer East Germany.

Certainly each military action of Adenauer would lead to the Soviet entry into the war. And the superiority of the Soviets in Europe would be so strong that Germany and France and NATO would have no chance of success. NATO would have a total value of seventeen divisions (nominally there would be twenty-three divisions). And all other troops would first have to be moved from the west to the theater of war. The Soviets would have forty-five excellently equipped divisions. The French journal *Match* recently printed a very objective article about a war between Germany and NATO versus the Soviets and concluded that the Soviets would remain the absolute winners. There is also the question whether the German parliament would be for a war against East Germany. Therefore, a war-like action on behalf of Adenauer vs. East Germany would be an adventure without a chance of success.

America would probably resist this "adventure." It is questionable whether Adenauer would dare to do this, in spite of his big speeches. Whenever America finally agrees to East Germany's freedom, peace will be maintained and a better state of affairs will be created in Europe than currently exists. This is strictly between us, because I normally do not comment on the Berlin question. I only concern myself with disarmament and peace. The U.S. should have concerned itself with East Germany's independence and the peace treaty between the Soviets and East Germany, instead of letting the unsolved problem of Berlin continue, which is troubling the whole world.

Thinking of you,
Sincerely,
Albert Schweitzer

When it was announced that the U.S. would resume atmospheric testing, I cabled Dr. Schweitzer urging that he immediately send his objections to President Kennedy. His cable response was terse:

IMPOSSIBLE FAIRE CE QUE VOUS DEMANDEZ. LETTRE EN ROUTE. [Impossible to do what you ask. Letter on the way.]

Lambaréné, Gabon
October 30, 1961

Dear friend:

I cannot do as you ask. I did not insist that Khrushchev halt the resumption of tests and I have never publicly denounced him (though in my heart I have denounced him absolutely). I cannot ask Kennedy by telegram not to take up testing in turn. They would say in America that I am meddling as a stranger in trying to influence the president of the United States.

My role is to make appeals to enlighten public opinion in all countries as to the situation in which we find ourselves and to explain what must be done to avoid war and to achieve peace. In attempting to address myself directly to Kennedy, I should do harm to the influence I might have in the U.S.A. The peoples of today are very susceptible to voices coming from abroad.

The resumption of large nuclear tests was in preparation for months in the East and the West. Some members of the American military are demanding that nuclear testing be resumed aboveground as well as underground. Since they left off attending the conference for the cessation of nuclear testing at Geneva, the Soviets have been meditating on the resumption of testing, judging that their nuclear arms were not equal to those of the United States. And in America the military set itself the task of calming public opinion by repeating constantly that the Soviets were more advanced in the construction of satellites, but that American nuclear weapons were far superior to the Soviets', or something of that order.

In this situation the resumption of nuclear testing was the temptation to which East and West had to succumb. The Soviets were first to succumb. It was they who shocked the world and who shall bear the consequences in world public opinion. The U.S.A., in resuming tests, can say that the Soviets made it a necessity.

Thus what has happened is what necessarily had to happen. It was inevitable after the breaking off of talks on a test ban. The continuation of the perfecting of weapons necessarily entails the resumption of nuclear tests. These tests are necessary for the creation of arms superior to those in existence.

It is deplorable, it is terrible, it is agonizing. We are sinking ever more deeply into inhumanity by the resumption of tests. For thousands of men are condemned to suffer and to die from nuclear radiation, and generations of newborn children will continue in increasing numbers to be deformed, incapable of living.

All this is happening because public opinion the world over has treated lightly the dangers of nuclear radiation. It thought that radiation did not hasten the necessity of the renunciation of tests and nuclear weapons. It let the military and the diplomats be, as if it were a question of ordinary politics. . . .

Will public opinion awake to the situation created by this negligence? I have been working for months on the wording of a new appeal! But it is impossible to finish it and to publish it. The situation of nuclear politics never ceases to change. It is never stabilized. Therefore one cannot judge nor advise. The text that I made a month ago no longer corresponds to reality. It is outdated by events. I am watching and when I think I am able to criticize and to propose, I shall speak.

My hope is that, by the gravity of the situation created by the resumption of tests, men throughout the world will understand that they must arrive at a solution to the problem of the terrible danger in which humanity is placed. They can no longer let things go, as they have been doing. We must understand that we are risking the terrible catastrophe in which humanity will perish.

You see, dear friend, how I follow my path, and how I am faithful to you in my work. . . .

So let us struggle.

With kindest regards,
your devoted Albert Schweitzer

1962

Despite Dr. Schweitzer's reservations about communicating with President Kennedy, he wrote the following letter.

<table>
<tr><td></td><td>Stamp:</td><td></td></tr>
<tr><td>PERSONAL</td><td>THE WHITE HOUSE</td><td></td></tr>
<tr><td></td><td>APR 30 9:52 AM '62</td><td></td></tr>
<tr><td></td><td>RECEIVED</td><td>Dr. Albert Schweitzer</td></tr>
<tr><td></td><td></td><td>Lambaréné, April 20, 1962</td></tr>
</table>

Dear President Kennedy,

Would you have the great kindness to forgive me, old as I am, for taking the courage to write to you about the tests, which the United States, together with England, want to carry out when Russia does not accede to your request that an international inspection on their territory takes care that no tests will take place.

I take the courage to write to you about this as someone who has occupied himself for a long time with the problem of atomic weapons and with the problem of peace.

I believe that I may assure you that, with the newest scientific inventions, each test carried out by the Soviets can be detected at a distance by highly developed instruments, which your country possesses and which protect the United States.

I also take the courage, as an absolutely neutral person, to admit

that I am not quite convinced that the claim that one state can oblige the other to tolerate an international control commission on its territory is juridically motivated. This right can only exist after the states agree on disarmament. Then a new situation will have been established, which will put an end to the cold war and which will give each state the right to know, through international inspection on each other's territory, that each country meets its obligations to disarm according to the agreement. The same international control will see to it that no test can be carried out.

An urgent necessity for the world is that the atomic powers agree as soon as possible on disarmament under effective international control. The possibility of such disarmament negotiations should not be made questionable by unnecessary appeals for international verification of the discontinuance of testing.

Only when the states agree not to carry out tests any more can promising negotiations about disarmament and peace take place. Also, when this cannot be achieved, the world is in a hopeless and very dangerous state.

I take the courage to draw your attention also to something that concerns you personally. The terrible discovery has been made, as you surely know, that the children of parents who were exposed to radioactive radiation, even a slight one, are normal in the first and the second generations, but from the third and the fourth generations on horrible deformities occur. The children born then are in danger of having deformed feet, hands, and organs, of being blind or of having deformed brains.

These sad happenings are caused by the great sensitiveness of the cells of the reproductive organs to small doses of radioactive radiation. The effect of this radiation is hereditary *and increasing*. From the third and fourth generations on the children are no longer normal but deformed. People do not like to talk about these facts and prefer not to give any importance to them. But nobody can declare it non-existent.

It is possible that the tests carried out in these times give less fallout than those made before. But this smaller amount of fallout

will still cause men and women of our generation to receive radiation through radioactive milk, radioactive vegetables, radioactive water, or in any other way. The smallest doses of radiation on the so sensitive cells of the reproductive organs are sufficient to cause the future misery in the third and fourth generations.

It depends on you, dear President, if this horrible misery of future human beings will be realized, when new atomic tests will be carried out. You are, by the position which you have in the present world, the personality who will be burdened with this responsibility.

Please, do consider, if you will take this responsibility by insisting on not absolutely necessary conditions for the cessation of atomic tests or if this terrible responsibility will move you to let the time come in which tests belong to the past and in which promising negotiations about disarmament and peace are at last possible.

It was not easy for me to draw your attention to the great responsibility you hold to protect future generations. Please, forgive me; I could not do otherwise, not only for the sake of humanity, but also out of consideration for you personally.

Yours devotedly,
Albert Schweitzer

EXECUTIVE June 6, 1962
ND 21-1
PC 1
HE 6
FO 9
CO 303

Dear Dr. Schweitzer:

I read your letter on the nuclear testing problem with interest and sympathy. I can assure you that no decision I have taken in my Administration has given me more concern and sorrow than the decision to resume nuclear testing. It was a tragic choice; and I made

it only because the alternative seemed to me to offer even greater dangers to or hopes for world peace, to unborn generations to come, and to the future of humanity.

If I had any assurance that the Soviet Union would not test again, I would never have directed that our tests be resumed. But it is impossible to believe that our refusal to test would have deterred the Soviet Union from initiation of a new test series whenever it suited their plans. The Soviet leaders have shown their contempt for world opinion in the past, and deference to this opinion is not likely to constrain them in the future. If the Soviet Union had been able to launch a new series without intervening tests on our part, it is conceivable that a grave shift in the world balance of power might have resulted, with fateful consequences for all our hopes for peace and freedom.

From the start of my Administration, I have tried to negotiate an agreement with the Soviet Union outlawing all nuclear tests. As you know, the Soviet Union has shown little interest in having such an agreement. Until the Soviet Union accepts a meaningful test ban agreement, I can see no choice, as the man responsible for the future of my country and my people, but to take necessary steps to protect the security position of the United States.

You raise the question of the need for international inspection. At present, national systems are able to detect seismic shocks but not reliably to identify them—i.e., they are not reliably able to distinguish an explosion from an earthquake. Until detection methods improve, there can be no alternative to some limited form of on-site inspection. Obviously such inspection would apply to the United States and Great Britain as well as to the Soviet Union.

I need hardly say that, as the father of two children, I share your concern over the pernicious effects of radioactivity. I can only say that I had to weigh this against the alternative—that is, unlimited testing by the Soviet Union alone, leading to a steady increase in Soviet nuclear strength until the Communist world could be ready for a final offensive against the democracies. I believe that the Soviet leadership includes men genuinely devoted to the cause of peace.

Our strength reinforces them in their arguments with their extremist colleagues. It would seriously undermine their position if their county were permitted to acquire decisive nuclear superiority.

Nothing lies closer to my heart than the hope of bringing about general and complete disarmament under conditions of reliable international control. You are one of the transcendent moral influences of our century. I earnestly hope that you will consider throwing the great weight of that influence behind the movement for general and complete disarmament. I am happy to attach an outline of the basic provisions for such a treaty. I also enclose a study by our Arms Control and Disarmament Agency on "The Detection and Identification of Underground Nuclear Explosions" and a copy of my speech of March 2 setting forth the considerations which led me to conclude in favor of the resumption of testing.

<div style="text-align: right">

Sincerely,
John F. Kennedy

</div>

<div style="text-align: right">

October 1, 1962

</div>

My dear Dr. Schweitzer:

The purpose of this letter is to report to you about events in the United States.

Perhaps the most serious thing that has happened is that the sources of indignation over nuclear testing are drying up. People who were in the forefront of effective protest three or four years ago against nuclear testing seem to have been numbed by events. The unilateral action of the Russians in breaking the moratorium on testing drastically weakened the ground on which opponents of testing were standing. In any event, there is now a curious sense of general acquiescence or rather resignation to the unremitting program of tests.

Several months ago, I visited the White House with several other concerned citizens to express our apprehension over the plan to explode nuclear bombs at a high altitude. We told top advisers to the

president that we felt the United States had the obligation to call off the tests until such time as the very serious objections raised by such eminent foreign scientists as Sir Bernard Lovell could be thoroughly studied. For the upper atmosphere is not the property of the United States. The concern of other peoples over the tampering with the environment had to be respected by the government of the U.S. Moreover, the United States had the obligation to make known to world public opinion such facts. On the other hand, if the United States possessed clear proof that such tests represented no environmental danger, it had the opportunity to make this proof available to the world. In either case, the U.S. could not proceed in blind disregard of the rights of the world's peoples.

The reply of the Administration spokesman was that they were certain that no danger existed. When we asked why they then did not make this fact abundantly clear to the public, they said they did not feel it was necessary.

Most shocking of all was the reply to my statement that the high-altitude tests were inconsistent with President Kennedy's assurance that outer space would be kept for peaceful purposes. They said that these tests were part of the peaceful-military program.

Ambassador James J. Wadsworth, who formerly represented the United States at the Geneva disarmament talks, has now become the most vigorous critic of the government policy, which, as he says, is being increasingly shaped by military influences.

Meanwhile, everything we hear from the Soviet Union indicates that the internal situation there is rather ominous. The unilateral decision to resume nuclear testing, thus breaking the moratorium, was a direct reflection of the increased influence of the military in the foreign policy decisions of the Kremlin.

In short, day by day the military factors on both sides pile higher and higher. Soon the point will come when one side will believe it can afford to wait no longer. Worst of all is the desensitization that seems to be taking place on both sides. People seem to drift from day to day, separating themselves totally from the large reality on which their lives depend. The Church, which ought to be involving itself in this issue as it has never been involved in any issue before,

manages to express its concern now and then but it has not made
any dramatic connection with the problem; it has not made peace
the central and overriding objective. If this war comes, as I have said
many times, it will not be a war between nation and nation, or be-
tween man and man, but a war against God, for man will be de-
stroying the things that are God's—the vital balances that make life
possible; the grand design of the natural environment; the spiritual-
ity of life; the ability to respond to beauty and noble thoughts. All
these are now in jeopardy and the Church has not fully seen the
issue for what it is. But you have, and that is why my thoughts are
so much with you these days.

My own spirits, as you can probably tell from this letter, are
somewhat less robust than they were when last we spoke. The ter-
rible sense of a lowering cloud is with me constantly. I know that
whatever hope there is resides largely in the energy that our hopes
will furnish, and I try in public to avoid saying or doing anything
that will dampen the confidence of others. I know I can do more
than I am doing but I confess that it is increasingly difficult to mo-
bilize myself constantly. It is the old story, I suppose, of the adren-
alin running low after having been primed constantly.

At any rate, I am definitely planning to come to Lambaréné in
January. I am still heartsick about the miserable combination of cir-
cumstances that made it impossible last time for me to complete my
journey to Lambaréné after having come so far. This time, there will
be no other obligations. It will do me good to be with you.

<div style="text-align: right">Sincerely,
Norman</div>

<div style="text-align: right">October 22, 1962</div>

Norman Cousins

Dear friend:

At last I am getting down to replying to your letter of October
1st. You are sad that those who are fighting against nuclear arms

may be tiring and may be becoming less enthusiastic than in the first days of the struggle. I have gone through the same experience.

But I think, however, that people are beginning to doubt that there will be a future for nuclear weapons and are realizing their danger. After the events that have taken place, they are beginning to understand that the unlimited production of nuclear weapons can be ruinous to the economy. One can no longer go into the construction of nuclear arms in order to maintain one's supremacy. The economy will no longer permit it. Nuclear weapons are beginning to be a grave problem, one that will continue, year after year, to undermine economies.

People are also beginning to understand that politics between East and West, where one wants to surpass the other, are stupid, and that it is simpler to live side by side in peace. Dear friend: time works for those of us who wish to abolish nuclear weapons. The world will see that nuclear weapons are a burden of which we must relieve ourselves.

And the idea of peace is also on the march. I have taken the trouble to inform myself about the meetings at the congress in Moscow. They are dominated by the conviction that nothing is in the way of peaceful coexistence in the world. We live in a time where the problems of Cuba and Berlin are the only ones under discussion between the East and West. They are, at heart, small problems. That will be realized more and more, as soon as reason takes hold.

So, let us continue our struggle against nuclear arms; let us not be discouraged by the weariness of former companions in the struggle.

Yours devotedly,
Albert

P.S. I have at present a proposition to make: In the U.S. it has been decided to use nuclear arms for the questions of Cuba and Berlin. This is a new and serious decision. I should never have thought that the government would dare to take this decision, such a serious one. And I am of the opinion that we must not accept this decision without protesting. *To start the debate, I think it might be useful for me to*

write an open letter to [Secretary of Defense] McNamara, to whom the United States government has made known that in a conflict over Cuba and in the case of Berlin it might use all its forces, which would mean nuclear arms as well. I am sending you this open letter, most respectfully in which I am presenting to him the gravity of the government decision with which he is charged. I attempt to explain to him the gravity of the decision and the terrible responsibility that he will have to bear vis-à-vis humanity. I am sending you the text of the letter in German, with the translation by Mademoiselle Ali Silver, the nurse who helps me with English correspondence. You may change the translation if you believe it can be improved.

Can you find an American magazine that would publish this letter? If you find a magazine would you simply wire me "Magazine found" (journal trouve). Then I will also try to have the letter published in European magazines. I hope that you will be able to publish the letter in several American magazines. Also offer the letter on my behalf to the American-German review *Aufbau* in New York. The editor in chief is an old friend of mine.

So I await your telegram. I hope that you are of the same opinion as I. Also send as soon as possible twelve copies (tear sheets?) of the open letter in English. I shall use them for Japan and India and England. We must fight. We will not let nuclear war come so simply into the world today. Let us struggle. I shall also send the English text to Lord Russell.

So I don't forget: Of course I shall be very happy to have you in Lambaréné and for as long as possible! I am delighted at the prospect of having you with us.

 Fondly,
 Albert

P.S. Please telephone Mrs. Erica about the open letter.

The proposed open letter from Dr. Schweitzer to Mr. Robert S. Mc-Namara, Secretary of Defense of the United States of America (October 1962):

Dear Mr. McNamara:

I learned from the newspapers that the government of the United States gives you, in your function of Secretary of Defense, the permission to undertake, in the question of Cuba as well as in that of Berlin, everything which you consider necessary. You are also allowed to decide for a war, fought with all kinds of weapons, also atomic weapons, when you judge this necessary.

Your government does you the honor to give you permission to make a decision in this so serious matter.

The fact that the government of the United States in the present situation leaves to somebody the decision about peace or war also caused consternation in the world, as the government makes known herewith that it came to the resolution to leave the decision in the Cuba question and the Berlin question to an atomic war.

This has never been clearly stated before. All over the world an atomic war has been considered as something so exceptional that, because of its horribleness, it could not be earnestly considered and risked.

Where you have been entrusted to decide for an atomic war, does this mean an unexpected, very serious aggravation of the political situation in the world?

A war, fought with atomic weapons, is something so horrible that not even military people, or the scientists, concerned with the real significance of atomic weapons, can have a full notion about it.

First of all, it no longer has the character of a war. War up to now has meant that through the use of weapons territory can be conquered or can be defended against enemies and that through the use of better weapons one can have a superiority which forces the opponent to surrender and to make peace.

A war with atomic weapons is very different. During such a war no territory or fortress can be conquered, no territory or fortress can be defended. The only possibility is mutual, senseless, unlimited destruction. Destruction will take place over vast territories, far over the borders of the combatants, because of explosions, fire, and a terrible poisoning of the atmosphere and soil. A great part of many populations will perish woefully.

Atomic war also has nothing to do with two belligerent nations, but with the whole of humanity. He who decides for an atomic war takes a terrible responsibility toward mankind. Nobody can release him from this responsibility.

Do leave us the hope, dear sir, that you are conscious of the terrible responsibility which would burden you in the case that you should decide to risk an atomic war because of the Cuban or Berlin question.

And, moreover, may you be confident that both of these problems can be much better solved by quiet, positive negotiations which try to maintain peace than by a war.

Politics of strength are in our time not the right ones, because they are provocative and poison the atmosphere.

I kindly ask you to excuse me, dear sir, because I have decided to write to you about this matter. I cannot do otherwise. I feel compelled to do so because of the great danger in which the human race finds itself.

Yours devotedly,
Albert Schweitzer

I sent a wire to Dr. Schweitzer expressing the viewpoint that the situation with regard to Cuba was very complicated and that he might wish to reconsider his proposed letter to Secretary McNamara.

October 30, 1962

Dr. Albert Schweitzer
Lambaréné

HOLDING UP YOUR MCNAMARA STATEMENT. TURN OF EVENTS IN U.S. MAY REQUIRE CHANGES. LETTER FOLLOWS.

Best Regards,
Norman Cousins

Lambaréné
October 31, 1962

Norman Cousins

Dear friend:

Thank you for your wire. Naturally, we did well not to attack McNamara, given the grave turn of events, which I hadn't been able to foresee. But when peace is established, we must, in our struggle against nuclear weapons, criticize the fact that McNamara did something very grave in announcing that he would use all forces—that is to say nuclear arms as well—in a war over the problem of Cuba or of Berlin. If we are really fighting against nuclear arms, we cannot abstain from criticizing McNamara, severely and publicly. Otherwise, we fail in our duty. We cannot make concessions. Naturally, President Kennedy was in agreement with McNamara. But one doesn't make public attacks on the president.

But McNamara's decision to say that the use of nuclear weapons was a possibility was a world provocation that was stupid and very serious. We must talk very clearly about it when the crisis has passed.

Above all, that he should speak of the Berlin crisis. For me as for others who know the reasons for the Berlin crisis, this is a stupidity about which the Germans must be arguing among themselves. For those who know the problem, to think of an atomic war over Berlin is idiocy. The American secretary of defense ought not to be concerned with that. And if there is an atomic war because of Berlin, the first thing that will happen is that the two Berlins will cease to exist—thanks to the use of atomic weapons. The Berliners know it and are afraid of a war because of it. We Europeans find it strange that the American secretary of defense should take up the Berlin question and offer to the Berliners an atomic war as the solution to the Berlin problem. Berliners would rather stay alive. Forgive me for writing you to say how much the idea of an atomic war to bridge the Berlin problem seems idiotic. All this is entirely between ourselves.

Devotedly,
Albert

October 30, 1962

Dear Dr. Schweitzer,

Please do not regard this letter as an adequate response to your own letter of encouragement and reassurance which will be profoundly appreciated by leaders of the peace movement in the United States. Later I will write you more fully concerning their reactions. At the moment, I want to put before you certain facts that may have a bearing on your open letter to Secretary McNamara.

First, there is indeed an important segment of the American military which is growing in authority in the United States. It is important for you to know, however, that Secretary McNamara actually belongs to the moderate faction in the government. I don't mean to suggest by this that he is sympathetic to our point of view. But at the same time it may be important to distinguish him from the hotheads.

Another fact that may have a bearing on your letter concerns the events in Cuba. There was prodigious pressure on the President to invade Cuba willy-nilly or, at the very least, to bomb the missile sites in Cuba rather than try a more moderate course. The President had to walk a tightrope between two extremes. On one side he had to contend with the hysterical clamor for an invasion. On the other side he was confronted by the danger that if he did nothing at all the missile sites would be completed, thus giving Castro the power to start World War III. The President resisted both these pressures long enough to be able to have the kind of exchange with Chairman Khrushchev that removed the danger of an immediate nuclear showdown and that could set the stage for a highly meaningful meeting between the two men.

Another factor in the present situation has to do with the large-scale fighting that has developed between China and India. The position of the Soviet Union with respect to this conflict may have a great bearing on the question of world peace in general and Asian affairs in particular. Therefore, the Kennedy-Khrushchev meeting takes on additional significance at this time.

I feel certain that you are counting on me to hold up the publication of your open letter to Mr. McNamara if events since you wrote it changed in the meantime. In any event, I am ready and feel privileged at all times to seek the widest possible circulation for your views. In addition to *The Saturday Review*, we have some access to newspapers and braodcasting media and will, as in the past, make maximum efforts to bring your words before the American people.

In the meantime, an event of unusual significance has just occurred in the United States. A dozen or so prominent Soviet citizens have met with an equivalent number of prominent American citizens in a closed conference that lasted one week. The co-chairmen on the Russian side were Academician B. K. Federov, Chief of the Main Directorate of the Hydrometeorological Service; and Y. A. Zhukov, commentator of *Pravda*, Deputy of the Supreme Soviet of the U.S.S.R. The co-chairmen on the American side were Philip E. Mosely, Director of Studies, Council on Foreign Relations; and myself.

Other participants included A. G. Masevich, Doctor of Physics, Deputy Chairman of the Astronomical Council of the U.S.S.R. Academy of Sciences, Chairman of the KOSPAR Working Group for Observation of Artificial Satellites; S. V. Molodtsev, Doctor of Law, Professor of International Law, Vice Chairman of the World Federation of United Nations Associates; S. Polevoi, writer, Deputy of the Supreme Soviet of the Russian Republic; G. V. Shmeiko, publicist, member of the editorial board of the journal *Soviet Trade Unions;* and N. A. Talenskii, Doctor of Science, member of the editorial board of the *Journal of International Affairs,* General of the Reserve. American participants included Paul M. Doty, Professor of Chemistry at Harvard, member of President's Science Advisory Committee: Arthur Larson, Director, World Rule of Law Center, Duke University, formerly a White House advisor and Under Secretary of Labor; Margaret Mead, Adjunct Professor of Anthropology, Columbia University, Associate Curator of Ethnology, American Museum of Natural History; Louis B. Sohn, Professor of International Law at Harvard, advisor to U.S. Arms Control and

Disarmament Agency; and Herman Steinkraus, former president of the U.S. Chamber of Commerce, currently president of American Association for the United Nations.

I felt fortunate in being able to arrange this meeting and get the support of the Ford Foundation to finance it. We couldn't have met at a more ominous or propitious time. The Cuban crisis was at its height but we were in constant session and we were able to serve valuable liaison purposes with our governments in the attempt to avoid nuclear showdown. The date for the conference had been fixed many months ago and was, in fact, the outgrowth of two previous meetings, the first at Dartmouth College in October 1960, and the second in the Crimea in May 1961. Both these meetings had been successful, not in terms of agreements actually reached but in terms of the ability to clarify opposing positions, to submit to rules of order in debate, to subject facts to cross-examination, and to develop personal relationships that could be fruitful beyond the conference table.

But neither the Dartmouth nor the Crimea meetings took place under circumstances as somber and as unsettling as existed at the meeting in Andover. Within a day after the Soviet participants arrived, the Cuban crisis was in the headlines. Three days later, just after the group assembled at Andover, the radio was crackling with news bulletins about an imminent statement of major importance by President Kennedy. That same night, the President went before the television cameras and the microphones to announce a blockade of all military shipping into Cuba. The delegates from both groups watched the announcement on a TV screen; the tension and the uncertainty in the room were palpable and acute. The fact that their two nations were apparently on a collision course now created an atmosphere of gravity for their experiment that none could have anticipated and all could dread.

Shortly after the President's announcement, the delegates went to their evening session in the trustees' room which had been equipped with IBM simultaneous translating equipment. The Americans were mindful that their Russian guests, 5,000 miles from their homes and

families, were probably wondering whether they ought to leave the United States while there was still time to do so. It is possible that the Soviet visitors wondered whether the Americans felt there was any use in proceeding. At any event, the co-chairman of the Soviet delegation began the meeting by asking tactfully whether the Americans wished to go on with the conference. The American co-chairman said there was only one way to find out. He asked for a show of hands of those who wished to continue. Without the slightest hesitation, every American hand went up. The Soviet participants responded in equal measure and the experiment was sustained.

During the course of the week, the Cuban situation gave rise to the most detailed, direct exchange of views. There could be no doubt that all the elements of the problem, including many which had been crowded out of the headlines, were fully presented. Blunt questions were asked and just as bluntly answered. One of the items on the prepared agenda had to do with the role of the United Nations in dealing with tensions, and with the place of world law in the establishment of a durable peace. It was inevitable that the relevance of this topic to the Cuban crisis should have been stressed by some of the participants.

Other topics vigorously discussed included the problem of achieving general and complete disarmament under iron-clad safeguards; the responsibility of the large nations in undertaking a cooperative program for assisting countries in need of economic development; the problem of maintaining peaceable relations while maintaining diverse political systems; and ways in which the access of each country to the other could be kept open in economic, scientific, and cultural relations.

On some days the sessions ran from early morning until late at night. Each topic produced a substantial supply of information, not all of it familiar to most of the participants. And, as might be expected, few statements went unchallenged.

Where facts were incontrovertible, positions gained in proportion. Suggestions were made for constructive improvement, especially in

the area of cultural relations, and a number of them had no difficulty
in gaining a concurrence.

Perhaps the most interesting development of the experiment was
that, paradoxically, the delegates drew closer together on the per-
sonal level even as the issues that separated them grew more intense.
The international crisis deepened and the debates at the conference
table were correspondingly sharper, but the personal rapport mounted
from day to day. Whether this was because the participants were
becoming increasingly aware subconsciously of their underlying
membership in a human commonwealth, or whether, as they came
to know one another, they yielded to the magnetic pull of human
gravity, it is difficult to say. One thing, however, is certain: By the
end of the week there was no awkwardness or strain in raising any
question, however severe, or in venturing any response, however
pointed. It was possible to be forthright without being caustic, im-
passioned without being abusive, severe without being cutting. You
could disagree and still retain your respect for the person you were
disagreeing with. Just in the process of working and living together,
those at the conference had been able to transcend what until then
had been their purely national identities and were recognizing the
implicit existence of a human agenda for their deliberations.

Moreover, there seemed to be a sense among the participants that
they were sharing in a privileged experience at a critical time. An-
dover was probably the only place in the world during the Cuban
missile crisis where Americans and Russians, albeit unofficially, were
talking things out together on virtually a day-and-night basis. This
increased and enhanced their sense of somber responsibility. It
made many of them recognize, too, that they were there not just for
the purpose of proclaiming but for the purpose of legitimate self-
examination.

In all these respects, the experiment was a success. The People-
to-People Program, so fully supported by the U.S. government, has
had no more striking example than Andover of the validity of its
underlying thesis. For if the human experiment represented by the

meeting at Andover can succeed under the circumstances and pressure that obtained at the time of crisis then almost nothing can be considered implausible or impossible in the field of unofficial contacts.

<div style="text-align: right">

With continued devotion,
Norman

</div>

<div style="text-align: right">

Lambaréné
November 11, 1962

</div>

Dear Friend:

Thank you for your letter of October 30th. First, the McNamara question. You say that he is on the side of the moderates, and yet he announced coldly, proudly, with Kennedy, that if war should come he would use atomic weapons. Where is the moderate? The moderate acted like an extremist, with unbelievable frivolity, as did President Kennedy. This is something very grave for the world, for one must think also of the world and of humanity, who will have to submit to an atomic war, for an all-out atomic war becomes immediately a world war. And it is necessary to point out to those who declare that they will use atomic weapons their responsibility vis-à-vis the world. I wrote to Lord Russell that I am against making public reproaches to Kennedy, because he is chief of state. A chief of state must be criticized in public only if absolutely necessary. Therefore, one can only criticize McNamara. And as the crisis has passed, I feel that I shall give up the idea of criticizing a military leader of the U.S. I will withdraw the letter to McNamara, as you suggest. But will you, an American, denounce this frivolity, so that the American military authorities may realize their responsibilities not only to America but also to the world? You know how much I love America. I am profoundly saddened when I hear that the newspapers are talking about a war hysteria brought on by the Cuban

crisis. And what would have become of you, and of us with you, if Khrushchev had not put aside all question of prestige and simply offered to surrender. Great peoples haven't the right to abandon themselves to hysteria.

And that McNamara and Kennedy would have declared that they would use atomic weapons as well if the Berlin question gave way to war. The Berlin question is a European one. It can be settled easily if the two Germanys begin to look for a solution. Basically, it is merely a question of formalities. If the U.S. wants to help solve it, the most useful thing would be simply to withdraw its troops from Europe as it promised to do by the Treaty of Potsdam.[*] It is abysmal folly for McNamara and Kennedy to think themselves obliged to fight a nuclear war over Berlin. A nuclear war cannot settle anything. It can only lead to inestimable destruction, as the military must know and must take into consideration. Nuclear war over Berlin means that within the space of one hour Germany will cease to exist.

Forgive me for being a bit strong. But I was terrified to hear that the head of the army and the president of the U.S. deemed it useful to consider a nuclear war not only over the Cuban crisis, which is their business, but as well over the Berlin crisis, which is not and which they do not understand. And in the U.S. everyone accepted this idiotic declaration about a nuclear war waged by the United States to settle the Berlin problem! Where are we going? You, the reasonable people in America, must educate your military and your politicians. The world must return to reason and give up these funny ideas that spring up in the imaginations of military men and politicians. We in Europe and you in America must see to this task. We must create a new state of mind if the danger of a ruinous catastrophe for humanity is to be avoided. So, I shall go to work in Europe

[*]The Potsdam Conference, held from July 17 to August 2, 1945, in Potsdam, Germany, met to consider military operations against Japan and procedures for peace settlements in Europe. Chief participants were the United States, Great Britain, and the Soviet Union.

with regard to these latest developments and shall give up the idea of criticizing, as a foreigner, American personalities. Things must be kept in order.

I am well, but my work is considerable and unceasing day to day. The amount of my correspondence is crushing me. It gets bigger every year.

With my best wishes, profoundly and devotedly yours,

Albert

P.S. In Germany, the Adenauer regime, anti-democratic as it is, becomes more and more insupportable. It is giving itself over more and more to the militarists.

1963

Beginning with the resolution of the Cuban missile crisis of October 1962, and ending with the assassination of President John F. Kennedy in November 1963, a spirit of optimism was at work in the world, signaling an upturn in the prospects for peace. Three men came to symbolize these new prospects— President Kennedy, Nikita Khrushchev, and Pope John XXIII.

At the initiative of the Pope, direct contact was established between the Vatican and the Kremlin. A specific result of this was the release, after years of internment in Eastern European countries, of two archbishops. I was asked to serve as emissary for the Vatican in negotiating the release of the archbishops with Premier Khrushchev. Learning of these meetings, President Kennedy asked that I convey a message to Premier Khrushchev, assuring him of the President's good faith in seeking a halt to the testing of nuclear weapons. In particular, the President was eager to break the impasse in the test-ban negotiations. In connection with these negotiations, I met with Chairman Khrushchev in April at his resort home at Gagra on the Black Sea. I wrote an account of this work in a book published in 1972 entitled The Improbable Triumverate.

The Cuban crisis provided evidence that the United States was eager to reach workable agreements on Berlin as well as the other basic issues. On May 27, 1963, a resolution calling for a treaty banning the atmospheric testing of nuclear weapons was presented in the United States Senate. In the long history of negotiations, the idea of a partial test ban had come up at various times during both the Eisenhower and Kennedy administrations, but

had not been supported by public and congressional opinion. With the support of some senators, President Kennedy could feel a gathering of momentum for the test-ban fight. On June 10, 1963, he was scheduled to give a commencement talk at American University in Washington, D.C. The President felt that some of the points from my report to him on my visit to Premier Khrushchev at Gagra might be incorporated in his speech, and he asked me to send him some notes for the draft.

The circumstances and timing of the President's speech at American University were auspicious. For at least twelve hours after it was given, no word appeared in the Moscow press about the speech. The Khrushchev government was required to make a fateful choice between publishing either the text of an open letter to the Russian people from Peking or the text of the Kennedy speech. The decision had far-reaching implications. Finally, the full text of President Kennedy's address was published in Izvestia. *Khrushchev's personal policy had prevailed. The Soviets halted production of strategic bombers, and it appeared that further measures of accommodations between Moscow and Washington would prevail.*

The positive response of the Russian press to President Kennedy's speech was followed by Soviet agreement to new terms for a limited test-ban treaty. But the treaty required ratification by the United States Senate, and the President was acutely aware of the need for a major campaign to obtain the votes necessary for passage. In order to get the arguments favoring a test ban across to a national audience, a comprehensive plan was drawn up. This included the preparation of full-page advertisements endorsed by prominent Americans.

June 24, 1963

Chairman Nikita Khrushchev
The Kremlin
Moscow, U.S.S.R.
Excellency:

I am enclosing herewith a full-page statement appearing in the *Wall Street Journal* June 24, 1963. You will note that it expresses the support for a test-ban treaty of many of the leading businessmen in

the United States. This statement is the result of the special program I spoke to you about during our meeting in Gagra.

In short, there has been a profound change in public opinion in this country. President Kennedy's leadership on this issue has been most effective. There can be no doubt of the sincerity of the U.S. in seeking a test-ban treaty.

Sincerely,
Norman Cousins

July 21, 1963

Telegram to Dr. Albert Schweitzer:

NUCLEAR TEST BAN NOW IMMINENT. YOUR ROLE IN HELPING TO AROUSE WORLD PUBLIC OPINION ON THIS ISSUE WAS A KEY ONE IN THE PRESENT RESULT. YOU ARE ENTITLED TO THE APPRECIATION OF ALL HUMANITY.

Devotedly yours,
Norman Cousins

October 4, 1963

Dr. Albert Schweitzer
Lambaréné, Gabon
Equatorial Africa

My dear Dr. Schweitzer:

Last Tuesday, in Washington, I was at a luncheon attended by members of the Congress and the staff of the White House. The purpose of the lunch was to celebrate in a modest way the victorious ratification of the test-ban treaty. There were several speeches. You would have been pleased, I think, to have heard the many references made to your role in bringing about a test-ban treaty. Everyone now recognizes that your appeal made this a world issue for the first time.

I think back to those early days of the fight for a test ban, when Dr. Libby of the U.S. Atomic Energy Commission tried to criticize you for your warnings concerning radioactivity in the atmosphere and in soil, food, and bones of children. I remember his public statements saying that the danger was so small as to be non-existent. I remember all the other efforts made to belittle your appeal. And now, everyone accepts the basic facts you presented more than six years ago. One of the chief arguments, in fact, in favor of the treaty voiced by both President Kennedy and Premier Khrushchev has been directed to the hazard of radioactivity.

One of my reasons for wanting to come to Lambaréné was to be able to report to you personally on various developments leading up to the test-ban agreements. I was involved in a modest way in the negotiations with Khrushchev, at the request of the President. My hope, as I say, is to be able to discuss this with you directly. In the meantime, I am enclosing a written report for your possible interest.

I think you know without my telling you how proud and privileged I have been to have been associated with you, however modestly, in the test-ban crusade. We still have a long way to go. The nuclear arms race continues. Underground testing continues. World tensions that could spark a nuclear explosion continue. But at least something specific that had to be done was done. History will give you your proper share of credit for this achievement.

<div style="text-align:right">

With all good wishes,
NC
</div>

The problem of nuclear weapons testing, discussed with Dr. Schweitzer at the Lambaréné hospital in 1957, was partially resolved as the result of the treaty outlawing atmospheric nuclear explosions. But underground testing remained a live issue as, indeed, did the entire question of the arms race. Dr. Schweitzer's letters in the two years before his death reflected his hope that the test-ban treaty might carry over to control of the arms race in general. Increasingly, however, his letters seemed to reflect some fatigue. He seemed to retreat into hospital matters. He wrote that he considered it a great privilege, in his nineties, to be able to continue working at his profession of medicine.

Epilogue

The compound at the Schweitzer Hospital in Lambaréné was a narrow rectangular affair grooved into the gritty hillside and flanked by the clinic and dispensary, both of them topped by deep red corrugated-tin roofing. On Saturday evening, September 4, 1965, the compound slowly began to fill up with people. Not on the busiest days of the hospital, when long lines of people waited to be treated, nor even at Christmas services or Easter Sunday, had the compound held so many people.

No call had been sent out. No one had said that this was the place to come to at just this time, but a loneliness settled over Lambaréné. For the great Doctor had been ill in his small room for more than a week and the word had gone out that his life was slowly receding. Everyone seemed to know somehow that the end was very near.

They came to the compound by torchlight. They came by canoe up or down the Ogowe River, or on foot from Lambaréné and the small villages, taking the road or the jungle paths. The sick ones got up from their slab beds in the wooden huts that served as wards. Patients came from the leper colony over the hill. And the doctors and nurses on the hospital staff left their quarters to join the Africans in the compound.

Some of the Africans began to sing hymns, in French, softly. More and more voices picked up the hymns and soon each person was joined to the other by the blending of human sound. Then, after the

singing, individual Africans or members of the staff spoke as they felt. By what they said, the Africans proved that Albert Schweitzer was not as detached from them as some of his critics had contended. "We have heard that some Europeans say he has done us no good," one of them said. "How do they know? They have never come here to see us. The grand Doctor, he came here and stayed for most of his life and gave us all he had to give, and that was a great deal."

An African patient stood up to say he understood that in Europe and America some people charged that the hospital was unclean and not very scientific. "But this is the hospital we come to when we are not well," he said. "There are other hospitals, but this one we know. We have known it for a long time. Our fathers came here when they were ill. It is for us."

Nurses and doctors joined in the witness. They told why they had left their own countries to work without pay in an equatorial jungle hospital. There was nothing self-serving about them as they spoke of their purpose. They had come to Lambaréné because they hoped their offer of help might be accepted. They also spoke of what it was that Schweitzer meant to them. And everyone knew without anyone having to say it that the work of the hospital would go on. This was what the commitment to Albert Schweitzer was all about.

The meeting in the compound ended and the people began to disperse. Then, at 11:30 P.M., the door to the Doctor's quarters opened and Rhena Eckert, Schweitzer's daughter, came out and said that her father had just died.

Two weeks earlier, Albert Schweitzer had called in his daughter and handed her a letter. In it, he was making known for the first time his wishes about how the hospital was to be run after his death. The letter said he wanted his daughter to be general head of the hospital and he named the doctors who were to be in charge of the medical services. Those who had been close to the hospital could quickly realize the good sense of the doctor's last request. Rhena had joined the hospital when her own children were fully grown. She had quickly established herself as a competent, conscientious, knowledgeable associate to her father.

So the hospital at Lambaréné survived its founder. But this did not resolve all the questions about Albert Schweitzer's life and work— questions that had been raised for half a century. The people who raised the questions contended that the hospital was the creature of extraordinary publicity, and that the Doctor had squandered his talents in the jungle. They said that his theology, however impressive it may have been at one time, lacked sophistication. Or that his philosophy was borrowed too heavily from Hegel. Or that his reputation as Bach authority or organist or organ builder drew on the public's capacity for being impressed by extraordinary versatility.

But all these questions missed the main point about Schweitzer. The main point has nothing to do with the sanitation at Lambaréné or Schweitzer's alleged autocratic attitudes, whether toward whites or blacks. Nor has the real point anything to do with the level of sophistication of his theology or philosophy, or his rank as musician or organ technician. There are solid grounds for according him high honor and distinction in all these professions and undertakings; but again, this is not really the central fact about Schweitzer.

The main point about Schweitzer is that he helped make it possible for twentieth-century man to unblock his moral vision. There is a tendency in a relativistic age for people to pursue all sides of a question as an end in itself, finding relief and even refuge in the difficulty of defining good and evil. The result is a clogging of the moral sense, a certain feeling of self-consciousness or even discomfort when questions with ethical content are raised. Schweitzer furnished the nourishing evidence that nothing is more natural in life than a moral response, which exists independently of precise definition, its use leading not to exhaustion but to new energy.

The greatness of Schweitzer—indeed, the essence of Schweitzer— was the man as symbol. More important than what he did for others was what others have done because of him and the power of his example. At least half a dozen hospitals in impoverished, remote areas have been established because of him. Wherever the Schweitzer story was known, lives were changed. A manufacturer in the American Midwest read about Schweitzer, sold his farm-implement man-

ufacturing company, and used the money to build a string of medical clinics in the Cameroons. A Japanese professor raised money in Schweitzer's name and started an orphanage. A young German medical school graduate, with no means or resources save a fund of inspiration, went to South America and started a hospital. Tom Dooley and his hospital in Laos became an American legend. A beautiful, talented young Dutch woman learned about Schweitzer and selected a medical career. Six years later she was chief surgeon at the Schweitzer Hospital in Lambaréné. She left later to found a hospital of her own, in southern France, carrying on in the Schweitzer tradition.

And there is the story of Larimer and Gwen Mellon and the work they did in Schweitzer's name in Haiti. At the age of thirty-seven, Larimer Mellon was making a career out of being a rich man's son. Just bearing the Mellon name was something of a full-time job. When he read about Schweitzer, the effect was explosive; it blasted him out of one life and into a totally different one. He returned to college to complete his undergraduate education, sitting in classes alongside students half his age. Then he enrolled in medical school. At forty-four, he received his medical diploma. With his wife, Gwen, he decided to found a hospital dedicated to Schweitzer. They selected Haiti not solely because of the high disease rate and the illiteracy of the people but because it was part of North America—very close to the most prosperous nation in the world. Some seventy miles north of Port-au-Prince, in Haiti, Larimer and Gwen Mellon selected the site of what was to become the Albert Schweitzer Hospital of Haiti.

Then there is the case of a young American named Fergus Pope. Traveling through Africa on a motorcycle safari, he stopped at the Schweitzer Hospital out of curiosity. That visit changed the entire course of his life. He returned to school, completed his undergraduate requirements, something he had not previously intended to do, worked his way through medical school in London, served his internship in a New Jersey hospital, and returned to Lambaréné as a fully accredited physician to make good his promise to himself. In the meantime, he had married and become the father of three chil-

dren. He brought his entire family with him to the Schweitzer Hospital. Dr. Schweitzer was overjoyed at the presence of the children at the hospital. The entire staff, in fact, was caught up in the adventure of a young American family on the hospital grounds.

What was it about Schweitzer that caused Larimer and Gwen Mellon, Ruth and Fergus Pope, and all the others to set their lives on a new course? It was the enduring proof Schweitzer furnished that we need not torment ourselves about the nature of human purpose. The scholar, he once wrote, must not live for science alone, nor the businessman for his business, nor the artist for his art. If affirmation for life is genuine, it will "demand from all that they should sacrifice a portion of their own lives for others."

Thus Schweitzer's main achievement was a simple one. He was willing to make the ultimate sacrifice for a moral principle. Like Gandhi, the power of his appeal was in renunciation. And because he was able to feel a supreme identification with other human beings he exerted a greater force than armed men on the march. It is unimportant whether we call Schweitzer a great religious figure or a great philosopher. It suffices that his words and works are known and that he is loved and has influence because he enabled men to discover mercy in themselves. Early in his life he was accused of being an escapist. He was criticized for seeming to patronize the people he had chosen to serve. Yet the proof of his genuineness and his integrity is to be found in the response he awakened in people. He reached countless millions who never saw him but who were able to identify themselves with him because of the invisible and splendid fact of his own identification with them. This is the measure of the man. What has come out of his life and thought is the kind of inspiration that can animate a generation.

We live at a time when people seem afraid to be themselves, when they seem to prefer a hard, shiny exterior to the genuineness of deeply felt emotion. Sophistication is prized and sentiment is dreaded. It is made to appear that one of the worst blights on a reputation is to be called a do-gooder. The literature of the day is remarkably devoid of themes on the natural goodness or even the potential goodness of

man, seeing no dramatic power in the most powerful fact of the human mixture. The values of the time lean to a phony toughness, casual violence, cheap emotion; yet we are shocked when youngsters confess to having tortured and killed because they enjoyed it and because they thought it was the thing to do.

It mattered not to Schweitzer or to history that he would be dismissed by some as a do-gooder or as a sentimental fool who frittered his life away on Africans who couldn't read or write. Schweitzer brought the kind of spirit to Africa that the dark man hardly knew existed in the white man. Before Schweitzer, white skin meant beatings and gunpoint rule and the imposition of slavery on human flesh. If Schweitzer had done nothing else in his life than to accept the pain of these people as his own, he would have achieved eminence. And his place in history will rest on something more substantial than an argument over an unswept floor in a hospital ward in the heart of Africa. It will rest on the spotless nature of his vision and the clean sweep of his nobility.

The tragedy of life is not in the hurt to a man's name or even in the fact of death itself. The tragedy of life is in what dies inside a man while he lives—the death of genuine feeling, the death of inspired response, the death of the awareness that makes it possible to feel the pain or the glory of other men in oneself. Albert Schweitzer was triumphantly and fully alive. His aim was not to dazzle an age but to awaken it, to make it comprehend that moral splendor is part of the gift of life, and that each person has unlimited strength to feel human oneness and to act upon it. Thus no man need fear death; he need only fear that he may die without having known his greatest power—the power of his free will to give his life to others.

The individual in today's world feels cut off from the large forces or movements that determine his future. This leads to fatalism and default. Schweitzer demonstrated that one man can make a difference. He had no specific prescription or formula. All he hoped was that the individual would be able to peel off the layers of hardened artificialities that separate him from his real self. Man's resources do not exist outside him. His responses must come from within. A

thinking and feeling man is not a helpless man. The sense of paralysis proceeds not so much out of the mammoth size of the problem but out of the puniness of purpose.

It may be said that only a Schweitzer had the knowledge and personal power to answer satisfactorily the question: "What can one man do?" Certainly we can't all be Schweitzers. But what should concern us is not what it takes to be a Schweitzer but what it takes to be a whole person. Nature has not been equally lavish with her endowments, but each person has his or her own potential in terms of achievement and service. The awareness of that potential is the discovery of purpose; the fulfillment of that potential is the discovery of strength.

For Albert Schweitzer, the assertion of this potential was not directed to charity, but to justice; also, moral reparations: "We are burdened with a great debt. We are not free to confer benefits on these people, or not confer them, as we please. It is our duty. Anything we give them is not benevolence but atonement. That is the foundation from which all deliberations about 'works of mercy' must begin."

As for the right time to act? The time, inevitably, is now. It can only be now. "Truth has no special time of its own," he said. When circumstances seem least propitious, that is the correct time.

Much of the ache and the brooding unhappiness in modern man is the result of his difficulty in using himself fully. He performs compartmentalized tasks in a compartmentalized world. He is reined in—physically, socially, spiritually. Only rarely does he have a sense of fulfilling himself through total contact with a total challenge. He finds it difficult to make real connections even with those who are near him. But there are vast urges of conscience, natural purpose, and goodness inside him demanding air and release. And he has his own potentialities, the regions of which are far broader than he can even guess at—potentialities that keep nagging at him to be fully used.

Albert Schweitzer was fully grown, fully developed, fully used. Did this make him happy? The question is irrelevant. He was less

concerned with happiness than with purpose. What is it that has to
be done? What is the best way of doing it? How does a human being
go about developing an inner awareness of important needs outside
himself? How does he attach himself to those needs? Is he able to
recognize the moral summons within him? To the extent that the
individual is unconcerned about these questions, or lives apart from
them, he is unfulfilled and only partly alive.

Index